THE DUPLICATING IMAGINATION

THE
DUPLICATING
IMAGINATION

Twain and the Twain Papers

Maria Ornella Marotti

THE PENNSYLVANIA STATE UNIVERSITY PRESS
University Park and London

Library of Congress Cataloging-in-Publication Data

Marotti, Maria Ornella.
  The duplicating imagination.
  Bibliography: p.
  Includes index.
  1. Twain, Mark, 1835–1910—Criticism and
interpretation. I. Title.
PS1338.M67 1989   818'.409   88—19560
ISBN 0-271-00650-1

To Jack

Contents

Acknowledgments

I wish to thank the people who encouraged and helped me in various ways in my work on this project. This includes: Professor Sergio Perosa (University of Venice), who suggested the topic of my "laurea" thesis, *Mark Twain's Fables of Man*; the late Frederick Anderson, former general editor of the Mark Twain Project, who offered me helpful suggestions; professor Agostino Lombardo (University of Rome, Italy), who encouraged my research on Twain during my years of teaching at the University of Rome; my dissertation advisers, professors H. Porter Abbott, Steven Allaback, and Garrett Stewart, who offered cogent criticism and helpful suggestions; the late John S. Tuckey, Robert H. Hirst, David Ketterer, and Paul John Eakin, all of whom read the manuscript with great insight when I submitted it for publication; Cherene Holland and Philip Winsor of the Penn State Press, who were involved in the publication process; my friend Betty MacDonald, who was of great assistance to me during the last revision of the manuscript.

Introduction

The time has come for an interpretation of the Mark Twain Papers. The publication of a portion of them, by the University of California Press, first in a scholarly edition and then in more recent times in paperback, has made them available to a reading public, as well as to scholars. Partly because of this publishing effort, some parts of the Papers are now receiving considerable scholarly attention; new critical works have suggested varied approaches to the quite bewildering mass of writing.[1]

The timing is right. Our own modern perception of the fragmentation of experience, so often reflected by contemporary fiction, and a prevailing philosophical concept of language viewing writing as a process have made available critical strategies that are useful for the unrevised, often unfinished, and mostly experimental writings which are the Mark Twain Papers.

The relevance of these writings can also be observed in relation to the main works. Not only do they add to the general knowledge of the author and his other works, but they also display tendencies that are latent in the better-known pieces. The more outspoken nature of the writing in the Papers might be partly the result of a temporary suspension of censorship. At least initially, parts of the Papers were not meant for publication and thus represent a form of private writing; even though some self-censorship was still at work, they provided a relief from the anxiety generated by the desire to meet the audience's expectations commonly associated with the published works. The role of the Papers can then be viewed as that of a lamp shedding light on the construction of the main and previously published works through the disclosure of a deeper and essential structure.

This study focuses on the experimental aspect of some of the fictional pieces of the posthumously published Papers—a selection from *Fables of Man, Which Was the Dream?, Satires and Burlesques,* and *The Mysterious Stranger Manuscripts.* Twain's recurrent experimentation in these writings stems from a concept of form as the result of the free-associative mind, which he formulated later in life while dealing with the construction of his *Autobiography.* He wrote:

> Finally in Florence, in 1904, I hit upon the right way to do an Autobiography: Start it at no particular time of your life; wander at your free will all over your life; talk only about the thing which interests you for the moment; drop it at the moment its interest threatens to pale, and turn your talk upon the new and more interesting thing that has intruded itself into your mind meantime.
>
> I'm not interested in getting done with anything. I am only interested in talking along and wandering around as much as I want to, regardless of results to the future reader.[2]

Even though in this quotation Twain is dealing specifically with the writing of his autobiography, his words reveal an attitude that can be used as an interpretive key to a large portion of his posthumously published works. What Twain seems to be describing here is digression as a formal principle. The mind creates thoughts through a process of free association: The text reflects this process directly. The text becomes an unmediated product, the result of an attempted symbiosis between word and thought. The wandering of the mind becomes the wandering of words in the text. Such writing, which can only be an ideal and a tendency, is meant to transcend the separation between written and oral performances, the oral (note Twain's insistence on "talk") being the unmediated thought becoming utterance. The ideal writing Twain wants to achieve is a paradox and a contradiction in itself: a writing that is spoken word, uncensored and unrestrained, and yet has the permanence characteristic of writing and not of orality.

This writing, which struggles to be spoken word, does not envisage an addressee, an audience, a listener, a reader: The written/spoken word is in fact thought. This is why the "digressive principle"—the principle of free association of thought extended to both written and oral performance—is a key to Twain's later conception of form. The ideal text resulting from this formal principle is a written/oral, conscious/subconscious text.

All the elements of this formal principle are relevant for our understanding of Twain's later works. It is a largely acknowledged fact that in his earlier career Twain was greatly influenced by the oral tradition of the southwestern frontier, of which he was one of the codifiers. This experience remained as a crucial fact in Twain's perception of the relation between oral and written language. He viewed the artificiality and the distance of the written form from the "original" as limitations. This attitude, so central to Twain's early training, is also a recurrent feature of his experimental phase. The other pair of opposed elements, conscious/subconscious, is strictly related to this conception of language; not only is the ideal text one in which the written equals the oral—a zero degree of writing, as the structuralists would call it—but it is one in which the difference between conscious and subconscious thought is overcome through a wandering of thought and voice that finds its unity and expression in the ideal written text.[3]

The merging of different styles, language patterns, worldviews, and literary genres marks such a text. The image that captures its essence is that of duplication (the frenzied duplication of both books and characters in "No. 44"), where the fragmentation of the self and the proliferation of signs and texts parallel each other. Duplication seems indeed the metaphor that crystallizes more powerfully the form and orientation of Twain's experimentation in his later and posthumously published works—hence the title of this study.

To whom would Twain's ideal text be addressed? To whom are the Papers addressed? Twain was often quite explicit in his statements about his wish to write for himself or for a distant posterity who could be the only appropriate audience for his message. This applies to a part of the Papers as well as to the *Autobiography*. Among various statements in his fictions, letters, notebooks, and interviews is a well-known letter to William Dean Howells, which Twain started on 12 May 1899, that refers to the writing of "The Chronicle of Young Satan":

For several years I have been intending to stop writing for print as soon as I could afford it. At last I can afford it, and have put the pot-boiler pen away. What I have been wanting was a chance to write a book without reserves—a book which should take account of no one's hopes, illusions, delusions; a book which should say my say, right out of my heart, in the plainest language and without a limitation of any sort. I judged that that would be an unimaginable luxury, heaven on earth. There was no condition but one under which the writing of such a book could be possible; only one—the consciousness that it would not see print. It is under way, now, and it is a luxury! an intellectual drunk.[4]

Twain was, however, quite inconsistent in both his actions and statements: He had part of the *Autobiography* published while he was still alive and sought publication for some pieces now included in the published Papers—more specifically in *The Fables of Man*. He also wrote letters expressing the intention of completing his unfinished works and having them published.[5] This ambivalence of behavior suggests a problem at the core of the writer's attitude toward his writing and his audience.

The impasse in which Twain found himself at the end of his career follows inevitably from the concept of language underlined above, as well as from the development of his middle and later literary phases. The idea of a form approximating the spoken word and the uncensored thought was at odds with the audience whose approval he had sought for most of his literary career, as well as with the family and literary censors whom he had elected to revise his work. In seeking that approval he had progressively moved from the codification of popular sources to the imitation of well-established and widely accepted genres. This is the literary distance that separates *Adventures of Huckleberry Finn* (1884) from *Personal Recollections of Joan of Arc* (1896). It is the distance, in other words, between a dynamic concept of genre and a static one, between the attempts to innovate literary forms through the mixture of higher and lower genres (the simultaneous presence of different levels of language) and the conformity to both the canon and the genres codified by a social and literary elite. However, even in Twain's conformist works, it is possible to find traces of the popular culture and oral utterance that had shaped his better and more original works. *The Prince and the Pauper* is based upon a fairy-tale fable; *Personal Recollections of Joan of Arc* is narrated by a personal witness to the events. In both "romances" a popular fairy-tale quality is preserved as a trace of the oral tradition.

It is clear that during the later successful, and yet minor, phase of his career, Twain found himself at an impasse: His underlying conception of language and literary form diverged from the language and form of the works he was having published. The audience whose approval he sought and conquered would not accept the wild streak, the satirical and outspoken tone, and the experimental extravaganza of his secret writings. His Papers, being a way out of this impasse, had to take the form of private writing. He must have conceived the ideal addressee of these writings as a distant posterity, an open-minded "other." Through this deferral of communication he tried to avoid the censorship that he feared might come for either political, moral, or purely literary reasons.

In this respect, the fictional pieces throw a better light on the writer's sentiment than any extratextual sources, which are quite contradictory on the specific issue. For example, in "The Secret History of Eddypus, the World Empire," Twain creates a character, Mark Twain the Father of History, personifying his concern with the problem of delayed publication; throughout the fictional pieces, and in particular in "No. 44," the recurring metaphors of writing and printing further attest to Twain's pungent interest in the creative process, the relation between author and audience, and the cultural impact of literary products. Like many fiction writers, Twain gives voice to his literary concerns in a less ambivalent, although more complex, way through his literary medium—fiction.

We can very well say that the private or semiprivate writings are often the expression of Twain's self-censoring attitude toward his later experimental production. He had a split awareness of his literary self, which was linked to an ambivalent yet keen perception of the expectations of the reading public; equally strong impulses to please and amuse his public, and to spite and shock it, tore him apart. Although the prospect of writing privately must have been appealing to him because it would allow him to enjoy a much sought-after freedom of expression, Twain, like any professional writer, must have found it difficult to give up altogether the idea of publishing the writings that he had been working on for so long and to reestablish a link with his own audience.

This accounts for the contradictory statements about publication made in letters, notebooks, and fiction. In any case, when dealing with this problem, one should keep in mind that eventually Twain did not publish a large portion of the works he had written during his later years. Twain's troubled and divided awareness found artistic expression in the Papers. Their history can not be told and understood without taking into account Twain's own attitude toward his unpublished work—an attitude of self-censorship that probably influenced his early editors and led them to censorship that excluded the posthumous material from publication for over fifty years; it might also have affected the scholarly approach and critical attention the Papers were given. The wheel went full circle: The social pressure that Twain had internalized was turned over, at his death, to his editors and critics. It is for this reason that a study of the Papers starts with a look at the history of their delayed publication, the scholarly work done on them so far, and the critical reception they received.

The Mark Twain Papers and the Critics: Self-Censorship and Censorship

Among the numberless conflicts that have characterized the troubled Russian-American relationship during this century, one particular episode is also part of the equally tormented history of the Mark Twain Papers: the patriotic exchange between the Russian critic Bereznitski and the American scholar Charles Neider.[6] On the occasion of the 1959 American Exhibit in Moscow, where Neider's edition of *The Autobiography of Mark Twain* was on display, *Literaturnaya Gazeta* (Moscow Literary Gazette) published a harsh criticism of that work. The charge against American literary scholarship in general, and Neider in particular, was that they had attempted to obliterate Mark Twain's true image through the suppression of his posthumous papers, which, almost fifty years after his death, had not yet been published. Neider himself was accused of omitting from the *Autobiography* parts in which Twain launched an attack on institutionalized religion and American politics, although he had included insignificant anecdotes.[7]

In his reply, published by *Literaturnaya Gazeta*, Neider, besides insisting on the absolute freedom of American criticism, defended his own method of editing. The basic assumption behind it was that "Mark Twain is essentially a great fabulist and not a great maker of political utterances."[8] He also pointed out that Bernard De Voto had already published Twain's political passages in 1940 in *Mark Twain in Eruption*.

Bereznitski's attacks in his answer were more specific and less personal than in his previous letter. He shifted the attack to American censorship of Twain's work. He came up with some facts: namely, the exclusion of *Adventures of Huckleberry Finn* from some Connecticut public libraries at its publication; the crossing out of *A Connecticut Yankee in King Arthur's Court* from the list of literature permitted for reading in the New York City public schools in 1949; the exclusion of *Huckleberry Finn* from these institutions (as demanded by Senator Joseph McCarthy and obtained in 1957); and the 1957 television production in which Jim was struck from the cast of characters in order to provide an "all-white entertainment."

Neider's second reply, which was not published by the Russian magazine, added only one new element to the dispute: the admission that part of the responsibility for the omissions had to be ascribed to Clara Clemens, Twain's daughter, who had opposed the publication of the chapters on religion in Twain's autobiography.[9]

The Neider/Bereznitski dispute, even though making news at the time, did not have any significant consequences and may seem only a minor episode. Yet this study of the history of the Papers starts with it because, from the chronological standpoint, the incident marks the end of an era; only a few years later the University of California Press started the publication of the Papers, a turning point that initiated a completely new trend in Twain scholarship. The Neider/Bereznitski incident could then be viewed as one of the last debates over whether to publish the still-unpublished manuscripts. However, some of the attitudes and opinions displayed by the two critics were not suddenly and totally superseded by the University of California Press publication.

Some of the critical tendencies that seem to oppose each other in this debate split between ideologically and aesthetically oriented approaches. Critics who favored the former often viewed the Papers as enlightening progressive documents revealing Twain's role as an American prophet and a social reformer; on the other hand, those critics who espoused an aesthetic approach were set back by the Papers' unfinishedness, their lack of apparent order, and whatever else could upset an already fixed image of Twain as *the* American humorist. Thus, while Bereznitski was essentially interested in Twain's philosophical attitudes, or even more specifically in his political opinions, Neider valued mainly those passages that suited his aesthetic taste. Both used a rather idiosyncratic principle in their choice and evaluation of Twain's work. Bereznitski, who had not read the Papers, was under the false assumption that all of Twain's opinions were critical of American society, its economic system, and its imperialistic expansionism. He ignored Twain's political and philosophical ambivalence. Neider's aesthetic evaluation was just as restrictive because it was based on a concept of literature and genre as totally unchangeable entities; he excluded what was not humorous in Twain because it would not conform to the generally accepted idea of Twain as a humorist; he discarded whatever was unfinished and fragmentary because it did not comply with his aesthetic ideals.

On the whole, Twain's early editors and critics were concerned with preserving a genteel image of the writer, and therefore censored whatever might upset such an image in readers' eyes. It must be said, however, that publishing Twain's posthumous works must have been a very difficult task. Paine, Twain's first editor, was left at the writer's death with thousands of pages in a state of indescribable disorder. In his editing of *The Mysterious Stranger, a Romance*, he used mainly what he thought to be the last version of the work and attached to it a final chapter that he pretended to have found later and to have assumed was related to that particular version. Apart from these falsifications, he also censored what seemed to him outspoken statements about religion and politics and deleted expressions that he found too crude or too rough. He applied the same principle to his editing of the *Autobiography*. Even though he followed the writer's order of writing and/or dictation, he excluded from publication the most explicit ideological passages. Later, De Voto endeavored to collect and publish these discarded passages in *Mark Twain in Eruption*. There too, however, a violation occurred: The material was organized by subject matter, a quite different principle from Twain's idea of composition based on the principle of association of thought. Furthermore, in his subsequent editing of *Letters from the Earth*, De Voto censored the sexual references in the text.

In the case of Neider's editing of the *Autobiography,* one should emphasize again his disregard of Twain's principle of composition. The reorganizing of the autobiographical material according to chronological order shows a total misunderstanding of an important aspect of Twain's activity as a writer—his formal experimentalism.

Among the various problems facing Twain's editors, the writer's self-censoring attitude was probably the worst. Twain's injunction not to publish some of his more outspoken words until many years, or even centuries, after his death can be found in various forms throughout his works and letters. One often-quoted example is included in a letter he addressed to Howells the day preceding the dictation of the chapters on religion that Neider had such a hard time publishing fifty years later: "Tomorrow I mean to dictate a chapter, which will get my heirs & assigns burnt alive if they venture to print it this side of 2006 A.D.— which I judge they won't."[10] Another example is his project to write a subscription book dealing with lynching to be entitled "History of Lynching" or "Rise and Progress of Lynching." Later on, however, Twain, ever mindful of the financial aspect of his enterprises, decided not to have the book printed, lest it might make him lose his southern audience.[11]

What made Twain so cautious? His religious doubts were shared by many of his contemporaries. Even in his discontent with capitalism and in his opposition to American imperialism he was not an isolated figure.[12] Yet he often expressed fear of the scandal that might ensue from the publication of his opinions. Was such caution due to Twain's image of his audience, or to his own self-image? In a public figure such as he was for more than half of his life the two images can hardly be separated. They merged into one persona consisting of a double personality: the image that he wanted his public to see in him and the image that he perceived the public saw in him. From this duality most of his ambivalence derived. Twain was fully aware that the public saw in him "the funny fellow," the public persona he had created and called Mark Twain.[13] To the very end he was tempted to challenge this public image and yet did not do so. It is likely that this restraint did not derive from excessive caution, but rather from a deep perception of his own separateness and fragmentation. The image that he had created for his reading public and his audience as Mark Twain was, as the name itself suggests, his second self—a self powerful enough, however, to obliterate his original, his creator. Quite often, when Twain wanted to give voice to the other self—his original and private self—he hesitated, suppressed his own expression through delaying publication, or went anonymous. An example of this is "The Curious Republic of Gondour," a utopian novella that he published under a different and fanciful name. The content of the novella was not at all scandalous, yet Twain did not dare use his name for publication because of the seriousness of the subject. He did not want it to be read and discarded as a comic story. Twain was aware of the readers' horizons of expectation, of the expectations that his signature created because of the genre with which it would be associated. This keen awareness certainly must have contributed to shaping the personal myth so central to the writing and the subsequent suppression of the Papers—Twain's personal myth of the suppressed artist.[14] The myth shaped the Papers into their fragmented and unfinished form. They voiced, at the same time, a need for expression beyond censorship and a need to be censored, suppressed, unpublished.

The censoring and self-censoring of his works created problems for his editors: Publication of what he had left unpublished might mean a violation of his will. They were, however, mindful that Twain himself was in the habit of contradicting his own declared intentions of suppressing writings by having them published, or by simply stating the opposite intention. This dilemma created by Twain's own uncertainty must have been aggravated by the external pressures created during the witch-hunting period of the fifties, when his main work became a casualty. In the sixties, a general change in the political climate, as well as a more rigorously philological attitude on the part of the scholars involved in the study of the Papers, eventually influenced the publication of all the major unpublished works by Twain.

The Mark Twain Project, under the direction of Frederick Anderson (fifth editor of the Mark Twain Papers, from 1964 to 1979) and then, after Anderson's death in 1979, under the direction of Robert H. Hirst, has expanded enormously. It has become both a thorough collection of all Twain's manuscripts and a publishing and editing enterprise that produces new editions of Twain's published works (in the Iowa-California series) and critical editions of his unpublished works (in the Mark Twain Papers series).[15]

To date, the Mark Twain Papers published by the University of California Press consist of five volumes of fictional material: *Mark Twain's Satires and Burlesques* (1967); *Mark Twain's Which Was the*

Dream? and Other Symbolic Writings of the Later Years (1967); *Mark Twain's Hannibal, Huck and Tom* (1969); *Mark Twain's Mysterious Stranger Manuscripts* (1969); and *Mark Twain's Fables of Man* (1972); three volumes of correspondence: *Mark Twain's Letters to His Publishers* (1967), *Mark Twain's Correspondence with Henry Huttlestone Rogers* (1969), and *Mark Twain's Letters* (1988); and three volumes of *Mark Twain's Journals and Notebooks*. The journals and notebooks from 1891 up to Twain's last years, numerous letters, and some fictional pieces are still unpublished.

The first two volumes of fictional pieces came out in 1967: *Mark Twain's Satires and Burlesques* and *Mark Twain's Which Was the Dream? and Other Symbolic Writings of the Later Years*. The former, edited by Franklin Rogers, collected burlesques that Twain wrote over a long period.[16] The other volume, edited by John S. Tuckey, concentrated on Twain's later fantastic stories, written between 1896 and 1905.[17]

In 1969, two more volumes came out: *Mark Twain's Hannibal, Huck and Tom,* edited by Walter Blair, and *The Mysterious Stranger Manuscripts,* edited by William M. Gibson. The former collection includes unpublished materials—except for the "Jane Lampton Clemens" biographical essay, part of which had appeared in Paine's edition of Twain's autobiography. The pieces were composed during 1876–84 and 1897–99.[18]

The other volume that came out in 1969 can be considered the major philological discovery brought about by the publication of the Papers. It follows, and is strictly connected with, John S. Tuckey's book *Mark Twain and Little Satan,* in which the Paine-Duneka edition of *The Mysterious Stranger, a Romance* is shown to be a fraud. The 1969 volume offered evidence of what Tuckey had found out and denounced in his 1963 book.[19] The University of California Press volume provides the three manuscripts together with Twain's working notes, a notebook entry about "little Satan, jr.," and a discarded page of a surviving manuscript included in the appendix.

The last volume of fictional pieces to appear was *Mark Twain's Fables of Man,* published in 1972 and edited by Tuckey. The unifying element in this collection of pieces written over a long period of time is the outspoken tone of the prose. Some of the pieces had already been printed by De Voto and Paine, but none had appeared in an authoritative edition.[20]

The merit of the Papers is obvious. Not only do they disclose a side of Twain's thought, but they also present the author at work,

experimenting with narrative devices, with motifs, and with the problem of form. Yet there has been resistance among the critics to deal
with the new materials: The scholarly work done on them is still slight
if compared with the wealth of scholarship devoted to the rest of Twain's
works.

A very explicit dismissal of the Papers comes from one of the most
brilliant studies of his work, James M. Cox's *Mark Twain: The Fate of
Humor* (1966):

> Tuckey's findings do not invalidate so much as they define
> Paine's text of *The Mysterious Stranger*. Though clearly edited
> by Paine, that text just as clearly is not going to be superseded
> by any future text . . . the point remains that there is no text of
> the story—that far from finding his intentions as he proceeds
> from version to version of his story (as De Voto wishes to believe),
> Mark Twain lost it. What he found instead was a new editor to
> replace the lost Olivia Langdon Clemens. . . . In the last analysis,
> Mark Twain discovered in Paine the editorial intention which
> he had lost: thus Paine's posthumous edition of Mark Twain's
> last work is the closest thing to Mark Twain's intention that we
> shall ever have.[21]

Tuckey's philological discovery is dismissed by Cox in the name of a
central concern of his critical method: the search for the authorial
intention. The Papers as a whole also are dismissed in compliance with
this approach: Whatever is not revised, completed, and published by
the author cannot be regarded as consistent with the author's intention.
According to this principle, the very center of the work resides in a
conscious act of will, which in turn implies the belief in a lucid center
in the text. This perspective inevitably excludes the possibility of the
existence of multiple and conflicting intentions and of different levels
of consciousness involved in creative activity. Experimentation cannot
be accounted for by such a vision.

Cox does not stand alone. As late as 1971, John May, in an article
studying the narrative structure of *The Mysterious Stranger,* also used
the Paine edition.[22] The rest of the Papers, with the exception of "The
Great Dark," have been given even worse treatment: either totally ignored or dismissed as the product of a period of failure. Only recently
have scholarly studies devoted to the Papers assessed their literary value.

What prevented the earlier critics and editors from paying due attention to the Papers? What is the critical prejudice standing behind this rejection of an important aspect of Twain's work, his formal experimentalism?

In 1920 Van Wyck Brooks's *The Ordeal of Mark Twain,* a work vaguely inspired by Freudian theories, set the tone for a discussion of Twain's last phase that extended over a few decades. Brooks ascribes Twain's despair during the last years of his life to the suppression of his artistic talent. A victim of the Gilded Age, of the commercialism and financial greed of the time, Twain, whose creative impulse had already been thwarted early in life by his sternly Calvinistic mother and by the illiterate vulgarity of the western environment where he grew up, became the victim of his wife's prudishness; in her censorship he found the substitute for his mother's strongly repressive role. Guilt feelings and the need to repress his natural vitality in order to conform to his mother's wishes and, later, to his wife's high standards of gentility created a bitterness in him, "the result of having transgressed some inalienable life-demand peculiar to one's nature."[23]

In *Mark Twain's America* Bernard De Voto reacts to Van Wyck Brooks's charge against the frontier by defending its culture.[24] This reassessment of the cultural heritage of the western frontier and its positive influence in shaping Twain's artistic production has been pursued in a series of works, such as Minnie Brashear's *Mark Twain, Son of Missouri* (1934), Constance Rourke's *American Humor: A Study of the National Character* (1931), Walter Blair's *Mark Twain and Huck Finn* (1960), Kenneth S. Lynn's *Mark Twain and Southwestern Humor* (1961), Daniel Hoffman's *Form and Fable in American Fiction* (1961), and, more recently, Walter Blair's and Hamlin Hill's *America's Humor: From Poor Richard to Doonesbury* (1978). Although quite different in approach, literary perspective, and conclusions, all these works follow a trend established by De Voto in his reaction against Brooks's denigration of the western background.

De Voto accounts for Twain's later pessimism in *Mark Twain at Work* (1942): He explains how a series of personal griefs and financial disasters brought the writer to the brink of despair and madness. In his work, mainly in some unfinished stories of the period, Twain tries to portray his personal experience in symbolic terms: His last works, far from being sheer failures, are the true symbols of his despair.[25]

Both Brooks's and De Voto's studies of Twain include seminal ideas. Brooks's concept of the suppressed artist is echoed forty years later by

Cox, who uses it as a starting point and then reverses the argument by showing how Twain, far from being the victim of his wife's censoring role, had internalized the myth of the suppressed artist and therefore sought the repressive role in others as the necessary constraint from which his humor would spring. We have also seen that De Voto's book on the influence of the frontier on Twain's art was followed by other studies of the tradition of southwestern folklore: Among these, a particularly interesting work is Lynn's *Southwestern Humor*. Just as Cox had eventually turned around Brooks's argument, Lynn turns around De Voto's. After showing the importance of the southwestern background, which he explores quite thoroughly, Lynn indicates how Twain, although influenced by that tradition, reacted against it and reversed both the ideological and formal terms of the frontier experience.[26]

Moreover, De Voto's perception of Twain's later symbolical writings as symbols of despair was echoed by Tony Tanner's "The Lost America—The Despair of Henry Adams and Mark Twain," in which the British critic, taking a sociohistorical rather than biographical approach, suggests that Twain's despair had to be ascribed to his difficulty in adjusting to the tremendous social and technological changes brought about at the turn of the century. In Tanner's opinion, "The Great Dark," rather than being a portrayal in symbolical terms of the personal despair of the writer, reflects the image of an epoch of change and upheaval.[27] De Voto's opinion is later followed and expanded by Tuckey's "Introduction" to his edition of *Which Was the Dream?*, where he explores the relation between the author's personal imagery and the symbolic images in his later works.[28]

Despite their intrinsic value and the vast influence they had for a long time over so many eminent critical works, Brooks's and De Voto's early books are also responsible for limits and flaws widespread among critics of Twain. First of all, both their approaches are essentially biographical. From their works one gets the impression that the value of a writer resides mostly in his life and personality, rather than in his work. Life then becomes the subject of analysis because the intention of the artist is sought in his life rather than in his works. Up to the sixties a large part of Twain scholarship followed that course. This kind of approach is limited because it rests on the presupposition that the failures of the work can only be explained by the failures of the life. The result is that the only way some of Twain's later works were read was in terms of his personal griefs and failures. Brooks emphasizes the role of early suppression and later censorship, while De Voto points out the disasters of the later years: Life is made responsible for art. Part of the critical dismissal the Papers were subjected to stemmed from the biographical bent of the early criticism. Their incompleteness and fragmentary form validated the aura of failure that had surrounded them from the very beginning.

The Papers were then neglected, forgotten, censored. Bereznitski was right. However, this neglect and dismissal can be ascribed only partly to political reasons. Even some of the major critical works written in the sixties touch but briefly on the Papers; when they do so, it is often solely to express a totally negative evaluation. In *Mark Twain: The Development of a Writer* (1962), Henry Nash Smith, for many years the custodian of the Papers, does not deal with the Papers at all and, when discussing rather briefly *The Mysterious Stranger*, mentions the existence of another manuscript version different from the one Paine had published. Yet he concludes: "The question is . . . not crucial, for in all the versions Mark Twain clearly intends to adopt the perspective of a transcendent observer in order to depict human experience as meaningless."[29] Thus the manuscript is dismissed and Tuckey's discovery of the four versions is undermined by one of the most eminent custodians of the Papers.

The same neglect of the Papers characterized other major works of that period, such as Pascal Covici's *Mark Twain's Humor: The Image of a World* (1962) and William Spengemann's *Mark Twain and the Backwood Angels* (1966). However, Lynn's *Southwestern Humor* (1959), Stone's *The Innocent Eye* (1961), and Salomon's *Twain and the Image of History* (1961) all discuss the Papers. Lynn points out the journey motif in Twain's later stories and suggests the influence of Poe's Gordon Pym on such "dream narratives" as "The Great Dark": "It is the sense that Twain's projected novel conveys of a world going out of control which brings the story of the Edwardses close to Poe."[30] He also suggests that the name of the protagonists, Edwards, might be an indirect reference to Jonathan Edwards. In fact, after reading *Freedom of the Will*, Twain had remarked, "the book seemed illuminated by the glare of a resplendent intellect gone mad."[31] In dealing with *The Mysterious Stranger*, Lynn discusses the three manuscript versions; however, he follows De Voto's assumption that the Eseldorf version is the third and final one. This is understandable, considering that Tuckey's discovery had not been made yet.

Stone traces the influence of contemporary works on Mark Twain's later phase as he observes the interplay of despair and sentimentality in *The Mysterious Stranger*. He deals with two versions, the Hannibal and the Eseldorf. In his discussion of the role of childhood in Twain's work, Stone touches upon an unpublished story, "Little Bessie Would Assist Providence," a satirical dialogue "wholly characteristic of the other side of his mind . . . the side that admired Jonathan Swift . . . and created Philip Traum."[32]

Salomon discusses Twain's historical vision. He devotes part of his study to "The Secret History of Eddypus, the World Empire," tracing Twain's evolution from an early progressive attitude to a later pessimistic cyclical interpretation of history that emerges clearly in the posthumously published short novel.[33]

These three works pay tribute to the Papers by showing that, in spite of the moods of despair they express, they are pieces of literature the critics can regard and study as powerful utterances of one side of Twain's genius. These studies tend to show the link with previous works in which patterns emerging in the Papers are already present. This reflects a substantial change in critical attitudes that once had either dismissed the Papers or regarded them as the direct mirror of the failures of life. In the 1970s, when most of the fictions of the Papers had been published (only *Fables of Man* came out in 1972) some scholars still resisted discussing the newly published material. J. R. May's study of the narrative structures of *The Mysterious Stranger* has already been mentioned. Hamlin Hill's interesting and iconoclastic biography of Twain's later years is a total dismissal of the artistic value of the Papers as well.[34] Randi Nelson's dissertation dismisses *The Mysterious Stranger Manuscripts*, though not the Papers as a whole.

Among essays that deal with parts of the Papers, Ellwood Johnson's "Mark Twain's Dream Self in the Nightmare of History" defines Twain's determinism in terms of idealism;[35] Stanley Brodwin's "Mark Twain's Masks of Satan: The Final Phase" deals with the existing relation between Twain's concept of the creative artist and the character of Satan.[36] In *The Mysterious Stranger*, Brodwin sees an attempt at a reconciliation of different and opposed philosophies. Two more works of the seventies need to be mentioned: Paul Delaney's "The Dissolving Self: The Narrators of the Mysterious Stranger Fragments"[37] and Richard Tuerk's "Appearance and Reality in Mark Twain's 'Which Was the Dream,' 'The Great Dark' and 'Which Was It?' "[38]

The major novelty in the criticism of the Papers in the seventies is represented by three outstanding books, of which two are devoted exclusively to their study. Gibson's *The Art of Mark Twain* (1976) devotes a final chapter to the discussion of *The Mysterious Stranger Manuscripts;* the focus, however, is on the first version, "Chronicle of Young Satan," which Gibson regards as the most successful artistically. He finds the last version, "No. 44," too fragmentary and unrevised, interesting but flawed. Sholom Kahn's *Mark Twain's Mysterious Stranger: A Study of the Manuscript Texts* (1978) supports a totally opposed view. The Israeli scholar makes the point that the third version is indeed the best one, the most artistically successful, the one toward which all of Twain's experimental efforts were geared. Kahn also sees the three versions as distinctive works, each with its own characteristics—not really three versions, but rather three works sharing some common patterns and similar traits, as is always the case with the works of a single writer. Mcnaughton's *Mark Twain's Last Years as a Writer* (1979) is a very accurate, interesting, and faithful reconstruction of Twain's literary activity during the last fifteen years of his life. To these books one should add David Ketterer's excellent article on Mark Twain's science-fictional motifs in "The Great Dark" and "The Secret History of Eddypus."

Kahn's work is the most useful for the purpose of this study. It marks a real turning point in the history of the criticism of the Mark Twain Papers, being a close reading of what can be considered the major work of the Mark Twain Project. Unlike previous books (namely, Tuckey's, Gibson's, and Mcnaughton's) Kahn's is not a philologically oriented study. With great assertiveness, he makes a clear break with the works that up to the sixties had contributed in various ways to one of the most powerful myths of American letters: the myth of Twain's despair in his later phase. He ignores this myth: He discusses the literary merits of the work of the writer and draws no hypothetical conclusions based upon Twain's life.

An interesting aspect of Twain studies in the seventies is the development of two groups of scholars supporting opposite views concerning the literary value of Twain's later writings. At the 1979 MLA convention in San Francisco representatives of the "idolators" (Sholom Kahn and John S. Tuckey) and the "iconoclasts" (Hamlin Hill and Lewis Leary) presented papers supporting their different perspectives.[39]

In the eighties, several important works deal, at least partly, with the posthumously published Papers. Susan K. Harris, in *Mark Twain's Escape from Time* (1982), traces Twain's recurrent escape patterns throughout his works, including the posthumously published material; a whole chapter of her study is devoted to "No. 44." Most of the essays in the collection *The Mythologizing of Mark Twain* (1984), edited by Sara de Saussure Davis and Philip D. Beidler, discuss the Papers while dealing with the various aspects of the writer's mythical attitudes. Robert Sewell's *Mark Twain's Languages* (1987) observes the solipsistic quality of the language in some of the posthumously published fictions. Finally, both Louis J. Budd in *Our Mark Twain* (1983) and Everett Emerson in *The Authentic Mark Twain* (1984) refer to and include parts from both the posthumously published Papers and the still-unpublished material at the Bancroft Library in care of the Mark Twain Project. Budd explores the complex implications of Twain's public persona, thus accounting for the ambivalence that surfaces in the later writings. In his biographical study, Emerson considers the more personal aspects of Twain's dark writings; he accounts for their unevenness, fragmentation, and incompleteness by the writer's tendency toward manic depression.

The Mark Twain Papers: Establishing a Method of Reading

The deferral is over: The message has reached its addressees. Yet are we the distant hypothetical readers of posterity that Twain had envisaged for the Papers? The message has indeed reached us, readers of the seventies and eighties, but we have no way of knowing whether we are really the readers implied in the texts, the posterity the author had in mind; we are faced with the impossibility of probing his intentions on this one point. We don't know whether Twain would have liked, instead, to wait longer before publishing his Papers. But as the texts have been published, it is our task now to decode their message. How do we do this?

As readers of today we see the text from a perspective determined by the knowledge we have of our present world and by the knowledge that our time assumes. We bring this awareness to the text, a text that was conceived with a dissimilar awareness, a knowledge and perspective linked to a different time. Our awareness, our knowledge, and our perspective make up our world of reference. There is, however, another world of reference—the world of the author—in this case, of Twain. His system of knowledge and belief relates to the world as it was seen at the turn of the century. Such a system is part of the text: It is its context.

A contextual perspective would lead us to explore the sociohistorical and philosophical background that may have influenced the author in the making of the text, while a reader-response approach would enable us to see the text as a verbal construct determined by the readers' horizons of expectations and world of reference. The formula encompasses two different concepts: the actual response that readers of various eras have given to a certain text and the internalized reader implied in the text, and born out of the author's awareness of the act of communication involved in writing.[40]

Even though nobody can deny the importance of a study of the historical and philosophical background of the work, which can provide further insights into the text, still one can assume that texts have enough autonomy to be readable without the reader's constant probing of the external context in order to understand the message. A relatively new trend in modern literary theory, the "new historicism," insists on the constant relationship between the text and its historical background. Without ever denying the existence of such an inherent link between a work of art and history, this study does not linger on it. One should note, on the one hand, that the connection between Twain's work and sociohistorical circumstances has already been explored exhaustively by other scholarly works with biographical and historical orientations. On the other hand, the text contains its context embedded in it. Because of its internal context, the text is related to the outer world—meaning not so much the world of events, but rather that of discourse. This openness of the text exists beyond time, because the text is not only meant for the readers of the time and place when and where it is written, but also for readers of any time and place. It is this openness to the future that legitimizes a contemporary approach to the text. In reading Twain, modern critics are entitled to use the knowledge of their time, their "encyclopedia," and their world of reference. If they look at the text through the perspective of theories conceived or codified after the time of composition, they do not do so out of disregard for the chronology and circumstances related to such composition, but simply because they do not see the text as a closed and finished product, limited to its own time and place of production. The literary text, because of the very nature of language, is not an antique to be relegated to a museum, but rather an antique being relocated, for everyday use, in an environment it shares with other objects from different times and places.

It is clear from what I have said thus far that, in this study, I regard the literary text as a product of verbal communication consisting of signs related to other signs. Its meaning cannot be contained in a single sign, but rather in a series of signs related as if in an endless chain or as a series of mirrors reflecting each other. Just as the signs in the text refer to more signs, so do the readers' interpretations of them. If the text is open to other texts, the present reading of it, which is not final, is likewise; it can only be a temporary closure.

The private character of parts of the Papers calls for further consideration of the concept of the implied reader. We have to keep in mind that, viewed as a speech act, the writing act is never totally private, never really solipsistic: It will always have an addressee. In spite of Twain's frequently declared exclusion of the contemporary reader from his intended later writing activity, a reader is nonetheless implied in the texts. We are then faced with the problem of deciding whether the implied reader of the Papers has to be limited to the posterity vaguely envisaged by Twain. His unconscious conception of an audience—any audience—was certainly based upon his perception of the contemporary audience of whose generic expectations he was aware. This unconscious conception must have inevitably influenced his conscious production. Furthermore, in spite of its exclusion and because of its denial, the contemporary reader is present in the Papers as a resurgent repressed element. The reader implied in the Papers is thus also the contemporary reader of the 1890s. Yet the recurring denials of communication affect the composition of the Papers, because the generic expectations connected to the contemporary public are often violated. If the role of the contemporary reader is somewhat downplayed, then the openness to the unidentified future reader is increased. Given this precarious balance, interpretation can only be an act of cooperation between author and reader, resulting from the meeting and overlapping of two worlds of reference as well as of two acts, the reading and the writing acts.

The text is the object of hermeneutics; it is viewed as a verbal construct of communication in which a message is sent by an author to an audience. In order to exist as such, the literary message has to refer to a system—that is, literature with its specific cultural codes. The activity of interpretation, as the present study suggests, should start from the purely denotative level of the textual message, should reconstruct the recurrent semantic elements—the isotopies—and explore the connotations until the global meaning of the text is revealed. In order to reach a full understanding of the text one should explore its signs, the interaction between signifier and signified.[41] Such a semiotic approach to the text is not only synchronic but also diachronic: It verifies the relation of the various parts of the text and also explores the evolution of codes of the canon. Related to historical evolution, these codes are embedded in the text.

Roman Jakobson's well-known definition of the process of communication and its six components—message, addresser, addressee, context, code, contact—inspires the concept of the literary text as a verbal construct.[42] The definition has often been used to explore the literary text, adjusting Jakobson's original scheme to fit the peculiarities of written texts. Following Jakobson's definition, we can say that the message is the object of the literary text (its core, its meaning, both its form and content); the addresser is the author; the addressee is the reader (all the readers that will read or have read the work); the context is any circumstance involved in the text; the code is the language in which it is written, as well as the literary conventions of the genre the work either accepts or reacts against; and the contact is the manuscript or typescript through which it is transmitted to the public.

The different components of the text respond to different functions that, in turn, are related to other hermeneutic activities.[43] These range from conventional close reading to narratology and deconstruction (study of the message); from biographical studies to early Freudian research based on the psychoanalysis of the author (study of the addresser); from inquiry into the reception of the work by the public to a reader-response approach (study of the addressee); from research into the historical circumstances surrounding the work to examination of philosophical and psychological systems of thought (study of the context); from research on generic discourse to that on literary or oral traditions (study of the code); and finally, to the philological study of the manuscript in its various forms (study of the contact).[44]

The appeal of Jakobson's definition of communication applied to the literary text is that it suggests a thorough conception of the text, legitimizing a vast number of critical approaches. One should add a further consideration: Neither the various functions of the literary text, nor the critical activities focused on each function, can be separated easily from each other. For example, an analysis of the message and of the functions of the various characters is related to that of the genres in which given functions are predominant; this creates a connection between message and code. Moreover, while dealing with problems of genre, one should consider the readers' expectations that determine the genre, and thus trace the relation between code and addressee. Nor should one separate addresser from code and addressee; the author's intentions are influenced by both generic conventions and the contemporary audience.

In this respect a very useful work is Henry Nash Smith's *Democracy and the Novel: Popular Resistance to Classic American Writers*, which traces the relation between the reading public and nineteenth-century American novelists.[45] Smith argues that Twain's choice, at the beginning of his career, to address himself to the subscription audience—a rather unsophisticated and lowbrow audience—resulted in a remarkable advantage. It allowed him "to free himself from the dominant literary conventions" and to find new forms of expression through "drastic revisions in existing genres."[46] Later Twain addressed himself to the middlebrow, genteel audience of the literary monthlies, especially the *Atlantic,* but he was never really at ease with that reading public. His works bear traces of the conflict. Several studies devoted to Twain's later phase investigate the author's attitude toward his work. Both Tuckey and Mcnaughton regard Twain's experimental attitude mostly as a series of failed attempts, some of them interesting; the writer seems to be searching for new material and a structural unity. Following a different approach, Cox explores Twain's open statements about his work, mainly his letters to Howells, and points out the inconsistencies in the writer's statements.

Though recognizing the value of the results achieved by these studies, it is possible to view the whole matter from a different perspective. First, the author's intentions are not an element separate from the text;

they can and must be found in the text. The studies mentioned above tend to give privilege to the out-of-the-text statement over the text itself. One should grant that Twain was often contradictory; for example, he declared that he intended to keep his autobiography unpublished during his lifetime in order to ensure his own freedom of speech; yet he had some chapters published by the *North American*. These discrepancies are highly meaningful. Cox reads them as one more hoax on the critics.[47] Another way of looking at such contradictions is to see that they simply testify to Twain's divided intentions; his ambivalence between a drive to be public and a drive to be private permeates his experimental works. It reveals itself in a chain of dichotomies running throughout the texts. The ambivalence emerges in the language, in its rhetorical figures. The discourse, which characterizes some trends in the neo-Freudian school of criticism, helps us investigate the problem of Twain's self-censorship. Such an approach regards the artistic text as the place where many repressed elements from the subconscious are allowed to emerge in a form acceptable to the conscious ego and/or to the society that has demanded their repression. As Freud describes it in *Jokes and Their Relation to the Unconscious,* what happens in the artistic product is similar to what happens with jokes: The societal and/or conscious repression is temporarily removed. The figures of speech reveal the trace of the repression, as well as the object of the repression.[48]

It is obvious that a censoring attitude accompanies Twain's entire career. As a matter of fact, some of the symbolical oppositions, so recurrent in the fictions of the Papers, are already present in his major fiction. However, because of the predominantly private, uncensored (although self-censored) nature of some of the Papers, and because of the game involved in the experimental activity, these traits are manifested more clearly in the unpublished works. It is not that, once the societal pressure is removed, Twain lets the censorship go; just the opposite—once the external pressure is removed, the play of internalized repression reveals all its force. Quite rightly, Cox remarks that the portion of Twain's autobiography that was not published during his lifetime is the least revealing of all.[49] From a more traditional perspective this reading appears to be inevitably true for other parts of the Papers as well; yet a semiotic reading gives opposite results.

The author's intention is not a monolithic expression. Twain himself described the ambivalence of intentions and the compound nature of

the work of art when, in a letter to Howells, he discusses the process
of writing the *Autobiography*:

> . . . an Autobiography is the truest of all books; for while it
> inevitably consists mainly of extinctions of the truth, shirkings
> of the truth, partial revealments of the truth, with hardly an
> instance of plain straight truth, the remorseless truth is there,
> between the lines when the author-cat is raking dust upon it
> which hides from the disinterested spectator neither it nor its
> smell (though I didn't use that figure)—the result being that
> the reader knows the author in spite of his wily diligence.[50]

In this passage Twain is describing autobiographical writing, a writing in which conflicting attitudes merge: The need for truth, which is
a convention of the genre, is set up against the need to hide, which is
a necessity of every private act. Because of the very nature of writing,
the trace reveals whatever is hidden "between the lines." In order to
describe the ambivalence implied in this kind of writing, Twain uses a
chain of powerful metaphors: creation/excrement, author/cat, hiding/
dust raking, revealing lines/revealing smell. Even though Twain is
dealing here with autobiographical writing (the entire process from
creation to fruition), what he says can be applied to his writings at
large, which are always permeated by the autobiographical act. In the
posthumously published Papers, the recurring awareness of writing in
a private form testifies to the presence of this act at the core of the
writing. The ambivalence, the divided intentions, are further affirmed
in the fictions of the Papers by the emergence of the image of the
"other," an ineffable, ephemeral character, sometimes a dream self,
sometimes a Superintendent of Dreams, sometimes a satanic child, a
visitor from another world, an image reminding one of Lacan's conception of the unconscious as the other.[51] It is an always repressed and
always reemerging presence.
    There is also another aspect of the "author-cat" metaphor that needs
to be mentioned: It shows Twain's self-referential attitude, his reflection upon his own writing. This is another predominant feature of the
Papers, especially of such fictional parts as *The Mysterious Stranger
Manuscripts* and the fantastic tales. The writing metaphor permeates
them: The dream work in "The Great Dark" is paralleled by the writing
activity, while in "No. 44," the third version of *The Mysterious Stranger*

Manuscripts, the duplication involved in printing is paralleled by the doubling and fragmentation of the self. With its limitless possibility for duplication, writing becomes a metaphor for subconscious activity.[52] From a reading of the main body of the Papers, the author's awareness of the subterranean link between the human psyche, with its fragmentation and unlimited possibility of expansion, and writing, as act of communication and artistic creativity, emerges as one of the most striking aspects of the later Twain.

Narratological, formalist, and semiotic perspectives can be particularly helpful in decoding the textual message. Gérard Genette's *Figures III,* a complete and widely encompassing analysis of narrativity that overcomes abstract models and defines a given text by exploring its literary structures, is important for an understanding of Twain's fictional experiments.[53] These are centered mostly on testimonial narrations (the characters narrate their own stories), which abound also in references to the narrative act. In Twain's fantastic narrations the mixed status of the narrators, who are also characters, increases the uncertainty inherent in the conventions of the fantastic genre.[54] Genettian narratology is helpful in the study of this aspect of Twain's later tales because it draws our attention to the narrative structures.

Because Twain's characters in the later Papers tend to respond more to mythical models than to conform to the conventions of fictional realism, they can be better described in terms of their functions according to Propp's definition than in terms of psychological connotations.[55] Through the analysis of the functions of characters inspired by the typology traced by Propp and Greimas, the paradigmatic reading of the three versions of *The Mysterious Stranger Manuscripts* reveals a similar model in the three versions, and thus reaches a conclusion different from the one suggested by Sholom Kahn's close reading of the text.[56] In spite of remarkable differences in the narration, the three versions, written over a period of eleven years, respond to a similar mythical model of binary opposition of forces. The persistent recurrence of similar models testifies to a unifying deep structure in Twain's fantastic narratives, which is related to collective archetypal thought and is another facet of the relation between text and context.

The characters' movements are an equally meaningful element in the definition of their functions in the text. Their relation to the

setting—either their mobility or their fixity—not only defines their
potential growth or their incapacity to change, but also describes the
relation of the text to the culture it is part of, and therefore of
message to context. Juri Lotman's semiotic model for the characters'
movements inside and outside of delimited spaces emphasizes the
relation between text and culture: The text is shaped by the model
of culture, while, in its turn, it provides a model—a secondary
model—for culture.[57] Cultures tend to view other cultures outside
them as uncivilized: The characters' movements from the inside to
the outside of a given, delimited space represent their voyages from
the civilized to the uncivilized world.[58] In Twain's "The Great Dark"
the opposition between inner and outer space marks the movement
of the characters during the dream/voyage of disaster: The well-lit
and cozy interior of the ship is the place wherein civilized life is
preserved, while the deck is where monsters and storms destroy any
relic of cultured life.

Lotman's concept of the modeling role of text and culture implies a
strict dependence of message upon both code and context. Not only
does the content of the literary message depend on the cultural context,
but its very form is determined by the evolution of the cultural environment. The Russian formalists emphasize such a concept, as does Mikhail Bakhtin; he points out that the evolution of genres is closely
connected to sociohistorical change and the transgression of codified
higher genres through both parody and the mixture of styles and levels
of language ("heteroglossia").[59]

A similar conception of cultural and generic interdependence and
evolution informs Lynn's *Mark Twain and Southwestern Humor*. With
its diachronic view of the humor of the frontier embedded in Twain's
writing, Lynn's work gives a clear sense of the innovative role played
by Twain. He adopts a form—the framed narration, typical of the
western tall tale—that used to be charged with conservative social and
political significance, and he turns its content around by changing the
function of the narrative voice, thus transforming radically its cultural
meaning. Rogers's *Burlesque Patterns* illustrates another aspect of the
relation of Twain's work to codified genres—the writer's early association with the San Francisco Bohemians and the persistence of burlesque patterns in his major works.

A study of the relation between message and code, another aspect of
the opposition between *parole* and *langue,* is the starting point of

the present research.[60] Twain's experimental activity in the Papers is shaped by both dependence on, and opposition to, the general system of signs provided by codified genres and social conventions. In the later experimental phase the literary burlesque is broadened to the point of encompassing social satire. The formal devices related to an estranged vision, which are so frequent in the early burlesques, persist in the later experiments. The parody of both higher genres and/or well-accepted social conventions is always done from the point of view of an uninitiated outsider. The vision of this outsider (who can be either a character or a narrator or a trace) is defamiliarized because he ignores the code of the literary text being parodied; his interpretation then can be produced only through a transformation of meaning because of the change of code, a transcodification. Transgression is the crucial element of burlesque, and it also accounts for Twain's transformation of the framed narration of the tall tale into the framed narration of his fantastic dream narratives. The transgression of the canon through transcodification in the early burlesques evolves into the violation of the rules of realism in the later fantastic stories. Both burlesque extravaganza and the uncertainty of the fantastic derive from the split vision at the core of Twain's experimentalism. As Henry Nash Smith argues, Twain's work is the product of the meeting and merging of two distinct cultural traditions, the west and the east, the vernacular and the genteel.[61] The synchronic presence of these two cultural backgrounds creates a duality in the text that is expressed either by the estranged outlook of the vernacular character/narrator facing generic and social conventions or by the uncanny "other" of dreams emerging in everyday reality. The duality, which operates at various levels—linguistic, psychological, and cultural—is the basis for both burlesque and the fantastic. Moreover, in the opposition between the two cultural poles of America, the oral and the written traditions are set up against each other. In Twain's Papers the opposition takes various shapes and is a recurrent theme.

Code and context are not easily separated. The fantastic narrations are determined not only by the code and context of the vernacular tradition but also by the philosophical thought of Twain's time. The discourse on dreams that Twain carries out in the Papers is paralleled by a similar discourse developed by William James.[62]

The contemporary context can also be associated with the expectations of the readers at the time. This brings us back to the problem of the code—that is, of the generic expectations of readers. Genres are determined by these expectations, which vary in time according to the changes in society. Also, in turn, genres determine such expectations. Twain's awareness of the expectations, his ambivalence (a desire to please and a desire to shock), his self-censoring attitude—all shaped the Papers. It is one of the aims of this study to explore such aspects of Twain's writing as they emerge in the fictional texts of the Papers. However, the intended private nature of some of the writings is also considered in relation to the implied reader. The private aspect does not exclude the function of the addressee in the text; it simply orients the text toward its posterity instead of its contemporary audience. The orientation increases the transgressive and innovative force of the text.

In exploring Twain's experimental work in the Papers, this study follows a partly diachronic development. Chapter 1, therefore, deals with posthumously published burlesques of the San Francisco period, as well as with the southwestern tradition; these are the starting points for a study of Twain's peculiar use of parody and burlesque. Already in the early works, the writer carries out a discourse on the relation between the written and the oral; he attacks the artificiality of written language. His ideal text seems to be oriented toward a utopian degree zero of writing where the written equals the oral. Many tendencies of the early writings can be found in the later satires, where burlesque patterns are developed and broadened, and where the literary burlesque becomes a tool for social satire. The texts analyzed in this chapter are included in the collections *Satires and Burlesques* and *Fables of Man*.

This discussion prepares the ground for the discourse on the fantastic developed in chapter 2, which is based on the textual analysis of two stories from *Which Was the Dream?* and reference to a few more. The analysis reveals that Twain's fantastic experiments transgress the well-established conventions of the genre of the fantastic, while, on the other hand, they are the result of the extreme development of the vernacular tradition: The framed narration of the tall tale is transformed into a "dream structure" in which the oneiric discourse equals the subversive speech of the vernacular character. The textual analysis traces the diachronic development of formal experimentation from "The Enchanted Sea-Wilderness" to "The Great Dark."

Chapter 3 analyzes and compares the three versions of *The Mysterious Stranger Manuscripts*. The similar functions of the characters reveal the existence of a deep structure, while otherwise the variants indicate the movement, in the third version, toward an increasingly more mythical way of thinking. The mode of "romance," with its mixture of levels and styles, seems to be the ideal noncanonical genre for Twain's last experiment.[63] *The Mysterious Stranger Manuscripts* marks a further development in the discourse on dreams initiated by the fantastic narrations; the rational, awake observer of the fantastic stories—himself the result of the transformation of the genteel narrator of the tall tales—becomes, in the later romance, an ironic voice and an uncanny visitor, the personification of the Lacanian "other."

Chapter 4 further explores the mythical aspect of the Papers. Twain displays a basic ambivalence toward both social and literary conventions. While he burlesques canonical genres through transgression and experimentation, he also paves the way for the renewal of form, and he anticipates a concept of writing that is modern. Similarly, while he attacks the myths of his society through mordant satire, he recovers a mythical mode of thinking through an exploration of the oneiric discourse and creates archetypal images quite consistent with the findings of Jungian psychology.[64]

1

Experiment

Although experimentation was part of Twain's routine activity throughout his literary career, during the later phase—in particular his last fifteen years—there was an intensification in the probing of form that resulted in the fantastic stories of the *Which Was the Dream?* collection,
The Mysterious Stranger Manuscripts, and some of the satires and anti-
utopian pieces contained in *Fables of Man.* These writings are the most
interesting part of the Papers. They are longer and more sustained efforts
in which experimentation becomes almost an end in itself. It must be
noted, however, that some of the formal peculiarities of this later period
can be traced back to Twain's early apprenticeship in burlesque.

Mark Twain's Satires and Burlesques includes these early experiments, which, although initially geared toward publication, were not addressed to a genteel audience. Not only are the burlesques an important
aspect of Twain's experimentalism, but they are also the ideal genre of
experimentation. Frequent estrangement procedures, the simultaneous
existence in the text of two genres set against each other, the use of
incongruous elements, the transgression of both generic and social conventions—all are elements that shape the burlesques and Twain's experimentalism as well.

Burlesques, in Twain's practice, convey the outlook of an outsider to
the world of well-established conventions: The familiar becomes unfamiliar through estrangement, while, at the same time, the unfamiliar,

the lofty, and the revered become familiar, lowly, and common through ridicule. A game of perspective is present in this literary practice, which in Twain's view involves the subversion of the order in which the world is expected to function. Time and space barriers are overcome, while incongruous elements from a different time and space are introduced into a given context, resulting in the shattering of the expectations raised by the genre itself. All these elements characterizing Twain's practice of burlesque are also relevant for a study of the later fantastic narrations, where the estrangement and incongruity of the burlesques are carried out and developed to a further extent, and where the duality of perspective results in the uncertainty typical of the fantastic genre.

Twain's early burlesques evince a transgressive tendency in his work, as well as an innovative energy he brought to American letters. In fact, burlesques, consisting of a parody of literary works and higher genres, while they upset the readers' generic expectations, also promote a renewal of form. This tendency points toward the later satires, where many devices of the burlesques are expanded and transformed: The higher genre that is parodied becomes an allusion to a mode of thinking which is the object of satire. The inherent pessimism of the later satires transgresses one of the most persistent myths of American culture, the myth of happiness and success that Twain himself seemed to impersonate. Through satire he also violated standards and rules for American letters contained in Howells's well-known statement asserting that the bright sides of experience are more appropriate for depiction in American fiction because they respond to the reality of American society.[1] In the Papers, Twain's transgression of Howells's ideas pertains not only to the semantic field but also to the domain of genre. While touching upon the least-bright aspects of both inner and outer reality, he also violates the conventions of the literary canon, which, in their turn, are determined by cultural expectations. Thus, understandably, experimentation and private writing, as a way of exploring ideas, became very closely linked in the writer's mind.[2]

Both transgression in satire and uncertainty in the fantastic are achieved through a dual perspective, which is also the basic device of burlesque. There the estrangement involves the existence of a point of view different from that implied by the genre that is the object of parody. This different outlook is provided by the presence in the text of either a character or a narrator coming from a different and separate cultural context. The game of perspective then becomes the confrontation between two views of the world, two codes, two languages totally opposed to each other. This literary device reveals the impact of the southwestern tradition and its literary expression. Later chapters of this study argue that the popular culture of the southwest is diachronically embedded in the narrative structures of the romances and fantastic tales of the later period.

The mixture of languages, styles, viewpoints, and conventions inside a single text recurs in both earlier and later experiments. This synchronic presence of two cultures in the text is related to a cultural phenomenon that Mikhail Bakhtin terms "polyglossia"—the phase of linguistic development of a culture during which the language and codes of a civilization are displaced by another emerging culture. The new language bears inevitably the traces of the linguistic and cultural struggle involved in its formation. This phenomenon, which Bakhtin observes in his study of the linguistic and cultural evolution of the European Middle Ages, is similarly observable in the cultural evolution reflected in Twain's work— his work is in fact the point of confluence in American letters of two cultural traditions, the eastern and the western. It is also the beginning of a new phase of independence from European literary practice. The meeting and overlapping of crosscurrents cause some radical change. Its trace is "heteroglossia," the mixture of levels of languages and genres that we find so often in the Papers.[3] The context of the southwestern frontier is the source for this cultural and linguistic heteroglossia, which finds its literary codification in the practice of burlesque and its further development in the later Papers.

Burlesque: The Discourse of the "Other"

Burlesque as a genre is widely considered inferior in the hierarchy of genres established by the Aristotelian categorization, in which burlesque, being related to comedy, must necessarily be inferior to such higher genres as tragedy. In his book on Twain's burlesque patterns, Rogers shows how Twain's critics, from Paine to Brooks, from Parrington to De Voto, underestimated his craftsmanship in burlesque.[4]

Rogers connects Twain's burlesque with literary burlesque as it was practiced during the nineteenth century, when it meant "a humorous imitation and exaggeration of the conventions in plot, characterization or style peculiar to a literary type or a particular book, play, short story or poem."[5]

Twain's connection with this tradition occurred through the San Francisco Bohemians, a literary group that originated in New York and then moved to San Francisco; it included Ada Clare, Bret Harte, Henry Webb, Artemus Ward, and Charles Stoddard. Through them, Twain became acquainted with the burlesque novel—the nineteenth-century form of burlesque. The main peculiarity of this kind of burlesque is the condensation that differentiates it from its eighteenth-century prede-cessor. Twain, whose previous literary experience consisted of humor-ous sketches in the frontier mode, learned a quite different literary skill from the San Francisco Bohemians. In the years between 1863 and 1871, the largest part of his production was in the burlesque genre. Later, like his British predecessors, he used patterns he learned from the practice of burlesque to structure his novels. Among Twain's major works, *A Connecticut Yankee in King Arthur's Court* is an example of a novel shaped by a burlesque perspective. Arthurian England is for Hank Morgan an unfamiliar yet familiar world; it is a reality that, although distorted by displacement of time and space, still alludes to the American setting. Here, too, displacement and ridicule shatter generic expectations connected to an ancient and revered legend.

As Shelley Fisher Fishkin argues, among early influences on Twain's apprenticeship in burlesque and parody one should take into account his experience as a journalist.[6] Journalism, as it was practiced in the 1850s and 1860s on the western frontier, provided the young Twain with an exposure to various literary devices and styles. In *The Innocents Abroad* (1869), for example, Twain parodies a widespread journalistic genre, the letter from a traveling correspondent. Even though not his first experiment in this kind of burlesque, it was his first extensive one.

Burlesque also becomes one of the forms of Twain's experimentation in his later and unpublished works. Its use conveys the writer's ambiva-lence toward codified genres, the higher genres most removed from the oral and popular tradition. In fact, burlesque implies a double perspective, that of literary model and burlesquing subject.

Mark Twain's Satires and Burlesques offers further evidence of Twain's use of burlesque in his apprentice years.[7] Left unrevised, most of the burlesques contained in this collection were discarded by Twain. In spite of a few different devices, most pieces of the collection point in the same direction: the unification of both technique and vision by means of an estranged perspective. Estrangement, as defined by the Russian formalists, is a formal procedure aimed at giving the reader an unusual perception of the reality described, a new and unforeseen image. This is achieved through both linguistic distortion and semantic displacement.[8]

In the earliest piece of the collection, "Burlesque, Il Trovatore" (1866), the narrator, who describes the performance of Verdi's opera by the Bianchi Grand Italian Opera Company, ignores all the conventions of this highly coded musical and theatrical genre:

> Down comes the X woman to her knees—but it ain't any use— the knight turns his back on her—and so she sets down on the floor and spreads her hand across her breast—ostensibly to feel her heart, but really to make up for the lowness of her lowneck dress—the knight (of course) comes and takes her round the waist and they sing. Enter the feather chap on, and she trying to faint and fall all the time and he holding her but at last she does fall and then all the soldiers leave—fat woman falls—flames show through cracks. (p. 24)[9]

The perception conveyed by the "Burlesque, Il Trovatore" is that of total absurdity; each sequence is disjointed from the following ones, and the movements of the characters lead to nothing. Clearly the narrator, absent from the scene and yet very present through an unmistakably rustic voice, sees no separation between art and reality: For him, gesture and thing are almost equivalent. The woman pressing her hands on her breast can only pretend to feel her own heart, while, in fact, she is trying to cover up her cleavage; in other words, she can pretend to feel what is inside in order to cover what is outside. The metalanguage of gesture of the melodrama reveals the opposition of cultures that is the core of this burlesque. Two codes, two cultures are opposed—the literal and the literary worlds. The discrepancy here is between the codes of the genre observed and the codes of the observer. The former is based upon the constant allusion to feeling through gesture; the latter consists of gestures meaning only gesture. The meaning changes as a consequence of the change of code; it is a transcodification. However, as in any case of transcodification, the addressee, as well as the addresser, must know the code of the original model. The addressee of the burlesque, in order to fully understand the parody, has to know the codes of opera. This involves a double perspective: the implicit literate view shared by addresser and addressee on the one side, and the illiterate view of the narrator on the other. The knowledge of the conventions of opera hides from the opera-goer the literal level of the signs he watches; in fact, the gestures themselves become unnoticeable in the long run. The estrangement, which the narrator's innocent view brings about, shows the usual and familiar aspects of the performance under an unusual and unfamiliar light; yet the opposite is true too. Through the ridicule brought about by the defamiliarization implied by the estrangement procedure, the high genre becomes common, usual and familiar. The gestures of opera no longer allude to the world of tragic passions; they become trivial gestures of everyday reality.

Just as in "Il Trovatore," in "A Novel: Who Was He?" (1867), a parody of Victor Hugo's novels, two codes—two cultural traditions—are played against each other: the romantic and the realistic trends in literature. Unlike "Il Trovatore," the object of parody and description in this burlesque is the verbal language of the "other," the romantic, as seen through the eyes of the realist. Through the description of its language, the worldview of the "other" is portrayed as well.

Here too, Hugo's style and the monumental dispersion in his novels are expressed through an estranged perspective consisting in given stylistic procedures isolated from the original text and from their contextual relations. The vagueness of Hugo's style is conveyed at first by the title itself ("Who Was He?"), next by the staccato paragraphs and the incontrovertible mock-syllogistic statements: "No man can be a man who is not a man. Hence Gillifat was a Man." The narrator's omniscience becomes mere triviality through the persistence of generalizing repetitions: "Such is life"; "Such is the nature of storms." Non-sensical pseudoscientific and historical digressions are interpolated in the narration:

> Storms always rise in certain conditions of the atmosphere. They are caused by certain forces operating against certain other forces which are called by certain names and are well known by

persons who are familiar with them. In 1492 Columbus sailed.
(p. 27)

Hugo's tendency to shift the focus of narration at climactic moments
so that the climax never occurs is also burlesqued:

> The two men glared at each other eight minutes—time is terrible
> in circumstances of danger—men have grown old under the
> effects of fright while the fleetest horse could canter a mile—
> eight minutes—eight terrible minutes they glared at each other
> and then—
> Why does the human contract under the influence of joy and
> dilate under the influence of fear? (p. 29)

The parody here is developed from a literary point of view, a stylistic
one: The ideal style, the ideal utterance and writing implied in the
worldview of the author, tends presumably toward *the thing,* the presence, and refuses the deferral and the rhetoric involved in the artificiality of Hugo's style. This tendency emerges clearly from one of the most
interesting peculiarities of this burlesque. At some point the code of
the writing shifts suddenly from finished product to work in progress.
To achieve this, Twain uses a double device. First, the omniscient
narrator, Victor Hugo, enters the story as a character and plays a
referential role: He starts reading his own novels to the characters/
observers. Second, the author himself, who voices his criticism of
Hugo's style while narrating the story, fills in the void in the narrative
function created by Hugo's shift from narrator to character:

> The dreadful climax was impending—fearful moment—when
> Victor Hugo appeared on the scene and began to read a chapter
> from one of his books.
> All these people and things got interested in his imminently
> impending climaxes and suspended their several enterprises.
> . . .
> When after several chapters the climaxes never arrived, but
> got swallowed up in interminable incomprehensible metaphysi-
> cal disquisitions, columns of extraneous general information,
> and chapters of wandering incoherences, they became disgusted
> and—

> Lo! a miracle!
> The *Croupier* up anchor and went to sea. . . .
> Victor was Victor still! (p. 30)

While commenting on Hugo's reading of one of his novels, the author/narrator refers to the burlesque itself; thus self-reference alters the code, while the whole piece is brought down to a narrative degree of nonartificiality. Moreover, Hugo's appearance inside the fiction not only shatters its fictionality but also establishes a relation with other texts of his that, in this case, bear the same peculiar anticlimactic structure. In fact, by inserting the presumed narrator in the story at a point of development when the reader would normally expect a climax, the real author creates a relation of intertextuality between the text he is writing and the model that inspires it—both texts are anticlimactic. A corollary of intertextuality is transcodification: The peculiarities of the text can be thoroughly understood only through a comparison with the model and its codes. The insertion of Hugo functions as an allusion to that model and code.

The characters' interruption of their activities in order to listen to Hugo's reading marks a further alteration of the fictional level, since the characters are defamiliarized and estranged from their given, conventionalized roles. This estrangement is even closer to the Brechtian theatrical conception of the *Verfremdungeffekt* than to the Russian formalists' postulation of it; the characters themselves join in the author's criticism of the text of which they are a part.[10] The conventions of fiction are thus temporarily suspended in order to allow the reader to touch upon some reality beyond the text.

The similarity shared by these early burlesques, despite structural differences, lies in a constant striving for the natural language, the reality. Such preoccupation becomes a recurrent theme in the later Papers. At the same time, one should note that this concern with language goes beyond language to touch on the worldview that language portrays. The discourse of the "other," the romantic, the sentimental, the affected, is in fact both language and thought. This is exemplified even more clearly by "The Story of Mamie Grant, the Child-Missionary" (1868). Here the parody encompasses the code, message, and addressee of the original model (*The Gates Ajar,* by Elizabeth Stuart Phelps, a diary-novel of religious and moral edification), an example of so-called temperance literature. The burlesque subverts the relation in the model novel between the mentor and the pupil. In this case the moral mentor is not the adult aunt, but rather the child Mamie, who at age nine instructs both her aunt and whoever she has a chance to talk to on matters of faith; in order to be more effective, Mamie hands out and summarizes various religious tracts to the several visitors to her house. Through this device Twain attacks more than one target; an entire genre is under fire. Despite the simplicity of the message parodied, this burlesque has a rather complex structure: Not only does the author establish a relation of intertextuality, but he also includes in the burlesque the addressees, the usual readers of Sunday-school literature. Thus the burlesque reaches out to its social context and through that to the world outside.

Presumably written during the same period (late 1860s or late 1880s), "Colloquy Between a Slum Child and a Moral Mentor" bears a few similarities to the "Mamie Grant" burlesque. It is a burlesque of Sunday-school sentimentality shaped as an instructive dialogue. A moral mentor sets himself the task of imparting moral and religious instruction to James, a slum child. During the dialogue, however, some crude realities of slum life emerge clearly. Even though the pompous mentor is unmoved, the trend of the dialogue subverts the goals of Sunday-school literature. The child character reveals the desperate poverty of New York slums; the moral mentor, on the other hand, appears for what he is—a sanctimonious hypocrite:

"Ah, naughty, naughty boy. You must not use slang. Where do little boys go who use slang?"

"Dono. I goes to the Bowery when shining's good and I've got the lush."

"Tut, tut, tut! Don't talk so. You make me nervous. Little boys who talk that way go to the—bad place!"

"No—but do they? Where is it?"

"It is where there is fire and brimstone always and forever."

"Suits crooks! I never ben warm enough yet, ony summer time. Wisht I'd ben there in the winter when I hadn't any bed kiver but a shutter. That Higgins boy busted two of the slats out, and then I couldn't keep the cold out no way. It had a beautiful brass knob on it, Cap., but brass knobs ain't no good, ony for style, you know. I'd like to ben in that place them times, by hokey!"[11]

The conflict between the two characters is continuously also a linguistic one. Not only does the boy's spicy vernacular stand out against the pomposity of the mentor's style, but it also signals his honest outlook; language and vision become equivalent. It is no wonder that the adult requests several times that James's language be kept under restraint. The linguistic opposition, so central to this burlesque, is the trace of southwestern humor, a literary tradition Twain became acquainted with before he started experimenting with burlesque. There, too, the linguistic opposition conveyed a cultural struggle. In the evolution of Twain's training in burlesque, "The Colloquy" marks a step in a direction that the writer will follow from then on. The burlesque is becoming social satire.

A further step in that direction is marked by "L'Homme Qui Rit" (1869), a burlesque of Victor Hugo's novel of the same title. A double model is involved in it—a literary text and a political situation. The result is a burlesque and, at the same time, a satirical allegory. The discourse on the artificiality of the written language becomes, then, analogous to the discourse on the hypocrisy and corruption of politics. Moreover, here Twain is clearly heading toward the heteroglossia, the mixture of genres and styles, that characterizes many of his later works. However, because it transposes and displaces codes from a different genre, "L'Homme Qui Rit" cannot be appreciated without knowing the codes of both the text model and the political context of both Andrew Johnson's presidency and that of the side Twain stood for—the Radical Republicans.

In Twain's major work of that early period we find many of the devices and literary concerns of the shorter, posthumously published burlesques. The model texts for *The Innocents Abroad* are both the letters from traveling correspondents and the travel books and guides, fashionable at the time, that had rendered Europe familiar to American travelers abroad and to American readers at home. Through a parody of such books, Twain portrays European mores and traditions under an unfamiliar and estranged light. Europe is, in fact, the object of burlesque description through the estranged eyes of an "innocent" observer reminiscent of the vernacular narrator of the western tall tales. Similar in this respect to the opposition of east and west, the conflict between Europe and America is here the clash between a basically literary, even bookish, culture, remote from the essence of reality, and a vernacular and partly oral culture still close to the core of human experience. This is the opposition between absence and presence. Europe is perceived, indeed, by its semifictional visitors as a series of signs referring to more signs, never really being *the thing*. Its core, that is, its past, seems to be unreachable and irretrievable. Because of its remoteness from presence, Europe is represented in *The Innocents Abroad* by relics and monuments, which are the trace of its past. The "innocents" do not recognize Europe as their origin; throughout, they view Europe as the "other" culture, totally alien from their own. Their response to Europe is marked by a series of disappointed expectations: Europe is always below its fame. The narrator has a fantasy of treating himself to a session in a luxurious barbershop in Paris. In reality, at the barbershop he visits, he faces near bloodshed. Notre-Dame itself appears to the American travelers as a picture that they have already seen. Europe at its best is like a picture of itself. The narrator finds misery, poverty, and human degradation hiding behind its myth of magnificence. This is because of Europe's artificiality—the artificiality of art products, which the narrator perceives as opposed to the reality and immediacy of life. The estranged perspective serves the purpose of laying bare the grim reality behind the fake myth.

In a burlesque of a relatively later period, "Burlesque Hamlet" (1881), estrangement is related to displacement of time and space; the contemporary world is present through an incongruous character, a foster brother of Hamlet, who comes from a different time and space. A book agent from Twain's contemporary world, he reasons according to the context and codes of the nineteenth century. This burlesque marks a movement from satire of contemporary mores to the genre of the fantastic. Time and space barriers are overcome, while an uncanny element is introduced. The book agent functions as Freud's "the uncanny"; he is, in fact, familiar and unfamiliar (*heimlich/unheimlich*).[12] He is a familiar face to contemporary readers but unfamiliar to the characters of the play, who in fact do not pay him any attention, never speaking to or even noticing him. He is also extraneous to the code and context of Shakespeare's *Hamlet* and to the readers' expectations of that play.

Just as in "Mamie Grant," through Basil Stockman the world of books is introduced in the text through its commercial side. With no success, Basil tries to sell his books, in Hamlet's Denmark. His presence provides the play with an "estranging" element and perspective, still leaving it untouched. Twain, as we learn from a letter to Howells, did not dare touch the "sacred" text, "for the sacrilegious scribbler who ventured to put words into Shakespeare's mouth would probably be hanged."[13] This gives us some insight into the transgressive aspect of burlesque. In more conventional burlesques, such as "Who Was He?," "The Story of Mamie Grant," and even "L'Homme Qui Rit," the transgression is kept under restraint by some canonical rules; that is, there is no alteration of the basic formal structure of the model text. Yet inside these rules the author is allowed great freedom. The form is kept; the content can be manipulated, so that the model is ridiculed through exaggeration. "Burlesque Hamlet" marks a deviation from the rules of conventional burlesque. Neither form nor structure is touched, except through the interpolation of an additional character. The transgression is thus avoided and perpetrated at the same time. In fact, the intrusion of the book agent inevitably alters the perspective; he finds himself out of place in the world of *Hamlet,* and his remarks betray his origin—his cultural code and context. Like the narrator in "Il Trovatore," he reflects upon the artificiality of the language while he reinterprets what he sees, thus transcodifying *Hamlet:*

> Well, I never saw anything just like this state of things before. They're the oddest lot of lunatics outside the asylum. . . . They're on the high horse all the time, then: they swell around and talk the grandest kind of book-talk. . . . It's the most unnatural stuff! Why it ain't human talk. (p. 69)

Basil is also aware of anachronism; for example, he realizes that smoking in Hamlet's Denmark is out of place. This awareness, the awareness of one's own estranged position, makes him similar to the characters of "Who Was He?," who give up their status as characters to become critics. Through estrangement, characters are transposed from one level of narration to another, from diegesis to metadiegesis, where they perform a metalinguistic function.[14] The ideal language for Twain's burlesque characters is the zero degree, as Roland Barthes would put it.[15] Their ideal is a language devoid of artificiality, totally equivalent to the spoken utterance in its spontaneity. Their estranged perspective overshadows many of Twain's views on the language of literature, just as the peculiar structure of the "Burlesque Hamlet" reveals his ambivalence and his cautious scruples when he has to subvert the well-accepted conventions of the canon.

In this respect, of greater interest is "The Autobiography of a Damned Fool" (1877), the first part of which is called "The Hellfire Hotchkiss Sequence," a work that kept Twain occupied for twenty years and was incorporated into "Schoolhouse Hill," the Hannibal sequence of *The Mysterious Stranger Manuscripts*. The germinal idea is in the biography of Twain's brother, Orion, who inspired many of his pathetic, unsuccessful, and naive adamic characters. "Orion's Autobiography," the initial project, soon became "The Autobiography of a Damned Fool." More fictionalized than an autobiography is supposed to be, it keeps, however, some of the basic features of the genre. It is written in the first person; it is the account of a life starting with early childhood—in fact, with family biography. It follows the trend of recollection; it traces the growth of an individual. The departure from the conventions of autobiography lies in the fact that it is written by a person who is not the character/narrator. However, this is the burlesque of an autobiography, and therefore a fiction.

The model text could be any classical autobiography; however, it is presumably *The Autobiography of Benjamin Franklin*. Not only does the character/narrator mention that autobiography, but also some meaningful details and facts of the burlesque correspond to the model text. For example, like Franklin, the protagonist starts his narration with family biography; he used to be an apprentice printer and lost his first job because of a fight with his master; he also shows interest in various ways of thinking. Keeping these considerations in mind, we can say then that the message is altered and reversed; instead of being the autobiography of a self-made man, this is the autobiography of a sad failure.

However, there is still another consideration. Initially, Twain meant this to be Orion's autobiography, and in spite of the fictionalization some of that intention remains. In this way, through the burlesque of an autobiography, he experiments with the codes of the genre. The most interesting violation is that of "the autobiographical pact," the transgression of the unspoken and implicit agreement between author and reader of the autobiography concerning the identity of the former as author, narrator, and character of his text.[16] In this respect, the experiment is somewhat comparable to Gertrude Stein's *Autobiography of Alice B. Toklas;* both texts accomplish a double violation. However, in Stein's autobiography, author and narrator do not share the same identity (Stein = author, Toklas = narrator, Stein = protagonist) whereas here, on the other hand, the violation of the autobiographical convention consists of the different identities of author and narrator/protagonist (Twain = author, Orion = narrator, Orion = protagonist). The different transgression is due to the different experimentation carried out by the two texts; Stein's is a mock autobiography, while Twain's is a burlesque.

"Autobiography of a Damned Fool" is not the only burlesque autobiography Twain worked on during the early phase of his career. "Burlesque Autobiography" (1871) anticipates, through digressiveness and willing omissions, the self-censoring omissions of his later serious *Autobiography*. After dealing at length in burlesque fashion with the supposedly remote ancestry of the Twain family, "Burlesque Autobiography" omits completely the life of its author: "it is simply wisdom to leave it unwritten until I am hanged," concludes Twain.[17] The main interest of these early attempts lies in their pointing toward an important aspect of Twain's experimentalism—the renewal of genre through the violation of its code.

A recurrent trait in the selection of burlesques that I have analyzed so far is a departure from some rules of the burlesque as it was practiced by the San Francisco Bohemians and their British counterpart, the group writing for *Punch*. One of the departures is the presence, sometimes acknowledged and sometimes implied, of an observer who introduces an estranged perspective. This aspect derives from Twain's apprenticeship in southwestern humor; the estranged perspective signals the cultural opposition implicit in that form. It also anticipates one of Twain's most recurrent literary traits: the tendency toward an ideal language, devoid of rhetorical codes, a writing that is like talk, stemming from the southwestern tradition as well.

Moreover, the interpolation of an incongruous character, as we have observed in "Burlesque Hamlet," anticipates the return of the uncanny in the later fantastic stories. This aspect, too, is related to Twain's transgressive tendency as shown by the practice of the burlesque, as well as by the violation of some of the established rules of the transgressive genre—a transgression of codified transgression. This tendency is, however, counterbalanced by scruples and fears, which are not limited solely to the literary field but also involve the social scene. These cautions might have determined, to a great extent, the deferral of the publication of the later satires, which share many traits with the early burlesques.

One of the best, most interesting, and longest pieces of the later phase is "The Secret History of Eddypus, the World Empire" (1901–2),[18] a burlesque of the utopian novels quite popular at the time of its composition.[19]

Like a utopian novel, "The Secret History" projects a future vision of society. Unlike its texts models, it is a nightmarish vision of tyranny and darkness. The history of the world Empire that Mary Baker Eddy founded, and of the many centuries of tyranny that followed, is written a thousand years later. The historical sources are found in a paper by a bishop who lived at the time, the so-called Father of History, a certain Mark Twain. Curiously, history from the end of the nineteenth century to the time of writing (a thousand years later) is incredibly similar to the cycle of world history that preceded it. Events and names are certainly confused and mixed together, but a cyclical tendency shows clearly, a principle of repetition Twain had come to view as one of the most persistent characteristics of humankind. For example:

> George Wishington fought bravely both by land and sea in the Revolution which emancipated his country from the dominion of England, and was drowned at Waterloo, so called on account of the looness or lowness (shallowness?) of the sea at that point, a word whose exact meaning is now lost to us in the mists of antiquity. (*Fables of Man,* p. 330)

As a matter of fact, many things are lost in the mists of time.

In this structure, the backward perspective, "The Secret History," reminds one of Bellamy's *Looking Backward.* However, even more than a discourse on the literary code of its model text, Twain's burlesque utopia is a satire of contemporary mores. The backward perspective fits into this purpose by creating a game of distance. The target is overt: Twain is leading a frontal attack on one of his favorite whipping boys, or rather, girls, Mary Baker Eddy, the founder of Christian Science. Burlesque becomes a tool for satire, as in "L'Homme Qui Rit." However, the contemporary referent is so overt that, even without a real knowledge of the history of Christian Science, it is possible to understand and appreciate this short novel. The ultimate goal of the satire transcends Christian Science and aims at humankind: Mrs. Eddy's power and her followers, the Eddymaniacs, are just one of the many examples of the human tendency toward dictatorship on the one hand and subservience and fanaticism on the other. Real progress is impossible because human nature never changes, and so the cycle of repetition is never broken. The age of darkness will always follow the age of light, and so on. The satire of current events, the rising star of Mary Baker Eddy, is only a pretext for larger philosophical statements.

The utopian model text serves a function similar to that of Hugo's romantic novels; just as the latter were burlesqued from an antiromantic perspective, so is the utopian novel burlesqued from an anti-utopian standpoint.[20] The optimism implied by the message of the utopian novel is defeated on philosophical grounds; history has proven that utopian societies do not exist. The message is reversed, but the code of the utopian novel remains. For example, events in "The Secret History" follow a rhythm of symmetry and repetition, creating a sense of order quite the opposite of the chaos we are familiar with in real life. This is similar to the order of Utopia, which is, however, meant to suggest harmony; the symmetry of Eddypus, on the other hand, suggests enslavement. The message is reversed by describing an inescapable tyranny rather than a freer society. Another point of similarity is represented by time and space, which in Utopia are outside the rhythms of experience. The setting is often in a remote and/or a nonexistent land; the time can be past, present, or future, but it is different from that of our experience. In "The Secret History" space and time are simultaneously familiar and unfamiliar. The displacement is achieved through the naming of both space and time. The names of places are deformed by means of two devices: They are renamed in the language of the new society; and their historical function is modified, while their connection with historical time is altered. Thus, according to Christian Science Historical Records (the records of the new society), Boston is renamed Eddyflats, and Rome Eddyburg. According to the secret history (a sort of alternative record of history), places lose the connotation they once had because the record is unable to locate the place we are familiar with. We read: "There was a Greek Empire, too, but we do not know when, nor just where it was located. Its capital was called Dublin, or Dubling" (*Fables of Man*, p. 326). Libraries were destroyed once Christian Science was constituted into an empire and subsequently merged with Catholicism, so there are no written records. Historical data are handed down through confused memories—from mouth to ear. "The Secret History" is meant to be a coded record; however, the code too is confused because the recipient of the letters recounting the alternative history has forgotten the ciphers of the code. The renaming of places and people is then further complicated by problems of interpretation and by ambiguous blanks of collective and personal memory. Because of this confusion, time is altered too. It still entertains a relation with the time of the real world, although it does not follow the same rules: The historical epochs are confused; the chronology is totally altered. Through alteration, a new conception of history is conveyed, and historical periods are divided into Ages of Light and Ages of Darkness. In general, in Eddypus the period from 300 to 1800 is regarded as the Dark Ages, to be followed by the Industrial Revolution, heralding the advent of the Ages of Light and American Civil Liberties. However, quite soon these liberties are betrayed by the American people, who start enslaving defenseless countries; soon Christian Science becomes the dominant religion and adopts the methods of the Catholic church during the Ages of Darkness. Freedom of speech is eliminated, any source of knowledge annihilated. The arbitrariness of time, a common trait in utopias, is reflected here by the burlesque treatment of history. In fact, the burlesque of utopian codes includes that of the historical records. The matter-of-fact tone, the certainty of facts that are totally obscure, the wild assumptions, the conjectures, the reconstructions based on scanty evidence—all put the entire historical activity under attack.

The continual allusions to facts and events of reality create a bond between the imaginary world of the burlesque utopia and that of Twain's time. Yet the society that is described is no longer a living organism, but rather a machine. In utopian novels this mechanism manufactures an ideal type of humankind. In "Eddypus," on the other hand, the mechanism, instead of creating a new humanity, annihilates it. This mechanism is not external to the human condition but is, rather, a law according to which human beings function. The cycle of history is in fact the cycle of human consciousness. The impossibility of the fulfillment of the utopian dream is not due to external circumstances, but rather to the reality of human nature. This is the core belief Twain discusses in "Eddypus."

As in the early burlesques, an external presence—a witness and observer—is introduced in the text: Mark Twain, Bishop of New Jersey, a prismatic figure and a source of historical records.[21] During his life-

time he witnesses an entire cycle of history: The pre–Civil War South
in which he was born is equated with the European Middle Ages, while
the advent of the Great Civilization—the Industrial Revolution and
American Civil Liberties—is a new Renaissance and a new Enlightenment, since all the major figures of those periods are born in that
compressed age. Mark Twain, the character, is then the witness, observer, and recorder of an entire cycle, which is equivalent to any other
cycle in history. Through this character of himself, Twain provides
the utopian burlesque with an estranged outlook; the presence of the
author, although disguised, suspends the disbelief, alters the narration
(the "diegetical" levels, as one would say in narratological terms), and
inserts the authorial (and extradiegetical) presence into the text. Although similar to the estrangement produced in the early burlesque
"Who Was He?" by the sudden appearance of Hugo among the characters, Mark Twain's presence as a character in "The Secret History" is
a slightly different literary procedure. It has a self-referential quality
alien to the earlier burlesque where the characters perform the role of
critics. This signals an evolution from the earlier experiments, which
might be due to a different relation between the components of the
process of communication. The function of the message acquires a
wider scope in the later satires than it had in the previous works, where
the code prevailed over the message. Also, the function of the addresser
is more predominant in the satires, whereas the addressee is deferred
in time and space; "The Secret History" contains an indictment of the
contemporary reader, who will not be allowed to read the writings of
the Father of History, Mark Twain. The explicit denial of an immediate
addressee alters a message that is not as dependent upon contemporary
events; the present situation functions as an example upon which a
general theory is built. The message is addressed to a distant, wider
audience. As a consequence, the function of the code is also different.
The model text is no longer a single text, but rather an entire range of
texts, representing both a genre and a context. Thus the burlesque
device provides a metaphorical allusion to a mode of thinking strictly
connected with the genre of the model texts.

In a later burlesque of Sunday-school literature, "Little Bessie"
(1908–9), a three-year-old imparts to her mother a reverse moral and
religious instruction.[22] All the beliefs upon which institutionalized religion is based are attacked; Providence is proven to be a malevolent will
ruling the universe. Unlike James, the slum child of "Colloquy Between

a Slum Child and a Moral Mentor," Bessie does not apprehend her bitter philosophy through direct observation of the surrounding reality; she has an adult initiator, a cynical mentor. The structural difference of this text from the earlier burlesques—"Mamie Grant" and "Colloquy"—is the presence of the third character who is indirectly active in the dialogue: Thus the child becomes a spokesperson for a pessimistic and deterministic view of the universe; her innocent outlook and stringent logic allude to the logical honesty of the philosophy she voices. However, the contrast between her age and the concepts she expresses creates a grotesque effect.[23]

The animal fables Twain wrote between 1900 and 1910 are just as satirical. The model texts are the animal fables of Phoedrus, Aesop, La Fontaine, and (in general) parables and fables addressed to children for purposes of moral instruction. The ideas satirized are Providence, cosmic vulturism, Western imperialism, and human subservience toward power. In "The Victims" (1900) the entire spectrum of creatures from microbe to man is shown at work in a cosmic plan of vulturism: Each animal eats someone else's child.[24] The cruelest of all is man, who kills "anything that might contain life and be helpless" (which of course includes blacks to be enslaved). Man, the Christian planter who buys the slaves, considers his act to be "the way to extend our noble civilization"; he will give the slaves Christian instruction. In "Goose Fable" (1899–1900), Mother Goose instructs her child to trust always, and under any circumstances, the god—that is, the human race; geese are supposed to bless mankind even when they are mistreated by them.[25] "The Fable of the Yellow Terror" foreshadows the history of Western imperialism.[26] The Butterflies (the West) want to bring their civilization to the Bees (the East), a happy people who do not want it. Not wishing to learn how to make honey, the bees refuse to buy it from the Butterflies, who at the time are the producers. So the Butterflies invent the story that the Bees are the yellow terror. This gives them the pretext to send in missionaries and instruct the Bees. Soon the Bees change their civilization, start to buy honey, and learn how to produce it themselves; it is rumored that they might start producing it at a price lower than that of the Butterflies.

The functions of the characters in these fables correspond in their main lines to Vladimir Propp's categorization of Russian fairy tales.[27] Propp argues that fables usually develop according to the following pattern: Initially the family and/or the hero are introduced either through a description or a simple mention of their names. Such is the case of the fables under discussion, in which, at the beginning, the names of the protagonists are mentioned. After this initial step, there is a second movement of separation in the form of either a departure from home or death, especially a parent's death. In "The Victims" Johnnie Microbe and all of the other youngsters of the various species leave home for a picnic, and in "Goose Fable" the death of the mother is impending; in fact, this final departure is foreshadowed by the departure of the geese: "The wild geese were flying northwards in a branching procession shaped like a harrow" (*Fables of Man,* p. 150). Departure is often either associated with or followed by a prohibition. Johnnie Microbe is not allowed to go to the picnic at first, and when he gains his mother's permission he is instructed. A fourth movement is that of the enemy undertaking some action in order to overcome the hero, as is certainly the case with "The Victims."

The similarity of functions between Twain's fables and Russian fairy tales is evidence of the writer's dependence on folklore, which in its basic structures follows similar trends in different cultures throughout the world. Moreover, ancient rituals are preserved in most fables and demonstrate the close connection between fables and mythical archetypes. Both "Goose Fable" and "The Victims" are initiation stories. In the former the code is a mythical initiatory ritual, while the message consists, instead, of the parody of a Sunday-school sermon. In "The Victims" the formulaic repetition of the code—similar to a popular rhyme—serves as a comment on the message describing the mechanical and deterministic laws of cosmic vulturism. These laws parallel those of human behavior in history. Man, however, rationalizes his predatory activities through religion and morals. While "The Victims" traces the chain of being from microbe to man, "Goose Fable" provides a metaphorical parallel to the relationship between man and God.

"The Fable of the Yellow Terror" alludes similarly to the world of current events. The fable is based on a relation of antagonism and on circularity of actions: At the end the oppressed country has developed enough potential to become the exploiter.

As compared to the earlier burlesques, these fables are less self-referential and less intratextual, since the form does not provide a discussion of the model text or genre. Here the satirical message refers to an external ideological context—American society and its belief system. The form of the fable alludes to the mythical roots of society, and to an ideal golden innocence totally opposite the situation described by the message.

In the later works there is undoubtedly an intensification of a satirical attitude, as evinced by a greater complexity in the system of signs. Each sign is related to another sign, which in turn is connected with a larger total vision. In "The Secret History," for example, we noticed how the burlesque of the utopian model is achieved through a reversal of that model—creating in fact a dystopian novel. The discourse on the code of the utopian model—the history retold—is related to a context of current events, Christian Science and its extraordinary success, which in turn creates an allegory of the history of humankind. This larger context, always present in some form in the later works, marks a difference from the earlier burlesques. At the top of the chain of being in "The Victims" is a Christian planter: The allusion to the slave system is overt. That system, however, parallels a larger system ruling both the world of history and the cosmic world. This larger context is implied also through the adoption of a model that is an entire genre rather than a specific text. The genre then stands to the single text as the cosmic vision stands to the specific current event or issue to be parodied. This deviation from the original burlesque pattern highlights much of Twain's attitude toward genre. Literary models stand for something beyond the purely literary work: The genre as a set of conventions alludes to the conventions of society, which in their turn reflect the rules of the universe. Human consciousness is the ultimate mirror in the chain of reflectors. Violation through burlesque acquires, especially in the later phase, the value of a larger and deeper transgression of fixed roles, both in the social context and in the context of the immutable laws governing the universe.

Estrangement is a form of transgression as well as one of the constant devices of both earlier and later phases. It is based on the presence of the "other" in the text. The "other" is sometimes simply implied; often it is an audible voice describing the unfamiliar reality that is observed; even more often the "other" appears as a character in a dialogue. It always provides a new and defamiliarized outlook on reality. In the later satires this presence in the text takes on the peculiar shape of an almost invisible character. It is Mr. Hollister in "Little Bessie," who, through his alienated perspective, shows the child the hidden cruelties of the order of things. It is the Father of History, Mark Twain, in "The Secret History," who carries out a function of revelation—he speaks from the grave, and thus can tell only the truth; from the grave he derives the authority that allows him to retell both his personal history and the history of humankind. Renaming, displacing, and breaking down the chronological order are all aspects of his estranged historical perspective.

The importance of the estranged outlook in the texts of the Papers is better understood through a study of *The Mysterious Stranger Manuscripts,* the subject of chapter 3 of this work, as well as from an exploration of the fantastic stories, the subject of chapter 2. For a better understanding of such a central and recurring narrative aspect in the Papers, one should also consider Twain's early apprenticeship in the tradition of the old southwest. The results of that experience are imbedded in most of his works and are a shaping structure in most of the Papers. The duality of vision, which is the very core of parody in the burlesques I have analyzed so far, is part of Twain's absorption in the culture of the American southwest and of his own very personal reinterpretation of that tradition.

The Vernacular and the Genteel: The Voices of the "Other"

A predominant tendency among Twain scholars who have studied the traditions that served as a formative influence on his development as a writer is to weigh his apprenticeship in burlesque against his origin as a writer in the southwestern school of humor. Two major works of the sixties, Rogers's *Burlesque Patterns* and Lynn's *Southwestern Humor,* oppose each other on the subject of Twain's development. Furthermore, Sloane's *Mark Twain as a Literary Comedian* downplays the importance of the frontier as compared to that of the San Francisco Bohemians, while Shelley Fisher Fishkin's *From Fact to Fiction* emphasizes the formative influence of Twain's early experience as a journalist in the west upon his literary career.[28] A more conciliatory attitude, however, had been taken already in 1962 by Pascal Covici's *Mark Twain's Humor: The Image of a World.*[29] The present study stands in a similarly mediating position and suggests that, while the apprenticeship in burlesque provided the young Twain with a literary code, the context of the southwestern frontier provided him with a vision that informed the message conveyed by that code.

As defined by Kenneth S. Lynn's study, the southwestern tradition was primarily based upon a game with point of view implying a distancing of the narrator from the object described. Lynn traces this tradition back to William Byrd II's *History of the Dividing Line*, a diary recording the colonization of Virginia that was meant for publication in London. Lynn emphasizes the style of the book, which reveals a particular attitude of detachment from the object observed "outside and above what is going on."[30] The literary model of this work is what Erich Auerbach has shown to be the literary ideal of such Roman historians as Sallust and Tacitus; they judged their subjects with extreme severity and their moral vision was defined in aesthetic terms. Grotesque and low characters were not allowed to speak for themselves. Lynn suggests that the development of the southwestern literary tradition followed a similar course. If, on the one hand, the development of the vernacular voice in the written text is one of the greatest achievements of that tradition, such development encountered great resistance. As long as literacy was the exclusive privilege of the upper classes, southern folklore was handed down orally, and its codification was done by southern gentlemen who believed in the elitist southern myth and defined their own image through style. The lower classes were then described with irony and were not given an audible voice. This obviously changed gradually as soon as the southern ruling class became less and less able to control the realities of its environment through an elitist myth: The vernacular voice became more and more audible in the works until it prevailed over the gentlemanly style.

The movement of southwestern humorists, which produced some of the most significant works in the first half of the nineteenth century, was centered in and wrote about what was then called the southwest, a region located between the Alleghenies and the Mississippi. Its members shared common literary and political ideals. Well-educated professional people, the southwestern humorists were conservatives who were often connected with the Whig party or the southern planters. They strongly opposed the principles and practice of Jacksonian democracy, which they saw as destabilizing the South. Not only did their political views seep into their writings, but they were, in fact, the essence of the message the writers wanted to convey. The southern upper class, in their view, was the only guarantor of order and civilization. Their message was directed to the whole nation, and its carrier was the magazine *The Spirit of the Times,* published by William T. Porter. The literary models for this movement were Walter Scott and Joseph Addison. The former's treatment of the Scottish past provided them with a mythical model: The glorious past of Scotland was equated with the South. Moreover, Scott's use of humorous low characters in relation to dignified aristocrats suggested a structural device. However, the literary model that contributed more powerfully to the shaping of the literary structures of their works was the Man of Reason, Addison's character/persona. The frame, an old literary formal device that was recurrent in Addison's essays in *The Spectator,* was adopted in order to create a needed distance between the point of view of the gentleman/narrator and the tall talk of the vernacular character (or second narrator). The narrator was thus kept separate from the comic talk and action he described.[31] In the frame (or intradiegesis, as it would be called according to a narratological perspective), the myth of the southern gentleman—an image of order and civilization—was established through an urbane tone of self-confidence and self-control. Within the frame (or metadiegesis), the tall tales of frontiersmen and backwoodsmen were recounted in vernacular by their protagonists.[32]

One of the purposes of Lynn's study is to show how Twain reinterprets in his works the southwestern tradition. The cultural context evoked by his study helps us define in clearer terms one important aspect of Twain's works that is diachronically embedded in the Papers: the duality and otherness expressed through language.

Parody is based upon the description of another's language and worldview.[33] As we have seen, this is the core of the burlesques of the early phase. Twain, however, employs a burlesque that diverges at some points from the practice of the San Francisco Bohemians. The departure consists of the estranged voices of narrators and/or characters, lending estranged points of view describing the language and worldview of the other. The peculiarity of Twain's literary burlesques is that the object of description is always the mainstream culture (the opera, Victor Hugo's novels, Shakespeare's most famous tragedy, the temperance literature), and the voices and/or point of view describing and observing are either implicitly or explicitly vernacular. Thus the literary procedure of estrangement is connected to the cultural context of the southwestern vernacular and conveys the literary ideal implicit in the oral tradition: the equivalence of the written and the oral—the zero degree of writing.

The emergence of the other in the text obviously shapes different texts in different ways. In the satires it creates a distancing that serves the purpose of irony. On the other hand, in the fantastic narrations the duality implied in the double narration of the tall tales evolves into the ambiguity and uncertainty characteristic of the fantastic genre.

In any case, Twain's literary innovation is shown by the evolution of forms from one text to another. The innovation consists mainly of the elimination of any mediation introducing, and somewhat censoring, the vernacular voice and point of view. This is most successfully achieved when the vernacular and the child character are combined, as in the case of Jim, the slum child, who is not only a vernacular character but also an interpreter of reality: In his speech, language and vision are equated. This is the case also of Twain's masterpiece character, Huck Finn, who, with his vernacular voice and innocent perspective, lays the facts bare. We can then say that the transformation of the function of the vernacular character/narrator from an object of description to a restrained voice, and eventually to a totally unrestrained voice and point of view, finds in Twain its most radical evolution.

It must be noted, however, that the other narrative function involved in the tall tale, the gentlemanly voice framing the vernacular story, evolves as well, often into the counterpart of the vernacular character. In this case the polite and urbane tone of the gentleman becomes merely pompous; it is the voice of artificiality in language and of hypocrisy in ethics. It is the moral mentor of the "Colloquy Between a Slum-Child and a Moral Mentor." It is his own voice, not description, that creates the parody. His worldview is expressed by his artificiality. In *Adventures of Huckleberry Finn,* the gentlemanly voice undergoes a different evolution; it is internalized by Huck. He allows this voice to emerge while debating his own choice to transgress the rules and conventions of a slave-owner society. His uncertainty is expressed by his language, which wavers between vernacular speech and a rather bookish and genteel diction that he has internalized.[34]

There is another possible evolution for the genteel narrator. He can disappear as a character and evolve into a mere narrative voice, such as the distant and ironic voice telling the fables of "The Victims" and "The Yellow Terror." Even though, in this case, it is not counterbalanced by a vernacular character, the function of the genteel voice is substantially unaltered as compared to the one in the tall tales, since it still provides a contrasting effect, through sophistication, with the naïveté of the mythical code of the fables.

A further and even more interesting evolution relates to the function of direction exerted by the gentleman/narrator toward the text. In presenting the speech of the vernacular character/narrator, the first (diegetical) narrator provides a mediation: The translator of "3000 Years Among the Microbes" functions as both mediator and director. In like manner, the secret transcriber of the "Secret History of Eddypus" recounts the muddled history of humankind on special papers on which the writing can be erased and reprinted at will; so, too, does the narrator who introduces the "bronzed and gray sailor" in "The Enchanted Sea-Wilderness." All three share a concern for language, a "metalinguistic" attitude; they know that language itself is a means of self-description for the objects of their texts. "Three Thousand Years Among the Microbes" is preceded by two prefaces—one dealing with the message and its veracity, the other with its code:

> I have translated the author's style and construction, as well as his matter. I began by reforming these, but gave it up. It amounted to putting evening dress on a stevedore and making him stand up in the college and lecture. He was trim, but he was stiff; he delivered strict English, polished English, but it seemed strained and artificial, coming from such a source, and was not pleasant, not satisfactory. Elegant, but cold and unsympathetic. In fact, corpsy. It seemed best to put him back into his shirt-sleeves and overalls, and let him flounder around after the fashion that he was used to. His style is loose and wandering and garrulous and self-contented beyond anything I have ever encountered before and his grammar breaks the heart. But there is no remedy: let it go.
>
> The Translator[35]

The translator of "3000 Years" deals with a written text retaining the style, voice, and personality of the original author; the narrator of "The Enchanted Sea-Wilderness" reports, instead, a message inscribed only in his memory. The original message is oral—the story told by the sailor. In fact, before starting the story the narrator says, "I kept it in my memory as well as I could, and wrote it down the next day—in my own language, for I could not remember his, of course."[36] The narrator of "The Secret History" exemplifies still another attitude toward the original text and its transcription. The entire history is meant to be private, addressed only to a limited audience of reliable friends; therefore both its contact and code are private—the paper on which it is written is erasable, and previously a cipher had been adopted. The latter, however, did not prove to be very efficient because the receiver had a hard time trying to decode it. The narrator is thus writing a history that is partly a reconstruction through memory of a written original he had heard about from other heretics who had read the original. Other sources for his history are books that had been written after the destruction of all books had taken place—confused evidence because most of the message in them had been handed down orally. The uncertainty of the message is matched by the lack of permanence of the contact; for example, the writing on erasable paper, which deprives writing of its traditional value of permanence and equates it to the instability and fluidity of oral performance.

The attitude of the narrators/translators reveals much of Twain's own attitude toward the written and the oral traditions. The narrators' ambivalence (attempts to restrain the oral performance and the subsequent realizations of the impossibility of such a task) reflects the diachronic development of the folktales of the Southwest up to Twain's own reinterpretation of that tradition. The codifiers of the southwestern tall tale—Longstreet, Hooper, Thorpe, Harris—worked on oral or semi-oral sources that had often been previously transcribed in the original vernacular by ghostwriters. This early transcription, which marked a first step in the passage from oral to written performance, responded to the needs of a changed audience: A reading public gradually replaced the campfire audience. A further development occurred when the publication of the stories reached a larger reading public through national magazines. The change of addressee entailed a change of code: A mediation between the oral vernacular performance and the reading audience was needed. The frame provided such mediation; it also added ambiguity to the message. As we have seen, different authors carried out this mediation in quite different ways. In Longstreet's work the genteel narrator is the focus of the story, while the oral performance is kept under control. The addresser receives the message as a written communication; the bond with the oral tradition is apparently severed.

However, under the impact of social and political change, the writers' attitudes changed as well: The vernacular character was again allowed autonomy of speech and a larger space in the economy of the story.

Twain's narrators/translators exemplify a dialectical attitude toward the oral tradition. Both the transcribers of "3000 Years" and of "The Enchanted Sea-Wilderness" try to restrain the oral performance that they intend to translate and mediate for their reading audience. In different ways, they are both unsuccessful in their attempt. Having tried to purge the language of the Microbe of its vulgarity, the translator of "3000 Years" gives up. He becomes aware that purging the language would mean to alter code, message, and addresser; thus he confines his censoring function to the apologetic prefatory note. The text he is dealing with approximates the oral text: It is an autobiography, and therefore, like Twain's own autobiography, meant to be talk. The prefatory note then reflects Twain's own attitude toward writing, showing his awareness of the impossibility of censoring the oral utterance, or rather the trace of oral speech in the written text.

The narrator of "The Enchanted Sea-Wilderness" displays still a different attitude. His manipulation of the oral text—because in this case he is dealing with a purely oral source—derives from what he perceives to be the limitations of his memory, which would not allow him to reconstruct the code of the original message. However, he delivers the story by imitating the utterance of the vernacular narrator; thus, the original utterance seeps into his performance and gives it the peculiar characteristics of oral speech—the repetitions, the anticipations of events, the conative function. Moreover, the mythic mentality of the vernacular narrator—his belief in a cosmic determinism—is just another token of the oral tradition. Thus, despite the unreliability of the vehicle of memory, the vernacular narration prevails over the genteel mediation.

The discourse on memory is developed even further in "The Secret History of Eddypus." There memory proves to be an unreliable vehicle for the preservation of evidence; yet in the midst of faulty and confused information—the effort at a reconstruction of history—the original trace (that is, Mark Twain, the Father of History) speaks from the grave:

> I see this page now for the last time; you will be the next to see it—and there will be an interval between. There is a tie between us, you perceive: where your hand rests now, mine rested last— you shall imagine you feel some faint remnant of the warmth

> my hand's contact is communicating to the page as I write—for I am writing this word of greeting and salutation, not type-writing it. . . ."[37]

The voice of the Father of History interrupts the flow of the burlesque historical reconstruction. It is the only authentic trace in the whole narration, in which faulty recollections distort both oral and written messages, creating a nightmare of confused identities out of the past. The origin is, then, the human voice, seeping into the writing and becoming presence. Through writing, the oral expression loses its transience and acquires permanence. Memory, the writing of the mind, is, on the other hand, pure transience: It is similar to the writing of the secret history, which, on erasable paper, shows itself intermittently. It is also like a cipher whose key has been lost and is hard now to decipher. It can only convey a faint image of the origin. Its relation to writing is that of an indefinite deferral.

Throughout the Papers these issues recur: the relation of the oral to the written text, memory as a fallible bridge between presence and deferral, writing as a form of presence. In the fictional experiments these issues emerge constantly and find their most thorough thematic development in the motifs channeled into the "No. 44" version of *The Mysterious Stranger Manuscripts*. Also, in the later fantastic tales, the opposition between states of consciousness—waking and dreaming—is the evolution of the dichotomy between written and oral performances. Because of its fluid nature, its subconscious origin, and its presence, the dream replaces the oral performance in the tales, whereas the waking state of consciousness approximates the frame of the tall tales— that is, the recording of experience through writing. Like the perfor-mance of the genteel narrator, the initial segment of narration in the fantastic tales (diegesis) results in an abortive attempt to restrain disor-der and create a logical order out of the apparent chaos of dream.

A related aspect of Twain's link with the southwestern tradition is fascination with the human voice. Vernacular characters appear throughout the Papers, and they are heard more than described. Their voices bridge the distance of centuries and of different cultures. Quite incongruously in "No. 44," a black character appears in the middle of a medieval castle and plays the banjo while he sings of his nostalgia for Africa. His voice has the evocative power to conjure up images.

The presence of vernacular characters is a constant reminder of an origin—often forgotten and erased—which, however, cannot be suppressed. They are a token of Twain's recurrent returns to his own personal origin, to the world of Hannibal and its imaginative material. A whole series of experiments (some of them published during Twain's lifetime) deal with a return to his famous heroes—Tom, Huck, and Jim—and the setting of St. Petersburg. Among the pieces collected in *Mark Twain's Hannibal, Huck and Tom* by Walter Blair, "Villagers of 1840–3," "Jane Lampton Clemens," "Tupperville-Dobbsville," and "Clairvoyant" are the most interesting because they provide us with an inside view of the world of Hannibal.[38] It is a world where written communication must have been almost useless, where everybody knows everybody else. By writing about this society, Twain codifies it, reverses its transience by fixing it in time. He also shows the roots of his own attitude toward the concept of community, his preference for the small community where individualities stand out. In "Villagers" he reconstructs from memory a good part of Hannibal's population. Each name triggers a story, a brief description; an individuality is re-created from distant memories. Thus Twain evokes a world of individuality and difference, as opposed to the unified world of writing and printing.

These semiautobiographical pieces suggest also the origin of Twain's repeated settings of small communities that reproduce in miniature the human community at large. Twain's whole conception of the microcosmos as the perfect sample of the macrocosmos is rooted in his memories, as well as in his romanticizing of the world of Hannibal.[39]

Oral communication also shapes the form of Twain's narration—the recurrence of dialogue, the mimetic mood, the tone of the spoken rather than the written word in his prose. This peculiarity can be considered a trace of the oral performance that remains as a remote ideal—an ideal rooted in both his early personal experience on the Missouri frontier and his later association with the southwestern culture.[40]

Polyglossia and Heteroglossia: The Dialogic Relation Between Old and New

Twain's work is often viewed as the meeting point of opposed traditions and cultures—the western frontier and the more sophisticated East

Coast. (Henry Nash Smith deals with this aspect in particular.) My study supports the view that Twain's work is the meeting point of languages—the language of the vernacular and the language of the genteel, the language of the oral and of the written traditions.

Mikhail Bakhtin, in *The Dialogic Imagination,* describes a linguistic and cultural phenomenon that he calls polyglossia.[41] It occurs often in the formation of a new culture when a dialectical interrelation between lower and higher languages is established. Polyglossia creates a dialectical tension in the literary text—a relation of opposition between languages, between the worldviews conveyed and represented by language. This tension, which we have observed as part of the diachronic development of the southwestern tall tale, is crystallized synchronically in Twain's work. In the burlesques each worldview, each language, looks at the other language and describes it through estrangement and ridicule.

The dialectical relation of language and points of view, because of the intercrossing of cultures, determines a related stylistic phenomenon characterizing Twain's experimental production: the stratification of different styles, idiolects from different social strata, and various genres in the text. It is what Bakhtin calls heteroglossia.[42]

This brings us to a crucial problem of hermeneutics. For the critic of Twain's Papers the definition of their genres is always problematic. Twain tries his hand at various genres inside the same text. The multiplicity of styles, languages, and genres results from a fragmented consciousness at work in the text. For this reason, not only does the text present problems of generic categorization, but it also poses problems of semantic interpretation. Where are the meanings of the text and of the author to be found? In the burlesques we can find them in the ironic consciousness emerging in the text. However, in the later and more complex fictional works of the Papers, the burlesque is only part of a series of genres at work in the text. For example, both "The Great Dark" and "The Enchanted Sea-Wilderness" are burlesques of other literary texts and fantastic tales. *The Mysterious Stranger Manuscripts* are romances that, however, contain burlesques of other genres as well as a straightforward use of genres and languages.

Heteroglossia is the true mode of Twain's experimentalism. It is the natural development of the binarily oriented structures of both burlesques and southwestern tall tales. In heteroglossia each element of style, each language, each genre, establishes a relation, some kind of dialogue with each other. The text acquires complexity and a precarious balance. Straightforward passages are followed by satirical ones, serious episodes are alternated with comic ones, stereotypical characters are interspersed with fully developed ones. The reader is faced with fragmentation. If the source of this duality can be traced back to Twain's early literary practice in the southwestern tradition and the subsequent apprenticeship in burlesque with the San Francisco Bohemians, the direction the fragmented texts of the Papers points toward is modern fiction, the open form, and the endless chain of signs.[43]

2

Fantasy

The duality at the heart of Twain's early burlesques and later satires also permeates his experiments in the fantastic. In the pieces that he wrote during the last fifteen years of his life, duality of perspective, estrangement, and distortion signal a connection to the early experiments in burlesque and southwestern humor that was never severed. These experiments in the fantastic, however, go a step further than his previous literary pursuits in that striving for the transcription of reality that I identified in chapter 1 as Twain's tendency toward the zero degree of writing. The search for the origin is not abandoned, but it is geared toward subjectivity, toward the exploration of the powers of human imagination.

In many respects, the fantastic experiments can be viewed as a development of the philosophical and literary discourse Twain had initiated with his early experiments in burlesque. The fantastic shares with burlesque parody an estrangement procedure, a defamiliarization of familiar reality, as well as a hyperbolic distortion of familiar objects. This is carried out through a dual perspective that, although present in both genres, is geared toward different results. While burlesques and tall tales achieve comic relief, the fantastic tales heighten the suspension of judgment. As Todorov argues, both narrator and reader, faced with supernatural events, hesitate between a naturalization of the supernatural and an acknowledgment of its mysterious trespassing of the laws of the physical world.

David Ketterer argues that, because of their heterogeneity, Twain's fantastic writings do not fit a generic categorization; in other words, they lack the homogeneity that characterizes genre.[1] I have already indicated in chapter 1 that Twain's heteroglossia, one of the most outstanding features of his early experiments and his later works, makes a generic study of the Papers problematic. This issue is further complicated by such writings as the experimental satires and dystopian tales, which are neither pure burlesques nor true fantasies, even though they include fantastic elements. The animal fables, for example, metaphorically allude to reality through distortion and reversal. Similarly, the dystopian aspect of "The Secret History of Eddypus, the World Empire" is based upon distortion of the data of reality and estrangement from familiar characters and events. A reversal through "gulliverization" occurs also in "3000 Years Among the Microbes," where the "landscape" of the inside of the human body mirrors the external universe. All along in these experiments the fantastic is mingled with comic and parodic elements.

It is similarly difficult to find a right categorization for the "voyage of disaster" stories that are part of the volume *Which Was the Dream? and Other Symbolic Writings*. As tales of imaginary voyages, they fall easily into the broad genre of fantasy, as defined by the all-encompassing categorization suggested by Rabkin.[2] Not only is Twain's fantastic hard to define, but the concept of fantastic literature itself, viewed either as a writing or as a genre, causes controversy and has been defined in various ways.

Rabkin's and Todorov's views stand at the poles. The former identifies the fantastic element in a variety of writings and genres and defines it as the reversal of the ground rules of any given text. This reversal occurs in the genre of fantasy, where the fantastic element prevails. Todorov, on the other hand, defines the fantastic not as an element present in other genres, but as an autonomous genre with precise features and quite narrow requirements.[3] Adverse criticisms of both approaches have already pointed out either the too loose generalization suggested by Rabkin or the too narrow definition given by Todorov.[4] It is not the purpose of this study to find the most appropriate definition of the fantastic genre, but rather to extract from other works on the subject suggestions that might illuminate the specific features of

Twain's experiments in this genre. Fantastic elements, as defined by Rabkin, abound in the later Papers; for this reason, the broader term "fantasy," suggested by his book, was adopted to entitle the chapter rather than the more restrictive "fantastic genre" proposed by Todorov.

A partial or total reversal of either inner or outer ground rules occurs likewise in the satirical fables, in the fictional historical dystopias, and in the various fantasies. Yet, a consideration needs to be added; the ground rules of the text should encompass the reader's horizon of expectation, which is inherent in the text. A similar consideration applies to Todorov's view of the fantastic: The hesitation that he views as a central feature of the fantastic should be considered also as the discrepancy between the reader's expectations of reality and the emergence of surrealistic events in the text. To say this is to suggest a broadening of the categorization proposed by Todorov so that the fantastic genre would encompass the contiguous categories of the marvelous and the uncanny. In fact, because of this prescriptive and restrictive quality, Todorov's definition excludes too many texts from the fantastic genre. In particular, Twain's experiments seem to combine fantastic, marvelous, and uncanny elements within the same texts. Only in the "imaginary voyage" stories does a suspension of judgment take place (through a game with double perspective). There the framed narration, typical of the southwestern tall tale, evolves into a form that generates hesitation in both the reader and the narrator/character. The evolution of the framed narration, which in three of the "imaginary voyage stories" takes the form of a framed dream narration, is the most outstanding formal characteristic of this phase and aspect of Twain's work. The framed narration is the very trace of the origin of Twain's writing, his source in the southwestern narration; it is the sign of a discourse at the core of his writing—the dialectical opposition between the world of writing and that of the oral tradition. It shows the continuation of that discourse and its evolution, while it also signals a mind that apprehends and describes reality through dichotomies.

Yet Todorov's method provides us with a framework and an interpretive key that help us view the fantastic as a series of variants determined by the variable game of the surreal in the text. It also highlights the subterranean relation between the phenomena of abnormal states of mind and the emergence of the fantastic. Both occur in opposition to a previously existing concept of normality. It must be noted, however, that according to contemporary trends in psychoanalysis the dissolution of the ego, occurring at the emergence of the irrational, signals a moment of truth in the evolution of the subject.[5] Similarly, in Twain's fantasies the emergence of the surreal, while shattering the previously established frame of normality, throws a disturbingly revelatory light over reality.

Indeed, the fantastic provides Twain with the possibility of exploring the subjective powers of the mind and of testing the possibilities of artistic language—in other words, of continuing the experimentation through transgression that he had started early on and that runs throughout his more private literary career.

In dealing with this aspect of the Papers, one should also keep in mind the writer's interests and concerns for the powers of the mind, and for dream psychology in particular. Entries in Twain's notebooks provide sure evidence of this interest and of the startling similarities between his perceptions of the structure of dreams and the more scholarly postulations of philosophers and psychologists, such as William James.

Tuckey takes a partially different approach to the relation between the text and the extra-text, pointing out its relation to the writer's homecoming fantasies in a period when he was compelled by financial disasters to travel and reside abroad.[6] Tuckey notes the use of the terms "voyage" and "ship" in both letters and notebook entries to designate life, home, and luck, and the persistent use of wish-fulfillment fantasies that resemble the plot of the "imaginary voyage" stories. Although Tuckey's point is well based and well documented, my study takes a different slant: Leaving aside any possible biographical references, it interprets the fantastic element more as a cognitive, even epistemological, activity than as a purely sublimating one. It is the persistent use of the framed narration itself that suggests this interpretation. Through the dual perspective implied in the double narration, the author inserts doubts in the text and has his narrators question the nature of the events they describe and witness. Was it a dream? Where does the dream end and reality begin? Is it possible that dreams can change the course of everyday reality? Not only do the readers share the hesitation of the narrators facing the dream, but they cannot evade the deeper philosophical and ontological questions implied in the narrators' doubts. Even though at the end it appears clear that it was a dream, one is left with one open question: What is the importance of the oneiric experience in human life? The real doubt, then, transcends the text and makes the reader ponder larger implications.

The fantastic provides Twain with an open field for the exploration of the powers of the psyche. Ketterer argues that Twain's power fantasies, as well as his interest in the power of fantasy, place some of his papers (namely, "The Secret History of Eddypus, the World Empire" and "The Great Dark") at the borderline between fantasy and science fiction.[7] In Ketterer's view, Twain's mind oscillates between a power fantasy, which would make him feel responsible for everything as well as immensely powerful, and the belief in the absolute power of fantasy, which would prove that life is a dream and thus provide him with an escape from responsibility. Twain's studies in determinism fostered this escapist attitude: If everything is determined, man is not responsible for his own destiny. On this subject, Tuckey expresses a quite different view.[8] He traces the two philosophical trends that interested Twain during the last twenty years of his career in two distinct groups of works: *What Is Man?* is based upon his deterministic beliefs, while the stories included in *Which Was the Dream? and Other Symbolic Writings* and *The Mysterious Stranger Manuscripts* mirror his interest in dream psychology and the powers of the imagination.

In my article "Mark Twain alle soglie della fantascienza" (1979) I suggest, as Ketterer does, that Twain, in his experimentation, moves toward science fiction.[9] The use of technological instruments as tools to provide enlarged vision and power to his characters, the personification of these instruments, and the pseudoscientific mentality shown by the first narrator in "The Enchanted Sea-Wilderness" seem to be elements suggesting a science-fictional attitude. I view these scientific elements as signs of Twain's fascination with both technology and deterministic philosophy. Unlike Tuckey, I trace in that study the writer's scientific trend, and his bent toward dream psychology, back to the same group of fictions: the fantastic tales. The two elements survive there together. The scientific attitude provides a referential structure, the world of logic and reason, while the fantastic resurfaces inside the framed story (metadiegesis) as a previously suppressed uncanny element.

The peculiar form of Twain's fantastic experiments finds its ideal narrative structure in framed and double narration. The opposition of points of view, of discourses, of grapholects conveys the opposition at the core of Twain's vision. Yet the two narrations are complementary, and so are the writer's trends, in spite of apparent discord. The introductory segment (intradiegesis), which depicts the reality, and the framed narration (metadiegesis), which contains the dream, relate to each other through subtle allusions.[10] This is proven, for example, in "The Great Dark" by the presence of an optical instrument as a tool for exploring the world of dreams. This presence reinforces the cognitive attitude, which is just another aspect of the science-fictional genre. Twain comes close to this mode in his later phase when he makes the connection between scientific discoveries and imagination.[11] Similarly, the two trends of Twain's philosophical thought—his determinism and his speculations in dream psychology—although opposed, distinct, and separate, entertain a relation to each other. If in fact human beings are determined by immutable laws in their relation to society and the physical world, so are they affected by the inner laws of the psyche. The dreams in which the protagonists of Twain's dream voyages seem to escape are in fact the nightmarish, darker, and innermost side of a constraining reality. There is no real escape in Twain's fantastic narrations; usually cognition replaces sublimation.

The framed narration provides Twain with a vehicle to convey his philosophical vision. It also allows him to continue the experimentation with language and form that he had started early in his career. The relation between written and oral discourse in the early burlesques anticipates what later unfolds into the relation between conscious and subconscious discourse. The two levels of the psyche function in their natural relation in ways similar to those of the genteel and vernacular narrators of the tall tales. In the fantastic stories the first narrator is involved in creating a framework of control and rationality, while the second narrator evades that control and, through a narration of dream and/or imaginary voyage, introduces an element of limitless freedom, irrational expansion, and unpredictable adventure. This reproduces at a symbolic level the relationship between the genteel and vernacular narrators. There too the second narrator evades the control of the first narrator and introduces through speech the unpredictable and the unruly. The vernacular speech evolves, in these later fantastic experiments, into the dream speech, the liberated expression that Twain had come to identify with superior artistic creation. Not only do the Notebooks point toward this interpretation, but "My Platonic Sweetheart," in which

Twain deals specifically with dream language, also indicates that he was seeking the source of creativity in the experience and language of dream. This liberated creativity could derive only from the uncanny element surfacing both in oral performance and dream language. He then gears his search for the source of creativity toward the inner self, which is expressed by the oneiric experience and the uncanny element emerging during that experience. In the fantastic stories, however, the emergence of the uncanny element contained inside the metadiegesis is not necessarily linked to dream; it can be related to an imaginary voyage or any other supernatural experience. Such is the case with "An Adventure in Remote Seas" and with "The Enchanted Sea-Wilderness," where surrealistic events occur during a voyage without return. The uncanny is an element subjected to a previous suppression that, in spite of and because of that suppression, gains a mysterious power. In "The Enchanted Sea-Wilderness" the repression of the emotional side of experience, symbolized by the elimination of the childlike dog, transforms the journey into a surrealistic, nightmarish experience. The dialectical relation is viewed here through a neo-Freudian approach to the text, in which art plays a role comparable to jokes in social interrelation. Art allows the emergence of previously suppressed drives of the subconscious in a form acceptable to both society and the superego. The trace of the dialectical opposition between the forces of suppression and the object being suppressed transpires in the formal structures of the text—in particular in the rhetorical figures. Twain's framed structure, in its earlier and later development, is one of the ways in which both suppressing and suppressed agents interrelate in the text.[12]

Although the framed narration is Twain's peculiar form of the fantastic, one should be aware that, in *The Mysterious Stranger Manuscripts* (Twain's last experiment in one of the forms of the fantastic, the romance), he abandons the framed narration.

As Louis Vax's study of the fantastic points out, the framed narration is not uncommon among fantastic tales.[13] It is a form that can be traced back to oral narration. Vax argues that the legend is the special kind of oral narration from which fantastic tales are directly derived. The legend in turn takes its origin from reality and experience. Three different phases mark the development from experience into tale. The first stage is simply a report by the witness of the experience; the second stage is a report of what the narrator has heard about the event;

the third phase relates what the tradition has recorded about the event. The frame would be a trace of these stages in forming the legend.

In adopting the framed narration Twain certainly followed a well-established convention of the genre.[14] Yet his peculiar use of the framed narration through the opposition of the written and the oral performance, the waking and the dream, is his *parole* in the *langue* of the genre. This peculiar use of the frame also defines his tales in terms of genre. In fact, the frame of a supernatural story provides a reference structure establishing the ground rules that, according to Rabkin, need to be reversed in order for the fantastic to occur. These ground rules of the text are later transgressed by the dream and/or imaginary voyage described in the metadiegesis. Yet the frame also ensures the return to the reality and ground rules that were established at the beginning. According to Todorov's theory, this return, by suspending the course of supernatural events, naturalizes the fantastic and places the whole tale almost beyond the realm of the pure fantastic genre, pushing it into what he calls "the uncanny"; yet the return to the world of normality does not mark the triumph of the real over the imaginary. Whenever Twain provided, in holograph notes, some ending for his fantastic tales, the return that concludes the adventure is hardly a reinstatement of reality. In fact, even the initial part of the frame, although reflecting the state of mind in a time subsequent to the events of the story recounted inside the frame, does not anticipate a closure. The dream, the imaginary voyage, has always affected the protagonists; normality has become somewhat abnormal. The emergence of the uncanny has changed the previous reality and reversed the ground rules forever.

At the risk of contradicting Todorov's definition of the fantastic, one must say that Twain's fantastic is an exploration of the powers of the imagination that leads eventually to the assertion of the power of dream over reality. In fact, the very existence of reality, as such, becomes doubtful. This is the conceptual turning point from parody—in the burlesques and the tall tales—to the fantastic. The conceptual breakthrough entails a change in the direction of the experiment with language. If the very existence of reality becomes doubtful, then its transcription will reflect this uncertainty. The transcription of the muddled and confused history of Eddypus is an example. Reality cannot be encompassed by writing. The origin is remote, and even though the origin is still the human voice—the voice of the Father of History and that of the sailor in "The Enchanted Sea-Wilderness"—this voice, this origin, needs the medium of writing in order to reach its addressees. However, the voice inscribed in the text transcends reality. It is from this awareness that the fantastic stems.

Even if it cannot be reached, reality cannot be totally evaded. The dream and/or the imaginary voyage allude metaphorically to the reality depicted by the referential frame. The fantastic then becomes another way of talking about experience, of describing it by displacing it, removing it from the constraints of the everyday. The fantastic becomes another way of reaching the thing, except that in the fantastic the thing to be reached is not part of the external reality but rather of the innermost self. The thing of the fantastic can be reached only through mirrors, alluring mirrors in which the self trying to reach its center has to lose itself and go through moments of terror.[15] We will deal with these mirrors and that terror in the discussion of the two stories that we have chosen to analyze from *Which Was the Dream? and Other Symbolic Writings*, "The Enchanted Sea-Wilderness" and "The Great Dark."

The discussion of the fantastic fiction will be preceded here by an exploration of parts of the Notebooks in which Twain expresses his interest in the fantastic, in dream psychology, and in the structures of the psyche. Through such notes it is possible to trace the genesis of the creation of the fantastic fiction.

The Notebooks and Fantasy

Twain's Notebooks of 1895–98 provide us with evidence of the writer's deep interest in various aspects of what we loosely can call the "irrational" or "the fantastic."

In the entries for 1895 and 1896 there is a recurrence of the idea of the journey. This can be related easily to the fact that Twain actually was traveling on a boat. However, what strikes us after having read "The Enchanted Sea-Wilderness" is how these notes anticipate the writing process. Sea and ship are often viewed in these entries as juxtaposed entities. The ship is an autonomous and self-enclosed microsociety, whereas the sea is huge, still and quiet, almost deprived of life. In the Notebook entry dated 6 January 1896 we read:

> What an eventless existence life at sea on a long summer voyage is. No life visible; now & then a school of porpoises; at intervals a solitary albatross; once a week a ship, far away; peace everlasting peace & tranquility.[16]†

And, a little further:

> However, a ship is a world of its own—one does not trouble himself about other world & and their affairs. (N & J 37, TS MTP, p. 2)†

And then again:

> The one difference between a river & the sea is that the river looks fluid, the sea solid—usually looks as if you could step out & walk on it" (N & J 37, TS MTP, p. 6); . . .†
> "but outside of the ship is no life visible but the occasional flash of a flying fish. (N & J 37, TS MTP, p. 7)†

The ship, inasmuch as it is a microsociety, has its own culture, its own traditions and legends that are handed down orally; the captain of the boat on which Twain is traveling functions as a collective memory, and he tells one anecdote after another. Twain is very much intrigued by the technical aspects of traveling, but he enlarges and expands them into the fantastic events that create a magic aura around the actual voyage. He has recollections of faraway times when there was no technically efficient machinery, the result of scientific discoveries:

> In the old times they used to heave the log in [ever] each watch; now the ship does it herself, by automatic machinery; heaves it day & night & all the time makes a record of the result. You don't have to watch it—it doesn't get drunk. (N & J 37, TS MTP, p. 34)†

He looks back with regret to the times when the world's distances were much greater, and writes a little further on:

No generation after the one now passing from the stage will ever
be able to appreciate how romantic it was; for the reason that
all-world-distances have shrunk to nothing now; [there are no
dim far-away lands, now, dreaming in a golden haze of mystery].
The mysterious & the fabulous can get no fine effects without
the help of remoteness; there are no remoteness, anymore. (N
& J 37, TS MTP, p. 37)†

On 4 September 1895 they cross the equator; in the entries that follow,
Twain deals with the electric currents that permanently affect the iron
parts of the ship, even modifying the proper and exact functioning of
the compass. On 6 September 1895, Twain refers to the compass in
terms that almost personify it: "A compass is a particular & fastidious
& wayward thing—gets wedded to habits & will not give them up" (N
& J 35, TS MTP, p. 43). This leads it to inaccuracies that the sailors
have to correct; eventually, when it has been adjusted, a load of iron
for the railways will unbalance it again. "It is much more capricious &
fussy than any woman," concludes Twain (N & J 35, TS MTP, p. 44).†
Under some specific circumstances even the most precise compass
can go crazy, and this can happen when the ship is crossing certain
spots at sea, mysterious places that, according to sea lore, do really
exist—

There are spots at sea where the compass loses its head & whirls
this way & that; then you give it up & steer by sun, wind, stars,
moon or guess, & trust to luck to save you till you get by that
insane region. (N & J 35, TS MTP, p. 44)†

As we have seen, "The Enchanted Sea-Wilderness" deals with a trip
through one of those "spots at sea." The Notebook entries seem to
prepare for the writing of the tale. The whole idea of remoteness is a
prelude to the development of a mental process leading to fantastic
literature; in the same way, the personification of the compass prepares
for the creation of the compass as a character in the tale. The juxtaposition between ship, seen as microsociety, and ocean, seen as impersonal,
huge, still macrocosmos, is part of the symbolic system of the tale.

A shift in themes in the Notebook entries of 1897 corresponds to a
shift in the fantastic narration: from travel, Twain moves to dream.
Reading the Notebooks written around 1897 and the beginning of

1898, one can notice the insistence of the dream motif: Twain takes notes about his own dreams, especially those that seem personally and professionally relevant and that can provide him with ideas for his tales. What interests him is how dreams develop in the human mind; he wonders about the relationship between the dreamer's personality during sleep and while awake. In the Notebook entry of 7 January 1897, he reaches the conclusion that all personality is double and refers to the literary example of Dr. Jekyll and Mr. Hyde (N & J 40, TS MTP, pp. 3–4). According to Twain, the human personality is organized in such a way that its two parts do not know each other; the dream part has, in his opinion, a total independence, which he calls "the spiritualized self." This idea is based upon discoveries made about somnambulists: A somnambulist, once awake, is unable to remember what he has done while in a trance state, unless a new trance is induced.

We are reminded here of the opposites in "The Enchanted Sea-Wilderness." Also, in such dream narrations as "The Great Dark" and "Which Was the Dream?," the separation between the waking and the dream states of the characters leads to the idea of the double personality, expressed also on the narrative level by the juxtaposition of the two narrators (the dreamer and the waking one) and of two separate worlds (the ship and the house). The separation between the two worlds is caused by the fact that the characters, while dreaming, lose memory of their waking state, which to them looks rather confused and unreal; a great confusion then arises in the characters' very concepts of reality (connected with the waking state) and of unreality (linked with the oneiric experience).

In the Notebooks, "the spiritualized self," besides possessing a "distinct duality," can go wandering on "mysterious trips" (N & J 40, TS MTP, p. 4). This is what happens in "The Great Dark," which, even from this point of view, can be considered as a further elaboration of "The Enchanted Sea-Wilderness"—from the story of a voyage to a dream voyage, from oral narration to dream structure.

The "spiritualized self" has enormous powers; it is free from the impediments of the flesh. It can do what the X rays can: penetrate deeply and see what the mere gaze cannot grasp. Again, we are reminded of the microscope in "The Great Dark" that plays such an important role by allowing the protagonist to acquire a deeper vision. The dream personality has a great capacity for movement—the possibility of moving around freely in space, of reaching the remotest places. There is no clear division between what we commonly call reality and unreality, between what actually happens in the field of reality and what happens only inside the human mind. It seems as if the prerequisites of the fantastic are present in the Notebook entries even before they become fiction; the barrier separating the real and the imaginary, the physical and the psychic worlds fades away. The mind creates and lives its own autonomous reality.

In one of the Notebook entries of that period, Twain records his dream of a black girl down south who offers him love and food and the sharing of the spoon she has been eating from. At the end, Twain comments:

> It was not a dream—it all happened. I was actually there in person—in my spiritualized condition. My, how vivid it all was!—even to the texture of her shirt, its dull white color, & the pale brown tint of a stain on the shoulder of it. I have never seen that girl before; I was not acquainted with her—but dead or alive she is a reality; she exists & she was there. Her pie was [not] a spiritualized [—it was just an ordinary physical pie, & real. Her] pie, no doubt, & also her shirt & the bench & the shed—but their actualities were at that moment in existence somewhere in the world. (N & J 40, TS MTP, p. 6; *Mark Twain's Notebooks*, p. 352)[17]†

Not only does Twain recognize the creative autonomy of the mind but also endows the "dream self" with a recognizable and visible appearance:

> The time that my dream-self first appeared to me & explained itself, (apparently I was for the moment dreaming) it was as insubstantial as a dim blue smoke, & I saw the furniture through it, but it was dressed in my customary clothes. (N & J 40, TS MTP, pp. 6–7; MT NB, p. 352)†

Again, as the compass of the Notebook entries is to be developed in the compass of "The Enchanted Sea-Wilderness," the "dream self" becomes the Superintendent of Dreams in "The Great Dark."

In an entry of the previous summer he had recorded a comic dream under the title "dream humor." A peasant bets the same sum of money on two horses competing against each other; his friends laugh and tell him that he thinks he is going to win both bets even though he won't win any. Twain comments:

> It seemed quite sane in the dream. And that is where dream things differ from waking-things—they can be thoroughly mad & incongruous without the dreamer suspecting it. (N & J 39, TS MTP, p. 30; MT NB, p. 311).†

Again a statement about the psychological autonomy of the dreamer: The dream follows its own autonomous logic, and this is why the dreamer creates an entire world independent from the waking one. The "dream self" bears some resemblance to the Christian soul; it is immortal. We read further on in the Notebooks:

> When my physical body dies my dream-body will doubtless continue its excursions & activities without change, forever. (N & J 40, TS MTP, p. 5; MT NB, p. 351)†

Twain thus expresses a hope in an afterlife, based, however, on a secular philosophy.

At the time of these entries, attempts at the analysis of the psyche multiplied in both Europe and the United States. Twain had spent many years in Paris, London, and Vienna, the capitals of research in psychology. Always interested in phrenology, believing in mental telepathy, Twain shared with his contempories an interest in psychology and metaphysics. He drew some of his ideas from his readings of books of psychology. His main sources were *The Principles of Psychology* by William James, *Herbertian Psychology* by Sir John Adams, and the writings of George Christopher Lichtenberg. The latter was an eighteenth-century philosopher and mathematician who believed that in a second one can dream events that prolong themselves for a considerable time, and who regarded the experiences of dreams as real events, "a life and a world,"[18] a view almost identical with Twain's own. Moreover, looking at Twain's working notes, it is clear that he meant to make one of his characters use Lichtenberg's arguments. Another coincidence of views involves William James. In some notes, Twain comments on the work of the famous psychologist and especially on his discoveries about somnambulism. James deals with what he calls the "spiritual self" and records experiences of some of his patients that have much in common with what Twain writes about his "dream self." When dealing with the connection between waking and dream states, James's statements are surprisingly similar to Twain's.[19]

In a short story of 1898, "My Platonic Sweetheart" (*Harper's Magazine*, 1912), Twain adds a new feature to the "dream self," which in the context of that tale becomes "the dream artist." Thus he clearly connects artistic creativity with dream. The "dream artist," whom he considers superior to "the day-thought architect" (the uninspired waking artist), uses dream language, a superior and uninhibited form of expression. Dream language resembles shorthand in its swift reproduction of thought. It is a language that suffers no deferral, a language that combines the immediacy of the oral and the accuracy of the written. It is the best vehicle for the "dream artist," who has enlarged powers of movement in space and of recall into memory.[20]

Together with those contained in the Notebooks, these postulations of the powers of the self and the origin of creativity throw a clear light on the experimental fiction centered on fantastic elements.

From the Tall Tale to the Fantastic: The Evolution of the Framed Narration

Written between 1896 and 1905, after the personal and financial disasters that compelled the writer and his family to live abroad, the stories included in *Which Was the Dream? and Other Symbolic Writings* share for the most part a similar "fable" recounting a fall from a position of luck and happiness to one of deprivation and loss.[21] A total uncertainty surrounds the tale. Neither narrator/protagonist nor reader can decide on the meaning of the experience told in the story. Twain's attempts at this "fable" follow a rather linear route. In "The Enchanted Sea-Wilderness" (1896) he experiments with the framed narration (metadiegesis) of an imaginary voyage. In "Which Was the Dream?" (1897) the imaginary voyage is replaced by a dream, while in "An Adventure in Remote Seas" (1898) the voyage motif is reintroduced. During the years 1897 and 1898, Twain started to work also on a story with a microcosmic setting, which would later develop in "3000 Years Among the Microbes." All these motifs are conveyed in "The Great Dark" (1898), where the framed narration (metadiegesis) consists of a dream of an imaginary voyage in a microcosmic setting. In the stories written after "The Great Dark" Twain experiments with these motifs separately. In "Which Was It?" (1902) the framed narration is a dream of disaster and adventure in a southwestern setting, whereas in "3000 Years Among the Microbes" (1905) a microcosmic setting and an imaginary experience are fused together.

This section deals in particular with "The Enchanted Sea-Wilderness" and "The Great Dark" because of their pivotal role; the two short stories are closely connected. "The Enchanted Sea-Wilderness" is in fact an earlier version of "The Great Dark," as well as a discarded part of *Following the Equator,* written probably during November and December of 1896. It deals with a ship captured in a circular space as a consequence of Nature's vengeance against its captain, who violated natural laws. It is based on the myth from which Coleridge's *Rime of the Ancient Mariner* derives, a story wherein the captain abandons a dog on a burning ship in spite of the sailors' requests to bring it with them. A few hours before, the dog has saved the whole crew by detecting the fire on time and awakening the captain. Even though members of the crew escape the fire and eventually are found by another ship, they are doomed. They will end trapped in a zone at the center of the ocean, between the Cape of Good Hope and the South Pole. It is a circular area divided into two parts. The first, "The Devil's Race Track," takes four-fifths of the zone's diameter and is hit by perennial storms, fog, darkness, and concentric currents that push the ship toward an inner circle characterized by the most absolute calm. In the middle of the second zone, "The Everlasting Sunday," there is a place lacking even the slightest breeze, and the glare of sunshine and the silence are eternal.

A survivor of the terrible adventure tells the story to an undescribed passenger of a ship, who retells it as he remembers it. The first narrator of this framed narration (the passenger) is learned and genteel and introduces the tale by the second narrator ("a bronzed and gray sailor").

The first narrator describes the situation in exact and precise terms:

Scattered about the world's oceans at enormous distances apart are spots and patches where no compass has any value. . . . The worst of these spots and the largest one is in the midst of the vast ocean solitudes that lie between the Cape of Good Hope and the South Pole. It is five hundred miles in diameter, and is circular in shape; four fifths of this diameter is lashed and tossed and torn by eternal storms, is smothered in clouds and fog, and swept by fierce concentric currents; but in the centre there is a circular area a hundred miles across, in whose outer parts the storms and the currents die down; and in the centre of this centre there is still a final circular area about fifty miles across where there are but the faintest suggestions of currents, no winds, no whisper of wandering zephyr, even, but everywhere the silence and peace and solemnity of a calm which is eternal.[22]

He also anticipates what he sees as the essential part of the story: "There is a bronzed and gray sailor on board this ship who has had experience of that strange place" (p. 77). This reveals his attitude toward the story, which he regards as an example to support his general theory. His logical, rational tone and the pseudoscientific data he provides help to establish the "ground rules" of the text. The extraordinary adventure—a puzzle for the scientific mind—can and has to be explained eventually in rational terms. He seems to suggest that nothing can, in the last analysis, evade the control of rationality. It is presumably for this reason that he decides to act as a filter for the oral narration of the sailor. He will provide a written transcription that, because of the fallacy of memory ("in my own language, for I could not remember his, of course," p. 77), should result in the suppression of the oral performance by the written. As a way of introducing a different attitude toward the pseudoscientific phenomena, he mentions the mythical names given by the sailors to the great circles of currents: "The Devil's Race Track" and "The Everlasting Sunday."

The attitude of the first narrator foreshadows a cultural opposition: The rational frame of mind is set against a mythical mentality. The former uses the language of genteel society; the latter is oral and vernacular. A cultural opposition, similar to that of the southwestern tall tale, permeates the story.

Even though the genteel narrator tries to silence the oral expression through a transcription, the attempt does not imply its disappearance. In fact, the transcription is done by using the sailor as second (metadiegetical) narrator. Moreover, the mythical mentality pervades the language of the framed narration (metadiegesis), and a clear-cut contrast is thus established between the attempt at scientific objectivity by the passenger and the mythical speech of the sailor.

In spite of this contrast, however, frame and framed narration (intradiegesis and metadiegesis) are interdependent both semantically and structurally.[23] In fact, the framed (metadiegetical) narration starts suddenly as a speech that has been previously cut and adjusted by the first narrator ("we got into that place by a judgment," p. 77). The reader knows "that place" through the description by the first narrator; however, without the frame, one would find oneself at a loss trying to understand the first sentence of the "bronzed and gray sailor."

The relation between the two parts of the story affects even more substantially a generic study of the tale. Without the frame (intradiegesis), the framed narration (metadiegesis) would be what Todorov calls the *merveilleux pur*—a fable characterized by extraordinary events, a world outside reality that remains unquestioned by the character. The interdependence between two parts (intradiegesis and metadiegesis) changes our perspective. The frame (intradiegesis) is, in fact, at the borderline of science fiction: Extraordinary events are presented, if not explained, as if they were scientific data. In contrast, the sailor, a typical exponent of the fantastic mentality, provides an explanation in purely mythical terms. Like mythical thought, the fantastic mentality rejects the meaningless in life. The opposition between scientific and mythic mentalities, present from the very beginning, is a source of ambiguity in the text. Both sailor and passenger face a mystery; yet, while the former accepts it in mythical terms, the latter describes it by using pseudoscience. The readers then face the dilemma of deciding whether what they are reading is part of empirical reality, or whether it transcends and transgresses its rules. This ambiguity is a fantastic element.

Since in the universe of this framed (metadiegetical) tale everything is meaningful, the devices that determine the events have to be full of meaning too. The dog whose elimination provokes the vengeance of Nature against the captain is portrayed as a person, a young sailor who helps the older sailors in their work, and as a child, "the pet of the whole crew," "full of play, and fun, and affection and good nature, the dearest and sweetest disposition that ever was" (p. 77). The captain also refers to him as a child and decides to leave him on the burning ship exactly for this reason: "He'd be more in the way than a family of children and he can eat as much as a family of children, too" (p. 79). Because the dog is clearly and strongly personified, his elimination, according to a mythical vision, triggers the vengeance of Nature. The universe, as it is perceived in the mythic vision of the sailors, is personified and, as long as its laws are respected, benevolent. The dog, an element of nature, is the object of an emotional projection for the sailors; its enlarged powers deriving from its instinctual nature allow it to serve the ship and save the men from the fire. After its elimination it is replaced by a mechanical instrument, the compass. It too is personified. Even in the first part of the tale, it is portrayed through a personification: The passenger notes that the compass, when it enters "The Devil's Race Track," "is scared, and distressed and cannot be comforted" (p. 76). The sailor says that once the compass enters the mortal circle, "it was gone crazy" and that "it had a soul."

These personifications let another important dichotomy emerge in the text. We have already seen that the first dichotomy opposes a scientific to a mythic approach; the second one is a corollary of the first. Two groups of characters are balanced against each other: On the one side are the sailors with their mythic vision, while on the other is the captain, with a rational and progressive mentality; the first group elects the dog as its totem, while the captain trusts the compass. The dichotomy opposing mythic and rational mentalities is best defined through the opposition between the tools of nature and those of science. Moreover, this dichotomy has a well-defined social feature. The captain is the authority in the microsociety of the boat, while the sailors are the object of such authority:

> Elliot Cable master, a rough man and hard-hearted, but he *was* master, and that is the truth. When he laid down the law there wasn't pluck enough in the whole ship to take objections to it. (p. 77)

The relation between these two sets of characters resembles that between the two narrators. The suppression by the captain of the sailors' emotional response would appear to parallel the suppression of the oral utterance by the first narrator. Both the first narrator and the captain seem to follow a scientific trend of thought: They tend to control reality through rationality. While the narrator tries to naturalize the fantastic, and to encompass the oral utterance by his own speech, the captain rejects mythical thought and exerts his repressive authority over the sailors' emotions. Through parallelism, a subtle link is established between the suppressive elements on the one side and the suppressed ones on the other. Thus a connection emerges between the world of the oral word and that of mythical thought, both objects of suppression in this text, and both resurfacing in various ways. Mythical thought finds, in fact, its terrain in the oral culture and its expression in the oral utterance.

The following scheme summarizes the network of relations in the text. In the frame (intradiegesis) we have:

$$\frac{\text{Suppression}}{\text{Suppressed}} \quad \frac{\text{Written transcription}}{\text{Oral utterance}}$$

The following scheme surfaces in the framed narration (metadiegesis):

$$\frac{\text{Suppression}}{\text{Suppressed}} \quad \frac{\text{Authority}}{\text{Emotion}} \quad \frac{\text{Captain}}{\text{Sailors}} \quad \frac{\text{Compass}}{\text{Dog}}$$

The entire series of relations in the text can be summed up in the following opposition:

$$\frac{\text{Suppression}}{\text{Suppressed}} \quad \frac{\text{Technological thought}}{\text{Mythic thought}}$$

For clarity's sake, one should note here that this scheme is not meant to define Twain's conscious intention or ideological position toward technology, but rather to unveil the symbolic relations in the text resulting from both conscious and subconscious drives. The opposition here suggested has no universal value. If science and, in particular, technology are here portrayed as repressing agents it does not mean that Twain considered science as a negative factor. Just the opposite. Elsewhere in his works Twain expresses interest and even fascination for technological progress and scientific discoveries: Both in "The Great Dark" and in *The Mysterious Stranger Manuscripts* the use of technological devices is part of a cognitive process. Yet the opposition resulting from the above scheme illuminates at least one facet of the historical relation between positivism and the literary imagination at the end of the last century. It helps define the liberating role played at the time by the fantastic genre in the impasse created by the deterministic trend in positivist scientific thought. As Todorov suggests, the fantastic was the guilt complex of positivism. As indicated earlier in this chapter, in Twain's fantastic tales it is possible to trace both a positivist and a symbolic trend—the fascination for progress and the drive toward liberated imagination. The two trends oppose and/or interact with each other in rather ambiguous ways. This applies quite clearly not only to these later writings but also to such better-known works as *A Connecticut Yankee in King Arthur's Court* in which the two trends work together to create an uncertain and somewhat contradictory message. Are we to believe in the liberating power of technological progress, or in its ultimate destructiveness? Is the entire fable just a persistent and hallucinatory dream, or is it a fantastic tale?

In "The Enchanted Sea-Wilderness" a mythic interpretation of the extraordinary facts is kept under control through the frame, wherein the narrator indirectly suggests the possibility of a naturalization of the fantastic element. Yet the uncanny emerges in the framed tale (metadiegesis). In the last analysis, the uncanny, arising out of the mythic interpretation of facts, is the disturbing element rationality fends off.

One example of the resurfacing of the uncanny is the recurrence in the sailor's speech of rhetorical figures that anticipate events (prolepses). A series of repetitions suggests that a "judgement" has been placed on the captain. This is foreshadowed by the first sentence ("We got into that place by a judgement—judgement on the captain of the ship," p. 77) and it is repeated at the end of the first chapter ("And deep down in our hearts we believed a judgement would come on the captain for this. And it did as you will see," p. 79). These anticipations (prolepses) represent the triumph of mythic perception over the captain's rationality and technological approach. The perception that had been repressed thus far resurfaces in the language and, through the language, states over and over again its prophetic power. Moreover, the anticipations (prolepses) are a sign of the emerging orality of the speech, the oral trace repressed in the transcription. They are the link connecting the oral trace and the mythic mentality originating it.

Besides the prolepses emerging in the speech, a series of anticipations of actions creates a parallel structure. The main theme of the tale is a journey toward death, and from the very beginning of the second chapter (that is, after the dog has been abandoned) death is foreshadowed: The encounter with another ship, interpreted by the captain as a sign of his inborn luck, turns out to be nothing but the foreshadowing of death. The ship *Adelaide* is the true double of the ship that had been lost in the fire. It is a twin boat belonging to the same company; its captain and some of its sailors have died. The crew of the *Mabel Thorpe* goes on board the *Adelaide* and the captain takes command. It is a clearly symbolic gesture: By possessing a ship that had been visited by death they take possession of their own death. After a few days of navigation they are hit by a violent storm and eventually lose their sense of direction. Darkness and silence envelop the boat. The sailors are quiet and they watch the compass carefully, but it provides no help; they are now in "The Devil's Race Track." They are corpses in life: Their ghost faces shine in the darkness of the perennial night. For nine days they cross the storm and the darkness, followed by big white albatrosses who themselves presage death and look like ghosts.

On the tenth day they reach a place of absolute calm ("into a calm sea and the open day and deep, deep stillness," p. 82): They are trapped in "The Everlasting Sunday." The horror of the discovery is such that the sailors, totally aware of their fate, keep quiet. This human silence, as well as the stillness of the sea, is paralleled by a constant indirect form of speech that, in the second chapter, replaces the frequent dialogues of the first chapter:

> The stillness was horrible; and the absence of life. There was not a bird or a creature of any kind in sight, the slick surface of the water was never broken by a fin, never a breath of wind fanned the dead air and there was not a sound of any kind even the faintest—the silence of death was everywhere. (p. 83)

In the midst of the silence and inertia something is moving; the crazed compass that

> whirled and whizzed this way and that way and never rested— never for a moment. It acted like a frantic thing, a thing in frantic fear for its life. And so we got afraid of it and could not

bear to look at its distress and its helpless struggles: for we came to believe that it had a soul and that it was in hell. (pp. 82–83)

After seven months, during which the boat is pushed with incredible slowness toward the center, other boats are seen at a distance. Yet it is an atrocious surprise; the ships are mere wrecks, and the sailors in them are mummified corpses, dead for twelve years. "It was our fate foreshadowed" (p. 85) concludes the "bronzed and gray" sailor, confirming through this prolepsis the parallelism of events in the story. After the visit to the death ship—an episode charged with comic and grotesque elements—the tale is interrupted. These grotesque elements are part of the heteroglossia we have been indicating all along as one of the main features of Twain's experimentalism. The grotesqueness is echoed also by the parodic attitude toward the model text, *The Rime of the Ancient Mariner*. Various details hint at that text, such as the appearance of the death ship *Adelaide* and the death-in-life state of the sailors entrapped in "The Everlasting Sunday." Comedy and tragedy, parody and straightforward narration intermingle in the tale.

A few other considerations are suggested by the names that denote the areas of death. Even though they oppose each other, both "The Devil's Race Track" and "The Everlasting Sunday" refer to the same cultural area. If "The Everlasting Sunday" recalls the puritan Sunday and the forced lack of activity (the absolute calm of the festive day), "The Devil's Race Track" brings back images of perdition in frenzied activities. The two terms oppose each other as do heaven and hell, the meditative stasis of religious life and the convulsion of mundane life. If seen in the perspective of this semantic area, another level of meaning is added to them: The tale can be seen as a huge cosmic hoax, a *Pilgrim's Progress* reversed, where the pilgrims go toward death and perdition instead of salvation. In this prophetic parable a sense of doom, deriving from puritan culture, pervades the scene. It is not uncommon to find such a mood in Twain's later works, where memories from an early religious training are intermingled with deterministic positivism to create the feeling of an encircled, mechanical, and hostile universe.

The description of the universe in "The Enchanted Sea-Wilderness" is that of a circle, a recurrent image in Twain's fantastic stories. In "The Great Dark," the dream ship travels in a round drop of water, moving progressively toward its center; in the first and third versions of *The Mysterious Stranger Manuscripts*, Eseldorf is described as the center of Austria, which in turn is geographically placed at the center of Europe. Absolute calm, even dreaminess, pervades the place, as well as lack of movement and cultural progress. All these concentric and circular images, of which the sea in "The Enchanted Sea-Wilderness" is the most clearly and graphically described, can be interpreted as mandalas. If the fantastic can be related and compared to the mythic mentality from which it seems to stem, another analogy is possible with psychic thought, which in turn adopts several aspects of the mythic mode of thinking.

The mandala and its symbolism were the object of an important study by C. G. Jung.[24] It is an image that recurs in the art of various civilizations. Jung collected the drawings of many patients in which this concentric image appeared and interpreted them in psychological terms. He concluded that this image recurs in personalities in a state of psychic dissociation. Such a pattern would serve the purpose of compensating the inner disorder through the construction of a central point to which everything would refer, and/or through the circular arrangement of different contradictory and unreconcilable elements (it is often divided into zones of light and zones of darkness). Jung called the mandala the archetype of completeness and saw in it the graphic representation of personality—conscious and subconscious—and the projection of the problem of opposites in human nature.

In "The Enchanted Sea-Wilderness," not only do the circular and concentric images reproduce the structure of the mandala, but so do the juxtaposition of light and darkness in the two zones of the ocean, as well as the series of dichotomies the text plays upon. We have seen how its symbolic system works; each term is either counterbalanced or followed by another that functions as its opposite, thus creating an almost constant binary structure: two narrators, two ships, two groups of characters, two totemic objects. If we connect this to the symbolic system of the psyche, as it is described through mandala symbolism, we can see how this tale reflects the opposites in human nature, with its unreconcilable conflicts and its different levels of consciousness. More precisely, a conflict arises between the progressive and the mythic aspects, between rationality and perception. The suppression of the second term creates a state of confusion (the loss of the sense of direction, the compass going crazy), followed by destructive and chaotic tendencies ("The Devil's Race Track"), and eventually the paralysis of the psyche, which is irresistibly attracted to the deep subconscious (the center of the ocean) and remains fixed in self-contemplation, producing stillness ("The Everlasting Sunday").

It is possible that, having achieved the description of a critical stage of the psyche, Twain could add nothing else to it. This might help to explain why he never finished the story. In spite of apparent inconsistencies, the tale has a coherence transcending the discrepancies of the plot. It is an exploration of a psychic state related to both the personal and the collective subconscious and, at least partly, might have served the function of self-therapy.

From Imaginary Voyage to Dream Voyage: A Further Evolution of the Framed Narration

A similar exploration is carried out in "The Great Dark," a further elaboration of "The Enchanted Sea-Wilderness." It is based on the same literary myth as *The Rime of the Ancient Mariner*. However, motifs that in the other story were predominant here become marginal (the judgment of the captain, for example). The adaptation of the original story is done in a more clearly antiromantic way through the use of numerous burlesque devices. From a letter to Howells it appears that Twain meant to write a story half, or even three-quarters, comic, with a tragic ending.[25] Having had it in mind for over a year, he wrote the tale during the summer and the fall of 1898.[26] The fable is as follows. A writer, Henry Edwards, after having played with a microscope that is a birthday present for one of his little daughters, falls asleep and dreams of being reduced, together with his family, to the tiny proportions of the germs in a drop of water that he has just finished examining. He dreams of leaving for a sea voyage, and the sea is made of the drop of water he had previously used for his experiment. Quite soon the ship runs into trouble. It is surrounded by darkness; sun, moon, and the gulf current have disappeared. The crew has lost its sense of direction, and the compass does not work anymore. When Henry moves from the cabin to the bridge he has new revelations: The Superintendent of Dreams, his oneiric double and the master of the dream world, tells him that what he is going through is not a dream but reality and there is no way out of it. His wife doesn't seem to be surprised; in fact, she has adjusted very well and has almost completely forgotten her past life on Earth—that is, her life in reality. Among the various events that occur during the trip are an attack from some strange marine monsters (the equivalent of the germs in the drop of water); the temporary disappearance of the protagonist's daughters, which creates panic and despair; an attempted mutiny, promptly repressed by the captain, who, in a Ulyssean speech, states the need to continue the journey even though the route is still unknown. At this point, the tale is interrupted. From the working notes of August 1898 and a Notebook entry dated 21–22 September 1898, it is clear that Twain had in mind the following development and ending: At a certain point, the ship falls under the light of the microscope and the sea dries up. Henry's family is taken prisoner by another ship, and attempts to save them fail; eventually, all die but the protagonist. He wakes up: "Looks up—is at home—his wife and children coming to say goodnight. His hair is white."[27]

From a holograph note, it is clear that Twain considered "The Enchanted Sea-Wilderness" as a first rough draft to be used later in the writing of "The Great Dark."[28] It certainly derives some motifs from the first tale: the sea journey, the broken compass and consequent loss of sense of direction; a domineering captain and a judgment on him; a talkative sailor who informs the protagonist of all the operational details of the boat; a zone of storm and complete darkness followed by a zone of light; the circular structure of the sea in which they are traveling; the repression by the captain of any revolt. There is also the transformation of some of the original motifs; the children replace the dog, who acts out a similar function in the other tale.

The main transformation in this sense is represented by the two narrators. While in the first tale the vernacular narrator is introduced by the genteel one, thus reproducing the same narrative situation of a typical tall tale, in "The Great Dark" the cultural opposition of "The Enchanted Sea Wilderness" is transformed into something more subtle and less sharply defined. There is role and sex opposition between the two characters/narrators—wife and husband, female and male. There is also an opposition in their function as narrators: While Alice reports a waking experience, Henry relates a dream. Through the frame, they establish the ground rules based upon domestic normality. This is because of both their status as narrators/characters (homodiegetical narrators) and the patent inconsistency of their statements in the summaries that constitute the frame of the tale. Through the unmediated speeches of both narrators, a violation of order takes place.

If in "The Enchanted Sea-Wilderness" the subversion of order attempted by the vernacular narrator is kept under control by the genteel narrator, in this tale the two narrators are given chances to talk directly without introductions: The first frame (the speech by Alice) is not meant to introduce Henry's speech, even though it does introduce Henry as a character. The lack of introduction results in a lack of distance, and this is a rather important deviation (*écart*) from the tall-tale structure of the first story. As a consequence, the unreliability of both characters is another deviation from the typical tall tale, which implies the reliability of one narrator; it is this deviation, however, that creates the element of doubt that, according to Todorov's theory of the fantastic, is an essential condition for the genre. It must be noted, however, that the unreliability, besides being based on their (homodiegetical) status, is also connected with the content and attitude of their speeches.

"The Great Dark" can be defined as a double-framed story. The framed tale (metadiegesis), the dream, is introduced by two frames in the form of summaries relating the same episode, or rather hinting at it, from two separate and different points of view, which oppose each other as two possible interpretations, one from inside and the other from outside. Without the first frame (Alice's speech), the tale would have been simply the story of a dream; this would not have allowed us to consider it a fantastic tale, since dream, if it is recognized as such, does not question reality and does not upset it. Henry's last statement (in Twain's holograph note)—"I think them dreams. Think I am back home in a dream."—without Alice's declaration would not have had the meaning of transgression of the limits of reality that it has. Alice begins with an anticipatory statement (prolepsis) that sounds vague and obscure: "We were in no way prepared for this dreadful thing."[29] Thus, she admits that what has happened (Henry's dream) has involved herself and her family; she admits that she has been part of the dream and is aware of it. In this way she recognizes that the dream is somewhat autonomous from the waking state and can create a reality of its own, which can ultimately be exchanged with the reality of the waking world.

If dream simply reflects everyday reality, we are still in the field of normality; but when we recognize the power of dream over reality to the extent that dream can upset and change it thoroughly, then the barrier between the physical and the psychic worlds disappears, and one of the prerequisites of the genre of the fantastic is fulfilled. This is what happens in the first sentences of the tale and the last sentence of the holograph note: The two statements echo each other and create a circular structure.[30]

The transgression of barriers finds its equivalence in the violation of codes on the narrative level, where we have an example of literature in process at the beginning of Book II. It starts with a hint at Henry's activity as a writer, an activity that does not stop with the dream—another example of the equivalence of dream and reality. Henry explains:

> I have long ago lost Book I, but it is no matter. It served its purpose—writing it was an entertainment to me. We found out that our little boy set it adrift on the wind, sheet by sheet, to see if it would fly. And it did. And so two of us got entertainment out of it. I have often been minded to begin Book II, but natural indolence and the pleasant life of the ship interfered. (p. 140)

By admitting that he has kept on writing, he transfers the activity from one narrative level to another, from frame to framed tale (from intradiegesis to metadiegesis). Since the two narrative levels correspond in the code of the tale to two different levels of consciousness, the shift from one narrative level to the other means, at the same time, the violation of the code and the transgression of the barrier between the physical and psychic worlds. As a matter of fact, this is more than an experiment of writing in process where the narrator, giving up his persona, violates the code of literary pretense and for one second allows the reader to see the process of writing as it happens, and when it happens: Here writing is shown as a stage of a total oneiric process, almost implying that its origin is in the world of dreams. This example shows how the dream structure is a crucial part of Twain's experimentalism, emphasizing the relation between formal experimentalism and fantasy. The first, through self-reflexivity, causes a breach in the levels of narration; the second, by trespassing the frontiers of the physical world, is a breakthrough in the levels of consciousness.

Another example of the parallel transgression of the levels of both narration and consciousness is represented by a short anecdote told to Henry by the sailor, Turner. It is about a certain Captain Jimmy, who has pledged not to drink anymore and has signed up with an antialcohol league. After three long years of abstinence, he eventually lands, goes to the league to have his name erased from their list, and finds that he has never been enrolled: All his efforts have been useless. This story (Twain uses it again in a different context in "The Refuge of the Derelicts") functions here as an exemplum, reinforcing the implicit meaning of hoax in the tale. It is placed at a point in the story when Henry is on the verge of having a revelation of the impossibility of waking up and going back to reality. The hoax, which is the overt meaning of the anecdote, by emphasizing the uselessness of human suffering, brings out the cruel deception implicit in the dream voyage, which can be seen in turn as a metaphor of the entire human experience. This is even more true since the anecdote also represents a transgression of the limits between dream and reality; it refers to a reality beyond the limits of dreams, although it is narrated during the dream voyage. It is a comment on the adventure of Henry, who leaves for a dream journey and finds himself involved in a real journey because life is a dream. Again the violation of narrative levels corresponds to the transgression of the levels of consciousness.

Looking at the text as a whole, we see that frame and framed narration (intradiegesis and metadiegesis) are connected with two opposed concepts. The two frames refer to the state of waking consciousness and evoke a feeling of order that is upset by the chaos brought about by the dream. If the code of the text implies the juxtaposition of reality and dream linked respectively with the formal juxtaposition between frame and framed tale (intradiegesis and metadiegesis), then the opposition of order versus chaos is part of that code. However, transgression is a rule of this text: In the order of the initial summaries (intradiegesis) there is already a hidden element of chaos. The house where Henry and Alice live seems to be ruled by the most absolute order, and Alice is its iron custodian. Nothing seems to be left to chance; from the children's games to Henry's writing activity, everything is planned. "It was the rule of the house," says Alice, creating the image of a convent or an army camp. Both Henry's and Alice's statements are full of feelings of surprise, ignorance, and discovery ("We were in no way prepared for this dreadful thing"; "We were experimenting with the microscope. And pretty ignorantly" [p. 103]). The microscope opens the way to a series of revelations; by changing the dimensions of things, and therefore altering their supposed order, it shows that real order never existed. The discovery of the germs in the drop of water introduces the true element of change in the everyday life of the Edwardses. Henry calls the germs "monsters" or "animals." The Edwardses had always lived with those monsters, ignoring their existence; the monsters were part of their inside; they were inside their home. Yet the couple's ignorance had made them believe that they were part of the world outside—both geographically and psychologically outside:

> I threw myself on the sofa profoundly impressed by what I had seen, and oppressed with thinkings. An ocean in a drop of water—and unknown, uncharted, unexplored by man! By man, who gives all his time to the Africas and the poles, with this unsearched marvelous world right at his elbow. (p. 104)

His observations suggest the complex symbolic relation the germs have to the rest of the household. While they are contiguous to the world of normality ("right at his elbow"), so that they could be considered metonymically related to it, they are also a metaphor for its hidden malaise. This symbolic displacement is the sign of the breaking up of the normal relation between space and characters: It is the movement from the normal to the fantastic space.

The mechanism of the dream is started by surprise and curiosity. During a short scene that marks the passage from the waking to the sleeping state, Henry, after meeting the Superintendent of Dreams, asks him to provide a ship so that he can leave for a voyage of exploration inside the drop of water. In order to take this trip the Edwardses have to be reduced to tiny proportions; in other words, to enter the world beyond the lenses of the microscope, they have to change their status from that of observing subjects, on the one side of the lenses, to that of observed objects on the other side. They have to find their reflection by crossing the threshold of a mirror. The dream is the place beyond the lens/mirror where they will find their inner reflection.

Dream apparently functions as the converse of the microscope since, instead of magnifying things, it diminishes them. The purpose, however, is the same: the discovery of an apparently unknown reality. Thus discovery, journey, and dream become equivalent terms. The interchangeability of dream and reality stems from this equivalence. The "monsters" that science (the microscope) allows Henry Edwards to see by magnifying them live, and have always lived, in the protagonist's reality, his house and his subconscious. The Superintendent of Dreams declares: "You came from a small and very insignificant world. The one you are in now is proportioned to microscopic standards, that is to say, it is inconceivably stupendous and imposing." (p. 123)

The oneiric cosmos is organized according to a binary structure: To each term another one of opposed sign corresponds. Thus the darkness that surrounds the boat is set up against the light inside the cabin; the storm on deck is balanced by the calm under deck; the loss of sense of direction is counterposed by the relevation that what is going on is reality and not dream; the disappearance of the daughters is followed by their reappearance; and the attempted mutiny is followed by the captain's victory. The ship is set up against the memory of the house; however, here a deviation occurs. The house is strictly connected with the idea of order and stability in the real world and the waking state, while the ship is connected with a sense of instability, movement, and the chaos of the journey in the dream world. Yet Alice, custodian of the order in the microcosmos of the tale, identifies stability with the ship where she has transferred her iron rules—and remembers the house as a transitory stage. This reversal is linked to the violation that governs the whole text. The cosmic disaster in a natural environment, where all the natural rhythms are suspended, is followed by the disappearance of the little girls, the destruction of the family, and eventually the mutiny. The past, the real (waking) world, is remembered but vaguely by both Henry and Alice, and this gradual loss of the past indicates a loss of identity. "I was indeed getting shadowy about all my traditions," says Henry. This almost suggests the dissolution of identity that has become a central aspect in postmodern fantasy.[31] The "land-past" is set up against the present in the sea, a present without end. The breaking up of the space-continuum—the normal relation between space and characters—is paralleled by the dissolution of the time-continuum—the normal order of events. The unending present time also reinforces the nightmarish quality of the tale.

Among the various dichotomies of the text there is that of opposing groups of characters. Alice, a stereotypical Twainian feminine character, functions as a custodian of order, respectability, and discipline; she is in charge of repressing any revolutionary tendency inside the cabin/

house.[32] The captain, on the other hand, is the custodian of order on the rest of the ship: Just as Alice dominates her daughters, her husband, and her servants, the captain rules the crew. While Alice struggles against Henry's tendencies toward laziness, disorder, and swearing, the captain struggles against the subversive tendencies of the sailors. Henry and the Superintendent of Dreams are their opposites. Henry masters the narration, while the Superintendent controls the dream. He is the trickster and plays all sorts of pranks on the crew: These represent the comic side of the tale. He is Henry's double; he is that part of his personality that tends toward playfulness, humor, and freedom. He is a symbol of the creativity of the human mind, of its capacity to create imaginary worlds; it reminds one of the archetypal image of the Spirit in its Jungian definition.[33]

This juxtaposition between two sets of characters, like that between order and chaos, is linked to the conflict between dream and reality: Dream invades the real, just as chaos exists inside apparent order. The narrative opposition between frame and framed tale (intradiegesis and metadiegesis) has a semantic equivalent.

The recurrent play of oppositions and the binary pattern that it creates can be regarded as a trace from both the previous tale, "The Enchanted Sea-Wilderness," and the structure of the tall tale. As we have seen, the cultural opposition between narrative discourses and sets of characters is carried on in "The Great Dark" as well. Just as in "The Enchanted Sea-Wilderness," where genteel speech tries to smother the vernacular by producing a version of it instead of letting the voice of the sailor be heard directly, the language of dream is here set up against two rational frames. However, just as the language of mythic belief somewhat affects the drive toward an exact scientific attitude of the first narrator of the previous tale, the language of dream and its logic invades the frames and, therefore, the world of waking reality. Finally, as in "The Enchanted Sea-Wilderness," the relationship between sets of characters is dominated by the same logic, a constant attempt at suppression. But what is eventually suppressed in the game of interpersonal relationships, as well as in the language? It is a series of drives toward the irrational, the subversive that Henry perceives through the microscope—reflected and made physical—embodied in the germs. Having started by discovering the existence of monsters in everyday life, he eventually discovers the "monstrosity" inside the human psyche. In fact, while the microscope allows the discovery of an invisible although physical world, the dream allows the exploration of an equally invisible although nonphysical reality. In order to reach the inner center of his psyche, metaphorized by the drop of water, Henry has to look at his own reflection—the reflection of his own inner self—in the mirror represented by the lenses of the microscope, and thus reach the oneiric state. Since the drop of water contains an entire world, with all its contrasts and divisions, cosmos and psyche become equivalent terms. This equivalence is the fantastic.

We have seen how the deviation from the original tall-tale structure (that is, the clear juxtaposition between reliability and unreliability, rational and irrational, genteel and vernacular) leads to a double structure and a double narration. The opposition, however, is not so clear-cut; just as the uncanny, in spite of all the attempts at suppression, is always resurgent, the unreliability is expanded to both narrators and narrative levels (intradiegesis and metadiegesis). This deviation is the turning point from the structure of the western tall tale to that of fantastic narration because it allows a geographically and historically restricted cultural conflict to move into a more general plane. A primordial struggle is portrayed here—one that is, at the same time, personal and collective, historical, and outside time.

The internalization of cosmic structures is also a rather typical Twainian attitude and can be related to a precise historic moment. In his *Autobiography* Twain says:

> The last quarter century of my life has been pretty faithfully and constantly devoted to the study of the human race—that is to say, the study of myself, for in my individual person, I am the entire human race compacted together.[34]

Such an attitude, that even in its narcissism is cosmic and prophetic, recurs in Twain's later works. We have seen how, in "The Enchanted Sea-Wilderness," this is rendered by the constant use of the first-person plural pronoun ("we") by the metadiegetical narrator; such usage creates an equivalence between the individual "I" and the collective consciousness. The mandala symbolism itself relates to both individual and collective consciousness. On the other hand, the internalized cosmos is a reflection of America in the 1890s. In the symbolical parable narrated in "The Enchanted Sea-Wilderness" one can see a generalized concern for the emerging great changes of a new society (the ship *Adelaide*) based on technological progress, and the destruction (through fire, a symbol of transformation) of the old society (*Mable Thorpe*), with its cultural signs and protectors (the dog) and its taboos (the beliefs of the sailors). The tale is a dramatization of the impossibility of such a substantial and sudden change: The irrational forces channeled into the totem are repressed and ignored by the new trend, which is efficient and purely rational; but eventually those instinctual forces explode and paralyze the new social establishment. A still different aspect of the 1890s is reflected by "The Great Dark": the medical discoveries that reveal the existence of germs in the human body (existence within existence); the optical discoveries that, thanks to the possibility of diminishing or enlarging or doubling an image, allow science to explore realities so far ignored; the discoveries of psychology that, by opposing the old positivistic theories, create an interest in the potential of the psyche and introduce the concept of the subconscious. In particular, optical discoveries, by providing an enlarged vision, function in "The Great Dark" as an all-encompassing metaphor, both for the exploration of the psyche and the fantastic text itself, which can be seen as an epistemological procedure. Moreover, the theoretical development of optics, argues Max Milner, allows us to find inside the invisible the manifestation of a visible other, avoiding the principle of reality and supporting the drives of the transhuman world of fantasy.[35]

Contemporary nightmares (increasing urbanization and industrialization, mass immigration and consequent social unrest, the growing power of revolutionary and anarchist movements) are here portrayed symbolically. Since the physical world itself is in doubt, contemporary reality becomes the product of the subconscious. To this purpose, the microscope/dream allows one substantial discovery: Whatever is suppressed (the irrational, the mythic, the monstrous) is pushed outside of a civilized life into some obscure wilderness, and will eventually emerge and invade that civilization. This anthropological and psychological discovery can be related to the particular historical moment. As the geographical frontier had by then been conquered, it was impossible to exile to it the savage and the primitive, which had to be, instead, recognized as a part of the human psyche and therefore of civilization itself. It is this relation to social and historical reality that places Twain's fantasies at the borderline between the fantastic and science fiction. The subtle allusion to reality stresses the cognitive aspect of the symbolic stories, which is one of the facets of the science-fictional genre as well. The external world is reversed and internalized. The binary structure and recurrent circular patterns that we have detected in the writings signal Twain's political and personal ambivalence. He was attracted to, and repulsed by, the future—that is, the changes of his time and the lack of permanence in life. He saw social and cultural phenomena as inextricably related to the inner self; thus, he merged his deterministic philosophy with his psychological and ontological vision.

Similarly, the experiments in the fantastic are the moment of fusion between his formal experimentalism and his exploration of the powers of the imagination.[36] Here he fuses motifs from the variants of the fantastic—the uncanny, the marvelous, and some science-fictional modes—as well as the parody of other genres. The lack of homogeneity is part of the nature of generic experimentation itself, as is the choice of such a noncanonical genre as the fantastic. In the fantastic experiments Twain continues the same trend as in his earlier experiments in burlesque and other contemporary experiments in satire. The estrangement procedure—the defamiliarization of the familiar—is central here too. The return of the uncanny, and the emergence of the surreal, stress the alienating quality of familiar reality. It is also part of Twain's search for the origin, which he locates in the surreal experience represented by the imaginary voyage or by the dream. Twain, anticipating in this respect some modern and postmodern perceptions, sees the core of the human condition in the displacement, the loss of identity, and the alienation occurring during the oneiric/surreal experience. This experience can be transcribed only through a language that is liberated from the conventions of the canon.

3

Romance

From a chronological point of view, *The Mysterious Stranger Manuscripts* are the last stage of Twain's experimental activity.[1] The writer worked at the three versions during the last eleven years of his career (from 1897 to 1908).[2] They develop further a spectrum of imaginary motifs and narrative structures running throughout the later Papers. It is this furthest development that unveils both the full range of potential, and the deadlock, of the writer's philosophical thought and experimental activity. His failure to recognize the total implications of his imaginative powers surfaces more clearly in this work than ever before.

As for the other fantasies previously dealt with, *The Mysterious Stranger Manuscripts* are approached at first from a generic perspective. The predominant mode of romance is here interspersed with fantastic, satirical, and burlesque motifs. However, the main concern of this study is not so much to define the diverse material in terms of genre as it is to observe Twain's game of transgression and experimentation, which leads to renewal of form through the search for folkloric and mythic roots. Throughout the three versions of the *Manuscripts*, experimentation is an evolving process. Inside the texts the various narrative elements—plots, characters, space, and time—form a symbolic network revealing doubling and otherness as recurrent features

and binding together literary experimentalism and philosophical specu-
lation.

In the *Manuscripts* Twain continues the play with literary genres
that characterizes his previous production. Through the parody of
higher genres, he satirizes both social and literary conventions.
Through heteroglossia, he introduces a variety of styles, languages,
and genres. The text expands beyond the limits of a given canon
to encompass modes and discourses that are traditionally viewed as
opposed to each other and, in any case, heterogeneous. An episodic
narration that is part of the digressive mode, and that the writer had
come to consider as his ideal form while working at his autobiography,
recurs in these writings. The proliferation of loosely structured episodes
parallels the variety of styles and discourses. This fragmentation of the
narrative structure corresponds to a fragmentation of perception, which
in *The Mysterious Stranger Manuscripts* finds its ultimate expression
and symbolic embodiment in the main character, Satan.

The fantastic elements to be found in many fantasies of this period
are present here too, usually in the form of a transgression of the
physical barriers of space and of the chronological limits of time. Here
too we have the imaginary voyage motif. The distant places and the
remote ages the protagonists visit allude, however, to reality as we
know it in our waking experience. The *Manuscripts* are often satirical;
when dealing with the world of fantasy, they refer to reality, and more
specifically to contemporary mores. The settings—a medieval castle,
an eighteenth-century Austrian village, a Missouri village at the beginning of the nineteenth century—reproduce in smaller dimensions the
structures of the external world. The world of fantasy and that of reality
intermingle. Contemporary history and science are displaced into an
imaginary context; likewise, fantasy invades reality.

As it did in the dream and imaginary voyage stories, the fantastic
element in the *Manuscripts* signals the exploration of the inner world.
The doubling, recurrent in various forms in the fantastic tales, alludes
also in these writings to the human psyche and its division. Doubling
here is a central motif, which, in the third version, develops into pure
fragmentation.

In many ways *The Mysterious Stranger Manuscripts* mark a further
evolution of motifs and structures used in previous or contemporary
Papers. In particular, the presence of "the other" at work in both burlesques and fantasies is embodied, here, in the satanic character. The

self-reflexivity of the text finds expression in the metaphor of the printing activity on which the third version is centered. Other significant aspects of evolution are the transformation of the framed structure of the fantastic tales through the elimination of the frame itself, and the expansion of the dream.

Yet the *Manuscripts* should be seen only as the last stage of development of a tendency already latent in Twain's earlier fantastic stories, rather than as a sudden shift in literary style. One of the earliest examples of dream structure is *A Connecticut Yankee in King Arthur's Court* (1889), where the frame, a segment of narration set in contemporary time, encloses a tale of adventures in the legendary England of King Arthur. Following the ending of the fable, the return to the waking state in the frame leaves the reader with no doubts as to the real nature of the events portrayed in it. However, what could be regarded as the dismissal of the unreal proves to be its opposite. The Yankee is unable to adjust himself to the reality of his time; he will not survive the narration of his dream. Thus the dream structure shows, from its earliest appearance, a basic ambiguity, a subterranean conflict involving opposed forces; the language of dream reveals an unsuspected power. A further step in this direction is marked by the stories in *Which Was the Dream?*, wherein the force of dream is expanded by both the lack of the concluding segment of the "rational" frame of the story and the traces of oneiric language and thought in the initial passage.

The evolution of narrative structures in Twain's fantastic stories seems to lead toward the elimination of the segment of speech signifying rational order; however, this tendency is not isolated. It is paralleled by an equivalent trend in previous works wherein the genteel narrator is eventually displaced by the vernacular one left in charge of telling the story. A clear example of displacement is *Adventures of Huckleberry Finn* (1884), wherein Huck, the vernacular character, is allowed to recount his story without any mediation. The only remaining traces left by the genteel narrator in *Huckleberry Finn* are Twain's editorial note concerning the various dialects used in the book, the burlesque proscription banning any interpretation, and Huck's allusion in the initial paragraph to Mark Twain, the author of a book entitled *Adventures of Tom Sawyer,* in which Huck himself appears as a character. The allusion is particularly significant because it temporarily alters the narrative level, bringing the text from the level of fiction to that of metanarration (from diegesis to metadiegesis). Huck transforms himself from character/narrator to critic of his own author and text. ("The book was made by Mr. Mark Twain, and he told the truth, mainly. There was things which he stretched, but mainly he told the truth.")[3] Thus, Twain challenges the authority of texts by mixing various styles, different levels of narration, and multiple frames.[4]

Chapter 1 of this study outlines how, in the later satires, the game of duality, typical of the southwestern tall tale and implied in the early burlesques, has evolved into a different and more complex duality: The genteel narrator has either become the pompous and sanctimonious counterpart of an outspoken vernacular character, or he has evolved into an ironic narrative voice. The gradual fading away of reality and logic in the dream structure is similar to the displacement of the genteel narrator by the vernacular. This parallel evolution in the posthumously published Papers shows a subterranean yet powerful link connecting oral performance to dream language; in both cases a violation occurs when this traditionally enclosed segment of speech predominates. Forces usually kept in a low position in both the social and the psychological scales are allowed to emerge and take over.

The similar development of these two sides of the writer's work can shed some light on the very nature of Twain's imaginary text. The binary opposition of values—cultures, languages, visions—that characterizes it is, at some point, overcome through the elimination of the most restrictive term of the two involved in the opposition. A yearning for freedom might partly account for the incompleteness of the posthumously published Papers: Twain's restlessness, so often pointed out by critics, could be an aspect of his work on the dream structure—an aspect of the development of that structure which led at first to the enframing of dream, and then to the destruction of the frame by the expansion of dream itself.[5]

The Mysterious Stranger Manuscripts is the last stage of this evolution, the result of the extreme development of the dream structure, leading to the absolute predominance of the imaginary. While in the dream tales the frame ensures the survival of the real as the opposite pole of the unreal, in the *Manuscripts* the lack of this narrative segment leads to the dissolution of the binary opposition. In the later work, a mixture of reality and unreality replaces the opposition of levels of consciousness—the waking and the dreaming states. In *The Mysterious Stranger Manuscripts* the dream is no longer opposed to rationality because it is part of the real world; there is no separation or transition from one phase to the other. Many signs indicate the presence of dream inside reality; Eseldorf's dreamy landscape and Satan (Traum in "The Chronicle of Young Satan") are among the most easily recognizable.

In the first chapter (shared with few deviations by two of the three versions of *The Mysterious Stranger Manuscripts*, "Chronicle" and "No. 44"), the reader is immediately introduced into an idyllic world, a dreamy atmosphere, a place remote from any form of technological progress or rational thought, far from the flow of history:

> It was 1702—May. Austria was far away from the world, and asleep; it was still the Middle Ages in Austria, and promised to remain so forever. Some even set it away back centuries upon centuries and said that by the mental and spiritual clock it was still the Age of Faith in Austria. . . .
>
> Yes, Austria was far from the world, and asleep, and our village was in the middle of that sleep, being in the middle of Austria. It drowsed in peace in the deep privacy of a hilly and woodsy solitude where news from the world hardly ever came to disturb its dreams, and was infinitely content. . . .[6]

In these passages, narrative levels interact through the use of two codes of language, referential and mythical. The historical and geographical data ("1702—May . . . Austria . . . the Middle Ages") are set against mythic nonreferentiality ("far away from the world . . . asleep . . . the Age of Faith . . . in the middle of that sleep"). Space and time references are thus interspersed with expressions denoting a mythic mode of thinking. The referentiality establishes the inner ground rules of the text, as well as a common ground with the "implied reader." The mythical pattern, on the other hand, causes a deviation, though not any reversal of these rules. Moreover, the narrator's tone conveys the feeling of a childlike innocence, transcending age—a permanent and unchanging state of mind:

> . . . by the mental and spiritual clock it was still the Age of Faith in Austria. But they meant it as a compliment, not a slur, and it was so taken, and we were all proud of it. I remember it well, although I was only a boy; and I remember, too, the pleasure it gave me.

> Eseldorf was a paradise for us boys. We were not over much
> pestered with schooling. . . . The priests said that knowledge
> was not good for the common people, and could make them
> discontented with their lot which God had appointed for them,
> and God would not endure discontentment with His plans. This
> was true, for the priests got it of the Bishop. (pp. 35, 222)

Looking back at his childhood and the past world and space of his
native village, the narrator does not show any critical distance, any
separation, any growth out of the "Age of Faith." The unending and
excessive naïveté shown by the narrator's initial speech causes him to
be regarded by the reader as an unreliable center of consciousness,
while another critical, though distant, consciousness is at work in the
text—the "implied author".[7] This voiceless presence establishes contact
with the "implied reader" through a subtle play with the point of view:
The feeling of a double vision is conveyed to the reader. This perception,
emerging from the text, could be viewed as the furthest development
of the double narration—its trace. The "implied author" functions as
the trace of the suppressed segment of narration: He replaces the
rational and restrictive frame. His role is later taken over by the character of Satan.

In all three versions, Satan appears in a small community as a child
and, through miracles, subverts the normal trend of everyday life; he
affects natural phenomena, stops time (even inverts its due course),
overcomes any space barrier, and moves around with frenzied energy.
The ultimate goal of upsetting normality is, paradoxically, the introduction of rational thought in the midst of belief. This is achieved through
the many dialogues between him and the Eseldorf youths whom he
takes on imaginary voyages through distant space and remote time and
thus tries to convert to his illuministic philosophy. In this way the
transgression of the rules of reality—in the form of movement beyond
expected limits—unveils the irrational essence of reality itself.

This is only part of a larger paradox. As the narration progresses,
Satan himself, the result of a preternatural way of thinking, becomes
the trace of the suppressed segment that the "implied author" represents in the first chapter. However, while he acts as the trace of the
previously existing narrative segment, Satan also prolongs the game of
"otherness" present in the previous Papers; here his role as the "other"

of the human protagonist of *The Mysterious Stranger Manuscripts* is defined through interaction with his human self.

By inheriting the role played previously in the text through the "implied author," Satan becomes his spokesman, as well as the result of the last development of the dream structure. The opposition of levels is replaced by their mixture, summed up in Satan's paradoxical character. Furthermore, his manipulations of the elements of the story—plots, characters, setting, and time—hint at the author's activity, his writing and rewriting of the *Manuscripts*.[8]

From "Dream Structure" to "Romance"

Upon moving from the distinctly marked opposition of reality and unreality, which characterizes the dream and imaginary voyage stories, to the blending of reality and unreality in *The Mysterious Stranger Manuscripts*, there is a shift from the genre of fantasy to that of romance.

Romance could be viewed almost as an intensification of the modes of fantasy; yet, even though these two genres share some common aspects, such as the overcoming of what the readers commonly consider to be the untrespassable frontiers of time and space, they also have separate features. The discussion of fantastic elements in the previous chapter shows that one of the prerequisites of the fantastic, according to Rabkin's theory, is the reversal of the ground rules of the text. Even though the narrator establishes some inner ground rules in the first chapter of both "Chronicle" and "No. 44" versions, and even though these rules, through references to space and time, acknowledge the existence of a common ground between narrator and reader, they are not separate from a mythic perception of life. Almost immediately the reader faces a perception of normality that is other than one would expect and that modifies reference itself. Scholes would aver that the world of Eseldorf presents a "radical discontinuity" as compared to the world of our experience.[9] It is certainly a place outside that experience, where the laws of nature are suspended to give way to those of imagination. Not only does the dreamy atmosphere suggest that, but the naïve description of life in Eseldorf, where prodigies, curses, and everyday occurrences intermingle continuously, does likewise. Nor does the supernatural ever raise wonder or doubt in the minds of the inhabitants. The lack of doubt also signals the shift from the fantastic to romance. We are here in the midst of the domain of the "marvelous," as Todorov would call it.[10] It is a world in which the rules of reality are suspended from the very beginning, and this causes neither hesitation nor doubt in the mind of the narrator. Moreover, readers easily recognize this world as other than theirs. The narrative frame then disappears because it would have no function here. The generic perspective—the view of *The Mysterious Stranger Manuscripts* as romance, rather than simply fiction—is one of the points on which my interpretation of this text differs most from Kahn's. Because of his critical orientation in his reading of "No. 44," Kahn has a hard time accounting for the final chapter, as well as for 44's identity:

> The ultimate mystery of Forty-four's identity is never explicitly solved, and I suppose it is theoretically possible to contend—as some critics using the Paine-Duneka text, with its ambiguous "Satan" angel, have done—that he is really the Devil, or a devil, in disguise or that he is just part of a dream or nightmare, as Gibson has suggested. But I think these solutions are incompatible with the entire "No. 44" text. . . . The idea that a dream, in and of itself, can set one free—and go on to exhort one to dream better dreams!—seems to me an inadequate statement of what August's story is about.[11]

It is likely that Kahn's problem with the conclusion derives from his unawareness of the generic mode of the text. Romance is strictly connected with the idea of dream and all its implications.

Reality does not disappear from *The Mysterious Stranger Manuscripts*. It is addressed and confronted continuously by Satan, who takes his disciples on excursions into the world of history, thus using the "real" world as an example to instruct them on the meaning of that world. Romance then takes on a didactic connotation. Moreover, the world of Eseldorf is a miniaturized image of the world of history and thus refers allegorically to the "real."

Didacticism and allegory go hand in hand in this romance. Reality is apprehended through broad generalization, rather than through detailed and individualized descriptions. The characters are archetypes; for example, the conflict between Father Peter and Father Adolf in "Chronicle" can be viewed as the clash between the good magician and the evil one. These archetypal traits are even more apparent in the presentation of the characters in "No. 44." The wise old man, the bad witch, the fairy godmother, the good blonde girl, the romantic lovers, the magician—these and many more are the romance characters of the last version. There, through adherence in some parts of the narration to the most trite conventions of romance, Twain achieves a parody that coexists with straightforward treatment of other aspects of romance, as well as with other genres, styles, and modes.

In general, the characters of *The Mysterious Stranger Manuscripts* are divided into enlightened and unenlightened. This is related to the quest motif that runs throughout, and which is a further evolution of the imaginary voyage motif of the other fantastic narrations. Satan's disciples are enlightened by their supernatural friend. Their youth makes them the ideal recipient of enlightenment, but the rest of the characters are, to a greater or lesser extent, ignorant. The sign of enlightenment is the knowledge of the true nature of the strange visitor, which he has revealed only to three youngsters in "Chronicle" and to only one in "No. 44." In the "Schoolhouse Hill" version the recipient is an old although young-minded person. The scope of the enlightenment is vast: It is the philosophical apprehension of the true nature of reality, of the essence behind appearance; it is ontology. As is often the case with this genre, enlightenment is achieved through allegory, didacticism, and a satirical mode coexisting with romance.

On this point, Northrop Frye's study of romance proves helpful.[12] His emphasis on the secular aspect of the genre is crucial for an understanding of the modes of romance in *The Mysterious Stranger Manuscripts*. Romance, according to Frye, is a secular scripture—that is, a tradition of writing that derives, like religious scripture, from a mythological lore. However, the secular scripture is based upon a different and separate corpus of mythology that has had a parallel, though distinct, evolution from the religious one. Romance also establishes a different relation to its audience than that of religious writings: While one relates to the public through parody, the other uses a mood of seriousness. Parody in romance often takes religious scriptures as model texts. In *The Mysterious Stranger Manuscripts* this is the treatment of the "adamic" and "satanic" motifs deriving from the Bible and other texts following its religious tradition, such as *Paradise Lost*. Since the model texts are illustrious, the parody acquires transgressive traits. It is also aimed at a target larger than the text itself; it attacks the canon. It satirizes the believers, the addressees of the religious scripture. Similar to Twain's early burlesques and the other contemporary satires, the *Manuscripts* allude to the society, the context, and the addressees of the model text.

In *The Mysterious Stranger Manuscripts* Twain traces the satanic motif back to its folkloric roots and develops it into a purely transgressive fantastic motif. According to the folkloric tradition, the narrator portrays Satan in the first chapter as a mischievous spirit who can only be kept under control through the authority of the Catholic church (as the episode of the assuaging of the Devil shows). As the story unfolds, he appears as a child character, later to be developed in the third version into a persecuted innocent, a Christ-like figure preaching a new, humanistic gospel. Thus Twain, through parody, transfers the satanic motif from religious mythology and related folklore to secular scripture. In shifting the satanic motif from one kind of scripture to another, Twain transforms it; he subverts the original meaning. The symbol of evil becomes a beautiful child whose voice is angelically musical and whose actions are not generally violent or destructive; he is not evil but merely neutral. Twain achieves this reversal of such a well-established folkloric and religious motif through a transgression that he aims at the belief system behind it. The appellation "epic of the creature," which Frye uses to describe romance, fits well the series of adventures the human protagonists of the *Manuscripts* are dragged into by Satan; these adventures are explorations of the current patterns of the human condition.

The human characters (Theodor/August) are representatives of the species, the inheritors of Twain's "adamic" theme, especially as it is dealt with in one of the posthumous tales, "The Refuge of the Derelicts." Here Adam is not a burlesque biblical character (as, for example, in "The Diaries of Adam and Eve") but rather the myth humankind has created, an object of emotional projection. His myth is discussed in the story by a group of sad failures gathered together in a sort of commune. They view Adam as the epitome of humankind: limited by his own nature, unable to be different from what he is compelled to be, he is cheated by an indifferent god. But he is also a child, a creature of nature, a noble savage and a potential rebel, who is defeated and condemned to repetition inside a mechanistic and deterministic cosmos. Theodor/August are adolescents who, like Adam, still preserve some signs of a primeval innocence; yet a tendency toward conformity shows in their behavior. Theodor throws a stone at a witch who is being burnt alive, and he does it out of fear and conformity. August too, although empathizing with 44, does not openly support him for fear of retaliation from the other printers. Satan is their counterpart and a perpetual rebel; he is the part of Adam that refuses to be enchained. In the *Manuscripts* he acts out his rebellion through his initiator's role, which consists mainly in revealing cosmic injustice to the young "everymen."

Because it emphasizes the deviation from traditionally accepted values, Frye's definition of romance seems to describe more adequately the *Manuscripts* than the "marvelous" suggested by Todorov's theory of the fantastic. Even though the readers are immediately introduced into a preternatural world, the ironic awareness conveyed to them by the implied author, as well as the deviation from traditional and sacred models, threatens the element of pure fable that one would find in the "marvelous."

The narrative structure that mostly allies the *Manuscripts* to the mode of romance is the episodic structure of the tale.[13] In the microstructure, this kind of narration uses frequent anaphoras (a series of sentences each starting with the same word) and anadiploses (sentences wherein the last word is repeated at the beginning of the following sentence, giving the impression of a chain, an incantatory rhythm of the word). In the macrostructure, episodic narration allows a series of digressions and a piling up of episodes, giving the impression of endlessness. The whole narration is a huge digression, a departure from logic, which usually generates plots; it is a plotless narration denying causality in action.[14] The lack of cause/effect logic in romance can only be viewed as a transgression of the rules controlling the world of the real, a transgression that parallels that of space and time. Another aspect of romance present in the *Manuscripts*, and one that Frye describes effectively, is a mixture of different levels of experience— reality and unreality, being awake and being asleep. In Frye's words, the "vertical perspective" is that of the *Manuscripts*.

The idyllic world of Eseldorf, the starting point for the story, presents elements of both reality and imagination. It is a happy space, a world of childhood, an idyllic world, connotated by sleep in its widest sense— a beatific sleep, but also a sleep of consciousness, a sleep of reason. The real (waking) world is both external and internal to the idyllic space: However, geographically external to it, it is reflected through the hierarchical structures of society it portrays. Brought about by Satan's presence, the world of adventures represents the other level, the one opposed to the still world of idyll. This world too is a mixture of the real and the unreal; while space and time barriers are overcome magically, on the other hand the conflict of history and society are described.

A further consideration relevant to the genre of the *Manuscripts* is suggested by the place science and technology take in the world of adventure. The *Manuscripts* appear to be a "romance" pointing toward science fiction—a genre that derives from romance and shares with it many thematic and structural elements. The futuristic perspective science and technology cast on the "old" world, as well as the presence of an alien (Satan) who comes from a different world and views every-day experience with a defamiliarized outlook, are the most outstanding features this text shares with science fiction. Twain's experimentation with the genre of romance points toward innovation, the renewal of form through the mingling of old and new elements. He introduces a new form of magic in the ancient form of romance: Technology replaces witchcraft. The replacement of the magician—a fake and worthless one—with 44 exemplifies the replacement of older and obsolete forms by newer ones. The flexibility of romance allows this game of substitutions, which anticipates the motifs later to be developed by science-fiction writers. As he went along, experimenting with one version or another, Twain developed these innovative features more and more.

The innovation resides also in his attitude toward romance. Unlike his previous adherence to the most sentimental conventions of this genre in his *Personal Recollections of Joan of Arc* (1896) and *The Prince and the Pauper* (1881), in the *Manuscripts* Twain mingles parody of the codes of romance with an exploration of the mythic roots of the genre. The difference from the later published works is most clearly on display in the third version, "No. 44." This may account for Paine's decision to publish the first version instead and call it *The Mysterious Stranger, a Romance*. The earlier version must have been easier to adapt to the trite patterns of romance as practiced by the genteel writers at the end of the last century.

The Trickster and the Holy Child: Two Aspects of the "Other"

One of the aspects of the renewal of form Twain carried out in the Papers is the use of folkloric and mythic motifs in an unusual context and code. He provides mythic characters with connotations different from those with which readers commonly associate them. Such is the case in the child motif, which is present constantly throughout the three versions. Not only is Satan a child among children, but the text itself is a recollection of lost childhood, thus placing great emphasis on that early period of life.

Twain's children often play an enlightening role. Their unconventional and neutral outlook allows them to defamiliarize reality and provide moments of revelation in the text. Their estranged viewpoint is comparable to that of the vernacular narrators of the tall tales and the burlesques, who expressed their "otherness" through a process of defamiliarization. Here estrangement acquires even more clearly transgressive connotations. The rebellious power of Twain's Satan lies mostly in his being a child.

We have already observed how Twain's Satan departs from religious mythology. The traditional malignity of Satan is transformed into neutrality and skeptical rationality: The rebellious dignity and stature of the Miltonic Satan is set against the boyish flippancy of a miniaturized devil. The only trait he shares with his antagonist—an invisible and almost absent God—is a similar indifference toward humankind. Twain explores the sacred mythology on which religious scripture is based, only to reject it through subverting it.

His imaginary concept of Satan is better allied to a folkloric, secular tradition describing Satan as a mythic trickster.[15] This tradition is referred to in the "Eseldorf" chapter:

> Ours was a beautiful and massive stone bridge of five arches,
> and was seven hundred years old. It was built by the Devil in a
> single night. . . . Always before, when he built a bridge, he was
> to have for his pay the first passenger that crossed it—everybody
> knowing he meant a Christian, of course. But no matter, he
> didn't *say* it, so they always sent a jackass or a chicken or some
> other undamnable passenger across first, and so got the best of
> him. This time he *said* Christian, and wrote it in the bond
> himself, so there couldn't be any misunderstanding. (pp. 38–
> 40)

However, in his final Satanic character Twain goes one step further:
His Satan corresponds in many ways to the Jungian archetype of
the child.[16] And this marks an interesting deviation from the Satanic
character in the first two versions of the *Manuscripts*.

As is the case for the child archetype, 44's birth is mysterious; he is
made the object of persecutions and eventually killed (in "No. 44" he
is burnt alive); he puts up a superhuman resistance; he is endowed
with mysterious powers over animals (44 befriends a vicious dog), with
whom he shares a subterranean link. He is an everlasting being, who
existed before the story begins and will presumably exist after it ends.
His origin is in the subconscious. Because of this mythic atemporal
quality, he is a bridge between past and future, between slowing and
accelerating tendencies. The accentuation of this mythic trait marks
a deviation from the folkloric Satanic character and allows both a
transgression of literary and religious conventions and a radical exploration of the Satanic motif itself.

Forty-four's existence is that of a persecuted innocent who pays
with his life for his being different; however, thanks to his dark
powers, his death is followed by a resurrection. The allusion to a
Christ-like pattern cannot be ignored. Like Christ, 44, after proving
through miracles his exceptional and godly powers, preaches his
own "gospel" to his only disciple; however, through 44's death and
resurrection, the only paradise that is regained for August is the very
earthly one of awareness and recognition. This enlightenment, which
comes only at the end, is strictly connected to the discovery of the
true essence of 44. The child Satan is part of August, his dream,
his subconscious, his unrecognized "other."

August is "everyman" and the heir of Twain's Adam. He is limited in his freedom of choice by his very human condition; he is not responsible for his flaws because he cannot be anything other than what he is; yet he feels guilty because he is enslaved by the "moral sense" that institutions and conventions of his time and society have made him internalize. Forty-four's initiating role is that of shedding light in August's mind as to the limits of his powers. He reveals to him the inconsistency of institutions, the hypocrisy of social conventions, the absurdity of the "moral sense," the impossibility of change. Forty-four's favorite target is the conformity of the "damned human race," which, after having been enslaved by an indifferent god and a malevolent nature, has accepted its own slavery through the deification of authority and the codification of social rules. The aim of Satan's transgressive action consists of defamiliarizing human behavior and shooting at the heart of social conventions. His didactic role acquires even more openly subversive qualities because of the associations that his archetypal patterns evoke in the readers' minds. The godlike child-hero, a mythic image recurring in many religions and usually associated with the sacred, is here Satan himself, normally allied to the violation of the sacred. More specifically, Satan the child brings forth the image of Jesus, the child of both folkloric tradition and the apocryphal Gospels.

In two tales ("The Holy Children" and "The Second Advent")[17] written twenty years before the *Manuscripts*, Twain had already satirized the Christian dogmas concerning Jesus' birth. In "No. 44," he goes so far as to probe the very essence of the sacred by creating a satanic "holy child." Myth is thus revived and subverted. Forty-four, Little Satan in a study trip on earth, sent by obscure forces, is a child Christ/Antichrist who preaches a new "gospel" based on solely human values. Theodor/August is tempted/enlightened by Traum/44.

The true essence of the fantastic is the violation of the rules of reality—the time and space barrier. In this romance the transgression is carried one step further: The target is myth, which, having been absorbed and transformed by institutions, has lost its original force. The transgression, through subversion and parody, is aimed at creating new myths and, through them, fostering new imaginative powers and renewal of literary form. The literary use of childhood brings into play subconscious powers aimed at upsetting the artificial order of superimposed social myths.

Plots and Characters:
A Study in Evolution

Throughout the three versions of the *Manuscripts,* the structural evolution of plot and characters parallels that of the protagonist, Satan. In dealing with the three versions of *The Mysterious Stranger Manuscripts,* critics follow specific tendencies. Some prefer the first version and insist on the basic similarities of the three versions, while others emphasize the differences among the three versions and trace the evolution leading to the third version, "No. 44."[18] Among the early critics who dismissed Tuckey's discovery of the three versions, Henry Nash Smith, when dealing with "Chronicle of Young Satan" (the first version), notices how the three texts are based upon the same fable. In his opinion, this proves that the first version is the one that mirrors Twain's intention most closely. Sholom Kahn, on the other hand, emphasizes the points of difference among the versions and focuses his study on the third rendering, which he finds more interesting. In this version Twain carries extravagance and fantastic experiments to an extreme. Kahn also argues that here the plot is more clearly focused on the confrontation between August and 44. It is doubtless true, as Smith indicates, that the three versions are based on the same fable— the encounter of a human being with a stranger who turns out to be Satan. And in fact, if the fable were the only element of a text in which the author's intention ought to be sought, we would have to agree with Smith's dismissal of the other versions of the *Manuscripts.* Yet other structures might be just as essential for the study of both the author's intentions and the text as such. A study of recurrences and deviations is often quite revealing of the direction authors take in their experimentation. It is particularly helpful, for this purpose, to look at the functions of the characters in the three versions—that is, the meaning of the characters' actions for the development of the narration—and thus determine the overall tendency in Twain's experimentation.[19]

In comparing the three versions we notice a persistent tendency to explore motifs, develop their inner potential, and later transform them into apparently similar, although more complex, structures.

An overall similarity of functions characterizes the three versions: Conflicting forces are opposed binarily.[20] In "Chronicle," the motif of the satanic seduction of the youngsters is developed through dialogues

displaying the opposition between two substantially different views of
life. It is correlated by the Father Peter/Father Adolf story, which acts
out the conflict between a nonconformist and nondogmatic Christianity
and the hierarchical, authoritarian, corrupt, official church. An append-
age to the story is the romantic motif represented by Marget, Father
Peter's niece, who shares the ups and downs of her relative's destiny
and, at the same time, impersonates the blonde-girl stereotype of romance—the innocent who is a pole of attraction for the young males
of the town.

Traum interferes at all levels of action through manipulations of the
limits posed by reality; he temporarily solves Father Peter's financial
problems by making him find a wallet full of money, but then, with
sovereign indifference, abandons him to his destiny of shame and
madness. He transforms Marget's cat into a continuous source of
wealth for its owner. In order to improve the plot, he stops and reverses
time whenever he thinks it necessary.

Similarly, in "No. 44," once the Eseldorf plot is abandoned, the large
and endless digression of the castle plot is developed through the
opposition of brute force and reason. On the ideological level, the
conflict between the interdiction of the church and free thought replaces here the opposition between the two views of Christianity characterizing the Eseldorf plot. On the level of action, it is extended to the
two groups of characters opposing each other: the printers who are
hostile to 44 and the wise master who protects him. The outcome is a
workers' strike that endangers the master; he may be ruined economi-
cally and be turned over to the justice of the church. Forty-four intervenes by creating strikers' duplicates who complete the unfinished
work. Here too, as in the first version, the romantic motif is an append-
age; the master's niece replaces Father Peter's, even taking over her
name—Marget. Forty-four interferes in this plot also: He uses the
duplicates to complicate the development of the love stories. The motif
of the satanic seduction—carried out by means of dialogues, trips, and
so on—runs parallel to that of the conflicting forces and represents, at
a different level, its double.

In "Schoolhouse Hill" the satanic motif is not counterbalanced by a
human plot; humans do not fight each other as much as they struggle
with the weather. Forty-four intervenes, rescuing people from a terrible
snowstorm. Coming out of the local school, where he shows his capacity
for instantaneous learning, he first encounters the local bully and beats

him up with no effort and no anger. This conflict presents a deviation from "Chronicle" that is carried over to "No. 44": The opposition of forces involves Satan personally. Forty-four is made the object of direct and hostile attack, and he reacts in a way that, while proving his enormous and unsuspected force, is devoid of aggressiveness. In other words, the conflict between the opposed terms—reason and brute force, or institutions and free thought—that we have identified as the structuring motif in the *Manuscripts* sees 44's direct involvement through personifying one of the two opposed forces—that is, reason.

Through such change of functions, the secularization of the satanic motif is completed: Satan is not any longer an external force acting upon human life, but rather an internalized element in human consciousness. This internalization, which is certainly the most important evolution from the earlier to the later satanic character, is intensified in "No. 44" by the creation of the duplicates portraying the fragmentation of the self.

The changes in name prove to be so strictly related to changes in character function that they are like the two aspects of one sign—its signifier and the signified. As soon as the name of Satan is transformed from Traum to 44, the function of the character varies. Traum always remains external to conflicts: In "Chronicle" his function is mainly didactic; he never becomes the personification of one pole of opposition. Instead, 44 is active in the plot and personifies one of the two opposing values. The two human protagonists follow an evolution that, in a different way, is also related to the change of name. August, the apprentice, develops to a fuller extent the initiatory potential of his predecessor, Fisher—a name suggesting quest.

The evolution of dream (Traum) to number (44) is certainly a significant element. While Traum (dream personified) is the offspring of Eseldorf's dreaminess, 44 (number) evokes the technological future inaugurated by printing; while Traum belongs to a timeless age of dream, 44 is rooted in time—the present and the past for author and readers, the future for the protagonist.[21]

This double perspective can only be approached by keeping in mind Twain's notorious ambiguity on the subject of technological and social progress. What does the shift from dream to number mean? Does Twain see in technology the ultimate liberation for humankind, the overcoming of delusions and dreams? Are the Dark Ages over in our epoch, which, with its unlimited possibilities of knowledge and pleasure, can eventually allow the human dream of happiness to come true? These are some of the problems the reader faces while observing the evolution of characters from one version to another.

The answers to these questions cannot be univocal. Much has been said about Twain's infatuation with technological and scientific progress, as well as about his awareness of its destructive potential. Both the infatuation and the awareness are illustrated quite clearly by Twain's works. The technological dream is not an idyllic state, as is proven by the final chapters of *A Connecticut Yankee* and by the nightmare induced by watching the germs through the microscope in "The Great Dark."

To the end, progress plays a liberating role in Twain's vision, distorted and perverted as it may be by the human tendency to repetition that makes human life an enslaving cycle. Progress is not an external element in the later Twain's terms. It can be read only as an aspect of the psyche that is counterbalanced by its opposite side—the retarding element. These two forces are at work in an everlasting conflict.

The evolution from Traum to 44 emphasizes the futuristic tendency of the satanic character, which is also suggested by the setting. However, there is no breaking up of the continuity between the two Satans; Traum's progressive potential develops naturally into 44. In turn, by acknowledging at the end his pure oneiric nature, 44 points out the Traum element of his identity. He then can only be regarded as the merging together of oneiric and technological tendencies, the slowing and the accelerating trends in human nature. He is the synthesis of the author's ambivalent attitudes.

The Space/Time Metaphor

Like a study of recurrences and deviations in plot and characters, one of space and time imagery can help us understand the aims and trends of Twain's experimental writing in the three versions. Neither space nor time is ever a purely minor embellishment meant to create an atmosphere. Space and time are always narrative functions that relate to the characters and help define, in turn, their function in the text. Here Juri Lotman's concept of the role of the space setting and imagery in the text proves to be particularly helpful.[22] The literary text, as

Lotman suggests, is a secondary modeling system based upon the general models of culture and becomes a model shaping culture at large. As a result of this strict relation between text and culture, the literary text, in shaping its own imaginary space, is influenced by the cultural concept of space. More specifically, the cultural perception of inner and outer space, of the movements inside and outside a given space, reflect symbolically the characters' psychological states in the literary text. Moreover, the characters' movements and their relation to the setting—either their mobility or their fixity—not only define their potential for growth or their incapacity to change, but also describe the relation of the text to the culture it is part of. Space thus provides a metaphorical model for the text. Viewed from this perspective, *The Mysterious Stranger Manuscripts* appear to be structured according to an anthropological perspective; the space defines the characters' symbolic development, while it also alludes to the shaping of the text itself.

In two of the three versions of *The Mysterious Stranger Manuscripts*, "Chronicle" and "No. 44," the same first chapter is repeated with minimal deviations; because of this insistence, the Eseldorf setting acquires a particular importance. A "topos" of the imaginary (at once remote and central to the wider world), Eseldorf is geographically at the center of Austria, the center of Europe, which in 1490 (the dating of the third version) was regarded in Europe as the center of the world. This central space is connected to the world outside through both mirroring and doubling: It is, at the same time, a mirror of the external world and a particular kind of double, the inner content of an external container.[23]

Centrality is a recurrent feature in the Twainian imaginary text, and it is always denoted by lack of movement; it is a place outside the mainstream of history, isolated from technological progress. In "The Enchanted Sea-Wilderness" it is the still zone, preventing movement, in which the ship is eventually trapped forever; in "3000 Years Among the Microbes" it is the body inhabited by the cholera germ; in "The Great Dark" it is the ship in the drop of water under the light of the microscope; in "The Refuge of the Derelicts" it is the Admiral's house.

This central space is, however, denoted in different ways in Twain and requires slightly different interpretations. For example, in the case of "The Enchanted Sea-Wilderness" the description emphasizes mainly the circularity of the space, while Eseldorf is depicted solely as a central space. Theories of interpretation of this symbolic space image diverge.

Some, like Jung, interpret the mandala as the symbol of totality, an ideal of completeness toward which humans strive. The circularity of the image reconciles the dichotomies at work in the psyche. Other scholars—among them some phenomenologists like Bachelard and post-Freudians like Rank and Durand—emphasize the aspects of intimacy of the image, which they read as the core and the essence of the inner being.[24] With no clear contradictions, these two readings highlight different aspects of the image. My textual analysis favors either one of these interpretive trends, depending on whether Twain's emphasis in any particular description is on the centrality or on the circularity of the image. In the case of "The Enchanted Sea-Wilderness," where the description emphasizes the circularity of the space, the Jungian archetype of totality seems to be a more appropriate model: The clear-cut oppositions at work in the text are reconciled in the mandala symbolism. On the other hand, the concept of an intimate core of being evokes the central space of Eseldorf. Its connotation of dreaminess allows it to be a point of departure toward the world outside rather than a closed circle. A return to the dream level and the stillness of Eseldorf is achieved at the end of the third version. This circular movement, however, is not a return to Eseldorf itself, but rather to what it stands for—the world where dreams come from, the human psyche.

As Juri Lotman points out, space functions as a description of the characters' inner changes; stillness and movement are connected either to psychological fixity or growth. This model describes the binary opposition of stillness and movement in the *Manuscripts*. No matter what theory Satan wants to prove concerning the repetitiveness of human behavior and the indifference of God, he does so by taking his disciples to remote times and spaces. More specifically, movement denotes growth, a process of initiation. For example, while in "Chronicle" the movement is always from the inner regions (Eseldorf) to the outer world of history, in "No. 44" the opposite trend is recognizable. This signals a change in perspective. The prevailing point of view becomes that of the world outside, the place from where the movement originates. The world outside, in this case, is often associated with the future (objects and characters from the future are introduced into the medieval castle).

It also must be noted that space and time are closely related: In the first passage of the story, time is allied to space in such a way that the central and remote space is also the "Age of Faith." Time and space mirror each other and function in a similar way. Eseldorf, which, in its connotation of unreality, is binarily opposed to the real, is also its center, as it is the center of Europe. Exactly in the same way, the "Age of Faith," as a mythic concept, is opposed to history and yet is its center, since it refers to the everyday history of ordinary people, also the center, the core, and the essence of the history of great events and great characters. As done for the space structure, we can talk of internal and external times, and we can also detect a relation of doubling and mirroring between these two dimensions.

Moreover, the opposition of stillness and movement in time parallels the structure of space. Satan can stop and reverse time, and evoke both past and future times in order to initiate his disciples into grown-up reality. Stillness denotes a state of permanent childhood, while growth and awareness come through projection toward past and future.

From a comparison between the first and the third version, a difference in the function of space stands out. The castle towering over Eseldorf, which was a secondary motif in "Chronicle," becomes of primary importance in "No. 44." In the first version, the narrator mentions the castle but omits its name, which he cannot recall; the motif is not developed further. In "No. 44," on the contrary, the castle represents a stage in the evolution of the main character. August leaves Eseldorf—which then becomes a secondary motif—and moves to the castle as an apprentice in the print shop. Because of the character's movement in space, the castle acquires a position that is external to the inner space of Eseldorf. It is a space wherein movement and change are possible; however, it is an intermediate space—placed as it is between Eseldorf and the external world of progress and change, between present and future, between inner and outer levels.[25]

Its description in the second chapter reinforces the connotation of intermediate position by combining disparate elements; it is a "topos" of the fantastic:

> It was a stanch old pile . . . the spacious chambers and the vast corridors . . . were bare and melancholy and cobwebbed. . . . In some of the rooms the decayed and ancient furniture still remained, but if the empty ones were pathetic to the view, these were sadder still. (p. 229)

Abandoned by the aristocratic family who owned it, the castle is in decay, almost empty yet inhabited by ghosts; it is likely that a treasure is hidden in its lower apartments ("the black deeps of the castle")—the last trace of past wealth. Opposed to all this gothic paraphernalia, the print shop stands in the tower. Like the treasure, but for opposite reasons, the print shop has to be hidden; it is a forbidden object that the church will not allow. The mixture of elements composing the castle creates the appropriate setting for Satan to emerge. While the gothic atmosphere—the forlorn place, the ghosts, the hidden treasure—is presented in burlesque terms, an allusion to the literary convention of the gothic genre that needs to create the setting for a plot full of mystery and intrigue, the hidden print shop is an allusion to the transgressive essence of the fantastic. Its location in the upper part of the castle is a sign of its connection with rational thought; conversely, the hidden treasure in the "black deeps" seems to be an offspring of the subconscious. Thus, this intermediate space mirrors, and is mirrored by, Satan, combining subconscious and obscure powers and a rational, progressive drive—elements of death and life, of unreality and reality.

The castle has in itself the potential for 44's adventures. Movement here not only proceeds from the inside toward the outside, but also vice versa: Forty-four trains his friend and disciple August to appreciate the cultural products of remote countries and different ages, and he brings these products to his room in the castle. The interchangeable movement, as well as the movement inside the castle, show this to be a space with quite a different function from Eseldorf. The print shop is the place with the most potential for growth: The activity of duplication developed there anticipates the duplication that is later extended to the characters of the romance. One last duplication occurs at the end, when Satan reveals to August that life itself is a dream, the quintessential duplication of the human mind.

The increased historical referentiality of "No. 44" marks a further deviation from "Chronicle." Already, in the first chapter, the dating of the story is set back two centuries to the very eve of the discovery of America. Eseldorf's backwardness thus becomes less conspicuous, while its centeredness in the world is accentuated. The historical referentiality appears again in the episodes of the Bibles to be sent to Prague and in the ban of the church. The main deviation between "Chronicle" and "No. 44" is the shifting of the setting from Eseldorf to the castle;

while this movement underlines the characters' potential mobility, it emphasizes the inner dependence between setting and character. The shift in setting allows the initiation motif to emerge in a more direct way.

Let us turn to the setting of "Schoolhouse Hill," chronologically the second version. Written while Twain was at work on the first version and had just started the third, "Schoolhouse" is a true digression in composition, plot, and setting.

The space, a Missouri village on the Mississippi River, marks one of Twain's many returns to what is commonly referred to as the "Hannibal Material," stories based upon his successful characters Huck, Tom, and Jim. They are set in Hannibal, or rather in its fictionalized version, St. Petersburg, and are based on Mississippi River folklore.

Following our discourse on the imaginary space we can try to trace the connection between this digression and what seems to be the main line of the Austrian setting. In spite of an apparent divorce between the two space images, there is a link: Both the Missouri and the Austrian settings present us with a small community that, apparently separated from the mainstream of history and the larger world outside, is a reflection of that history and that world. These small communities, recurrent in Twain's works, are modeled after Twain's recollection of the first small community he ever encountered—Hannibal.

This perspective accounts for the mixture of general and personal history; in other words, Twain's mythic vision of history results from his identifying the story of the small community with the history of humankind. This is why, in this respect, Eseldorf, Rosenfeld castle, and Hannibal function similarly. They establish a peculiar relation with the outer world of history: They mirror it by reducing it to smaller dimensions. They provide a miniature image of it that reminds one of Swift's Lilliput. Moreover, because of Eseldorf's centrality in the world, the relation of doubling between the small community and the larger world (of Austria, Europe, and the universe) acquires special characteristics. It can be described as the relation of two similar objects, one of which contains the other, as in a game of Chinese boxes. It is a *mise en abîme*.

Both historical space and historical time follow this pattern. In Twain's vision of history, the European "Dark Ages"—a rather chronologically undefined era—and the pre–Civil War south are seen as equivalent. This is clearly illustrated by "The Secret History of Eddypus, the World Empire." Previously, in *A Connecticut Yankee,* the slavery system in the south was alluded to when dealing with slavery in legendary and feudal King Arthur's England.

The "Schoolhouse" digressions should not be seen as a change of direction, but rather as a meaningful return to those roots that generated Twain's entire imaginary vision. It is a return to the idyllic space of childhood, a world of preternatural beliefs, the source of magic—in other words, the space of romance. Writing this digression allowed Twain to mediate, through a return to personal space and history, between the mythic unreferentiality of "Chronicle" and the increased time and space referentiality in "No. 44."

The third version, if compared with the other two, is more strictly related to a historical context, the pre-Reformation period and the discovery of America. At the same time, it is projected toward a future time and space—that is, America; food, magazines, and various objects of the future are used as educational tools by 44 in order to train his friend August to appreciate a wider world. This movement allows Twain to play with perspective, which hints at the relativity of point of view; whatever represents future dream in the text is in fact present, or even past, reality for both author and readers. This shifting perspective transforms space and time references into fantasy and myth.[26]

The Writing/Printing Metaphor

In spite of differences in their relation to time and setting, Traum and 44 act in similar ways upon the environment from which they stem. Forty-four is to the castle what Traum (dream) is to the sleepy Eseldorf (city of asses): He is its product, but also its disturbing element, the stranger. Because of this dual status, he reflects the internally contradictory elements of the surrounding space as he also introduces new elements into it.

While paying his dues to the magic of the gothic past by letting everybody believe that the power behind the fantastic events occurring in the castle is the buffoonish magician, 44 starts a duplicating process (of the Bibles) in the print shop, which he later extends to reproductions of the printers themselves. This entire act of duplication, while still retaining the essence of repetition, is an act of creation bearing the features of a larger and deeper transgression of the laws of human mortality. The duplication of the printing material and of the printers that 44 performs clearly alludes to the normal activity of the print shop: that is, writing and its technological extension, printing.

The function of the print shop in the castle becomes clearer and more relevant through 44's duplication. One could reverse the statement and say that 44's function is better defined by the presence of the print shop. And one could further say that 44 personifies the writing/printing activity through the duplication he creates and the duplication he represents. In fact, being a dream, he is the ultimate "duplicate" of the human psyche, which is the "original."

In this respect, "No. 44" carries the transgression of the rules of society and of the universe further than the previous versions, since writing/printing not only supports social and religious laws but, being the result of the human desire for transcendence, violates the laws of human mortality. In the Eseldorf chapter, writing is the exclusive prerogative of the church, a tool of manipulation used to gain control over the people: "Such things speak louder than written records; for written records can lie, unless they are set down by a priest" (p. 41). The printing of Bibles to be sent to Prague in "No. 44" is instead a tool for the Reformation and thus represents the taking over of writing by free thought.

To write and to print means to inscribe oneself; it is, at the same time, a death- and life-giving gesture. It means to transpose oneself in the dead characters of a print shop, but it also denotes a way of confiding one's permanence beyond life to the text. "No. 44" plays upon this paradox. Death and opacity ("dead languages" and "abstruse sciences") are counterbalanced by the liberation of the human mind through communication ("languages") and knowledge ("sciences"). Duplication itself sums up the contradiction: the creativity of the new text and the deadness of repetition.

Forty-four transposes printing from the level of reality to that of the fantastic when he extends duplication of the Bibles to that of the characters—the doubles of the printers, who, significantly enough, are called "duplicates." Their sudden appearance in the castle rescues the project of printing and sending Bibles to Prague, and allows a temporary victory of free thought and rationality over authority and obscurantism, but their arrival also creates a world of chaos and division.

Duplication frees unsuspected energy—the "duplicated" printers work like fiends—but it also creates conflicts and divisions; the "originals" do not recognize themselves in the "duplicates," and the two entities are never reconciled into a single identity. An amusing comedy of errors takes place. To make things even more complicated, each entity—"original" and "duplicate"—holds inside a further division: They are each divided into "waking" and "dreaming" selves, each enjoying a separate existence on separate time levels.

This division, besides mirroring the conventions of the world of romance, reflects Twain's psychological vision during the last twenty years of his life. The "waking self" in his conception of the psyche corresponds to what could be described as the conscious state, while the "dreaming self" bears some resemblance to the modern and Freudian concept of the subconscious. Kahn argues that Twain's psychological theory is roughly parallel to Freud's:

> The Waking-Self is clearly the ego; the Dream-Self, with its great imaginative freedom and tendency to chaos, points in the direction of the id and libido; and the Duplicate, with its complex suggestions of sensuality and fleshiness (implying also their opposites), points in the direction of the superego. Or, with a change of emphasis, one might see Forty-four as a dramatization of the problem of the superego—or conscience, in Clemens's terminology.[27]

The Twainian "dream self," however, has almost metaphysical properties; because of its immortality it resembles the Christian conception of the soul. On the other hand, it seems to be the personification of the fantastic because of its capacity to travel through time and space. The merging of a metaphysical and a fantastic vision is then achieved in the "dreaming self." Twain's play with the fantastic acquires the importance of a metaphysical quest; at the same time, the search for transcendence, through the persistent doubling, takes on psychological implications. The doubling also alludes to the relation between man and God implied by the Judeo-Christian tradition—a relation between self and other. However, the outcome of the story, by overcoming the separation between self and other, suggests the introjection by the self of god and universe.

The fantastic amounts to a total vision of humankind and the universe. The powers of human imagination are boundless, able to overcome the limits of the real. These limits are rooted in human nature; they are embedded in human repetitiveness, which leads eventually to the stillness and the trapped immobility of determinism. The human imagination is then a breakthrough in this cycle of eternal repetition. The capacity for transcendence is also rooted in human nature—it is the advancing, inventive, free-reasoning side. The metaphysical aspect of the fantastic lies in this capacity to transcend the immanence of human destiny. In this sense, in "No. 44" duplication is an element of the fantastic.

It must also be noted that duplication works in the text at a dual level: While it portrays symbolically the human psyche, with its contradictory and unreconcilable aspects, it also signifies the reflexivity of the text. In fact, the writing/printing metaphor is part of a literary discourse about the text that develops inside the text itself. Twain addresses there the problem of immanence and transcendence involved in writing and printing; thus he anticipates metafiction.

As we have seen, the "duplication" involved in printing creates a paradigm to which the "duplication" of characters alludes. In turn, the relation between writing and printing parallels that between "original" and "duplicate." In order to reach out and thus ensure its own transcendence, the printed text has to be separated from its source, its original, the moment of writing. This separation is acted out by the episode of the liberation of the duplicate. Just as writing and printing are aimed at creating a form of transcendence in human life through the permanence of the printed word, the "duplication" of characters creates doubles endowed with more spiritual, ephemeral, and powerful natures than their "originals." While the latter are trapped in the limits of their nature and the constraints of the real, the former are limited only by their connection to their "original." In one of the concluding episodes of the story, August's "duplicate," Schwarz, is freed from his fleshy connection to his "original"; once he is free, he disappears and becomes a pure spirit, a "dreaming self" forever:

> So he told Schwarz to stand up and melt. Schwarz did it and it
> was very pretty. First his clothes thinned out so you could see

him through them, then they floated off like shreads of vapor, leaving him naked, then the cat looked in, but scrambled out again; next, the flesh fell to thinning, and you could see the skeleton through it, very neat and trim, a good skeleton; next the bones disappeared and nothing was left but the empty form—just a statue, perfect and beautiful, made out of the delicatest soap—bubble stuff, with rainbow hues dreaming around over it and the furniture showing through it the same as it would through a bubble; then poof! and it was gone. (p. 381)

The Mysterious Stranger

The separation from the "duplicate" is the first step in a change of movement in the plot: the themes of ascent follow those of descent. The liberation of the duplicate and his return to the oneiric stage is an ascending movement; his "duplication" is a descent from the oneiric state to the waking one.

Similar movements occur in both "Chronicle" and "No. 44": A man is frozen into a statue, and a woman is transformed into a cat. These mark descents from the human level into either the inanimate or the animal worlds: The human image is captured and enslaved. The liberation of the "duplicate" starts the opposite movement—the ascending process that anticipates the conclusion of the romance.[28] The "duplicate" impersonates a need for freedom when he asks to be separated from his "original":

> I care nothing for that—it is these bonds—stretching his arm aloft—oh, free me from them; these bonds of flesh—this decaying vile matter, this foul weight, and clog, and burden, this loathsome sack of corruption in which my spirit is imprisoned, her white wings bruised and soiled—oh, be merciful and set her free! Oh, this human life, this earthly life, this weary life! It is so groveling, and so mean; its ambitions are so paltry, its prides so trivial, its vanities so childish; and the glories that it values and applauds—lord, how empty! (p. 369)

While hinting at the separation between dreamer and dream, his ascending movement anticipates the separation between 44 and August and the conclusion of the story.[29]

The movement of ascent/liberation, before the ending, is achieved through the spinning back of time—a procession of historical events separated from their historical, chronological, and geographical context, just as the "duplicate" was separated from the "original." Manipulation of time is a recurrent trait of Twain's fantastic works. For example, in a later posthumously published satire, "The Stupendous Procession," various historical epochs, movements, and ideological ideas parade outside the context of their time and space;[30] in *The Mysterious Stranger Manuscripts*, at certain points time is stopped, reversed, accelerated, or slowed down through various devices, among which is a character counting time according to a different unit. One of the conventions on which social order is based is thus attacked, while the freedom of human imagination is asserted. Forty-four's manipulation of historical time and space functions as a *mise en abîme* of the author's rewriting and experimentation—his rearranging of story and history. This last movement of separation between time and history foreshadows the reassertion of a mythical and cyclical vision. Also, through the breaking up of the relation that characters normally entertain with time and space, Twain anticipates one of the most outstanding features of postmodern fiction.

The last step is the separation of 44 from August, which occurs after the final recognition is achieved. Forty-four acknowledges his oneiric nature; his origin is in August's psyche. Once he has faded away he can be replaced by other dreams:

> "I myself have no existence, I am but a dream—your dream, creature of your imagination. In a moment you will have realized this, then you will banish me from your visions and I shall dissolve into the nothingness out of which you made me. . . ."
>
> "Dream other dreams and better!" (p. 404)

He reveals to August the essence of his own human nature:

> "I am perishing already, I am failing, I am passing away. In a little while you will be alone in a shoreless space, to wander its limitless solitudes without friend or comrade forever—for you

will remain a Thought, the only existent Thought, and by your
nature inextinguishable, indestructible. But I your poor servant
have revealed you to yourself and set you free." (p. 404)

In spite of cognitive and liberating power, dreams cannot save humans from their unhappiness. All is dream, but dream is nothing:

"Life itself is only a vision, a dream." (p. 404)

"There is no God, no universe, no human race, no earthly life,
no heaven, no hell. It is all a Dream, a grotesque and foolish
dream. Nothing exists but You. And You are but a *Thought*—
a vagrant Thought, a useless Thought, a homeless Thought,
wandering forlorn among the empty eternities!" (p. 405)

The nihilism of the final statement emphasizes the deadness of
separation from the double, the deadness of ascent that leads to the
void, the nothingness, as the sudden opening up of the space setting
clearly suggests ("empty eternities"). The series of denials ("no God,
no Universe") annihilates both transcendence and immanence, revealing the deadlock of Twainian thought. The freeing element in the
human mind, which Twain identifies in the satanic character, can only
lead to the recognition of a deadlock. Even though human thought
creates everything and survives all, it still cannot break through the
cycle of repetition that is the essence of human existence. Thus liberation is the awareness of having been the dupe of illusions; it is the
awareness of the powers of imagination, awareness of subjectivity in
the perception of what seems to be the real.

Twain's nihilism is born out of his incapacity to bring his beliefs to
their extreme and logical conclusions. The breakthrough that might
have come from either mysticism or political action is eluded. The
tragedy is born in the self and never goes out of the self. Solipsism is
the result of the missing exchange between individual and culture.
Everything is internalized; even technology—seen as a liberating element from the progressive standpoint Twain partly identifies with—is
internalized, becomes part of the dream instead of a tool of liberation.
The meaning of dream itself is subverted at the end. Dream is annihilated. Only cold, desperate reason is left.[31]

The writing/printing metaphor provides a paradigm. Just as writing expresses the human need for permanence and transcendence, Satan impersonates the human dream of liberation from cyclical repetition through the overcoming of rules limiting reality; just as printing is the technological extension of writing, which is meant to make the need expressed by writing possible, 44 is the technological dream of human-kind. However, just as printing, through duplication, reenters the cycle of repetition, 44's "duplicate" characters, even though they act out human potentials, end up by creating new enslaving cycles.

There is a lack of recognition of the other (duplicate/original) as part of a whole, part of the self. This lack of recognition accentuates the conflict between opposed elements and leads eventually to the disintegration of one element. At the literary level, we have observed the parallel disintegration of the frame. Here, at a semantic level, we see the disintegration of the spiritual part of being and, eventually, of any belief system. Material reality is not saved, and only rational thought survives in a vacuum. In Lacan's terms, the unconscious is perceived as the other.[32] This is how the "originals" perceive their "duplicates"; this is how 44 is perceived by the other characters of the story. He is the "stranger," the other, the disturbing element. In the conclusion of the *Manuscripts,* where the conflict between a deterministic view of the human condition and the breakthrough of dream stays unresolved, 44 is dismissed. He is the "other," the stranger that Twain fails to recognize.

4

Myth

Modern and contemporary discourse displays various approaches to myth.[1] Following the path of Jung's archetypal theory, Campbell's studies of mythic patterns and images, while observing similar structures and motifs in rituals in world religions and folklore, suggest a psychological interpretation; the recurrence is evidence of similar mechanisms in the human psyche and of the existence of a collective unconscious.[2] However, the structuralists, and in particular Claude Lévi-Strauss, concentrate on the relation between variant and invariant elements in culture and, in so doing, argue that myth should be interpreted according to the methods of structuralist linguistics, which is based upon the relation between *langue* and *parole*.[3] The variants of a myth constitute the *parole* of a given cultural group, while the invariant elements are its *langue*. Following this path, Roland Barthes examines the belief system and social rituals of contemporary French society as a specific *parole* in the *langue* of the Western world. He views myth as a mode of signification that "is not defined by the object of its message, but by the way in which it utters its message."[4]

By making burlesque of language, Twain shows a quite similar awareness. Not only is the existence of myth possible solely through its telling and retelling, but myth is also part of human speech; myth is language. In order to satirize myth it is necessary to burlesque its language. This is part of what Twain does in his burlesques and satires.

In both the early burlesques and the later satires, while experimenting with genre, Twain is indirectly attacking the well-accepted myths of his society, which he sees embedded in the codified genres where they find their linguistic expression. Opera, for example, is not only a highly codified genre expressed through an artificial language; it is also the myth of doomed passions, which finds expression through high-pitched tones of vocal utterance. Not only are Victor Hugo's novels part of a larger category that we can loosely label as romantic fiction, a genre with precise conventions and a distinctively vague and bombastic language, they manifest also the romantic myths of man's relation to nature and of the triumph of passion over reason and law. The language is myth itself since it reproduces the vagueness of feeling and the exultation of passionate thoughts. By parodying the language and the conventions of a given work or of an entire genre, Twain makes the belief system behind the form his target. This becomes even more evident in the later satires, in which the model texts are no longer specific works but rather a range of works, an entire canon. Moreover, in these later works there is the tendency to adopt forms that, like the fables, have an almost everlasting existence because they transcend the limits of a given culture through recurrence and repetition of mythical images. During the later phase, Twain is in fact concerned with belief systems pertaining to the entire human race rather than to a single culture at a given moment.

However, this is only one side of the coin. As soon as we turn to the later fantastic productions, namely, the stories of the *Which Was the Dream?* collection and *The Mysterious Stranger Manuscripts,* myths and archetypal images emerge from the texts. The Christian myths of death and resurrection, of fallen angels and fallen humankind, are intermixed with cultural myths of the wanderer, the curse of nature, the blessed and luck-giving animal, and the journey in the night, as well as such archetypal images as the child hero, the trickster, the wise old man, and, especially, the mandala symbolism, both in its graphic form and as a more abstract idea of perennial circularity. The presence of this mythical lore is further complicated, however, by its intermingling with persistent burlesque patterns, which not only emerge separately from the mythical elements of the texts but are closely connected to them.

For example, the myth of the child is first treated in a burlesque manner in the opening section of the first and third versions of *The Mysterious Stranger Manuscripts,* wherein the mythical innocence of the narrator is ridiculed through his own naive language. The widely accepted belief in children's innocence is later challenged in episodes in which children themselves are involved in the cruel social practices of the villagers. Quite soon in the story, however, the archetypal child image emerges and is impersonated by the young devil Philip Traum/44. The Christian myth of evil embodied in Satan is thus indirectly satirized through the very fact that the devil is a child—the symbol of innocence. Moreover, the young Satan's connotations are those of the child-hero archetype. This instance provides us with an example of Twain's complex attitude toward myth often on display in the Papers; his ambivalent attitude toward myth stands out and calls for our attention. Because of the contradictory elements in the text, we are compelled to view the writer's attitude as a problem. The question we face is: Is Twain a mythmaker or a myth-satirist? The texts we have analyzed so far point in apparently opposite directions.

While dealing with different attitudes toward myth, Roland Barthes describes three possible responses: the producer of myth, the mythologist, and the reader of myth.[5] While the producer is the very source of myth, the mythologist is an interpreter and a critic of myth who allows himself a distance from it; the reader is eventually the receiver of myth who applies myth to his own understanding of the mysteries of life. These three different responses emerge alternatively from the Papers and trigger questions. Are Twain's Papers the result of a mythmaking mind or, rather, the work of a perceptive critic of social myth? Are the Papers themselves mythical fables or satires? Is Twain a recipient of the social myths of his time as well as their critic? These questions are addressed in this chapter through a closer look at the mythical patterns in the Papers.

The Three Responses to Myth

Among the later longer narratives, one in particular illustrates Twain's relation to myth. Because of its direct treatment of myth, "The Refuge of the Derelicts" provides us with material for discussion.[6]

To honor the human race, a young poet conceives the idea of building a monument to Adam. He seeks the support of an eccentric retired admiral, who presides over a community of derelicts who in some way or another have failed in life. The poet is admitted into the community and, during his stay, keeps a diary. From his record we learn of the discussion taking place in the community on the subject of Adam. The father of humankind serves the derelicts as a mirror for their failures. The center of the story moves from a discussion of the monument to a series of sketches of the derelicts and their personal stories of failure. The stories follow each other in an endless chain of digressions, while Adam's character is subjected to various interpretations by the derelicts. In the final chapter of the unfinished narrative, a naturalist gives a lecture to the derelicts on Nature's benevolence; however, the images he shows to support his point disprove it completely by proving instead Nature's vulturism. The rhetoric of the lecture is defeated by crude reality.

Although unfinished and episodic, "The Refuge of the Derelicts" is tightly centered around the myth of Adam. In fact, all three of the possible attitudes Barthes envisages are on display in the story. The narration moves from the production of myth (the proposed building of the monument to Adam) to its interpretation (both the derelicts' personal response to it and the scientific dismissal of Adam by Darwinian evolutionary theory), and eventually to its integration into everyday reality by its readers through an inevitable evolution.

The monument—the initial segment of the tale—is meant to celebrate an abstract idea of the human race and to preserve the survival of it as idea. Darwinian evolutionary theory excludes Adam as source, as father of the human race, and belittles his origin. Since origin and essence are strictly connected, the poet (the protagonist) has to preserve the idea of Adam as father of humankind in order to preserve the idea of the human essence as something separate and superior to Nature. In preserving an old myth, and in fact elevating it through the monument to the attention of his contemporaries, the poet becomes a producer of myth. However, as soon as he moves from the outer space of abstract ideas—an unidentified setting at the beginning of the story—and enters the Admiral's house, myth changes substantially through discussion and interpretation. The idea of the monument is abandoned and even excluded from the story. The focus is shifted to the human experience; however, the burlesque sketches of the derelicts follow a definite pattern of loss, of fall from Eden that echoes Adam's fall. Once he has disappeared as an abstract concept and an object of deference, Adam reappears as a mirror in the derelicts' lives. His function is thus described by the Admiral:

> ". . . which would you take, Adam or the germ? Naturally you would say Adam is business, the germ ain't; one is immediate and sure, the other is speculative and uncertain. Well, I have thought these things all over, and my sympathies are with Adam. Adam was like us, and so he seems near to us, and dear." (p. 221)

Thus myth has some use for its readers even after it has disappeared as the official myth suggested by its producers. It can be incorporated into people's lives and save humans from their alienation. Adam mirrors the derelicts' lives, mirrors their failure to live up to the standards of society. Their lives in turn mirror the human condition at large; their loss, like Adam's fall from Eden, is the recurrent passage from a situation of initial happiness to that of failure. Adam, however, in the derelicts' personal interpretation, is not responsible for his own failure, just as they are not responsible for theirs. This idea is crucial to the evolution of the myth: Adam, who is initially viewed by the producer of the myth as the father of humankind, is later viewed by the derelicts as a helpless child. The two black derelicts voice the opinion with particular eloquence:

> "It's plain to me, dey warn't fa'rly treated. If de'was a Adam— which people say nowadays de'wasn't. But dat ain't nothin', justice is justice, en I want him to have de monument." (pp. 209–10)

> "Po' little Adam—po' little Eve! It was de same like my little Henry: if I say 'dah you is, a-snoopin' 'round'dat sugar agin; you dast to tetch it once, I lay I'll skin you! Cose de minute my back's turned he's got de sugar; 'caze he don't k'yer nothin' for the skinnin', de way I skun him. Yes-suh, I kin see it all, now—dey didn't k'yer nothin' for de skinnin', de way de good Lord allays skun'en befo'." (p. 209)

Adam's function is reversed: from Father of Mankind he has become Child of God, and as any natural child he is a rebel against institutions. Yet he does not expect to receive the harsh punishment he gets for his minor transgressions. The punishment is a cruel hoax, a sudden betrayal. The Fall is an accident, evidence of the alienated position of humankind in the universe. Slaves to their own nature—they cannot be anything else than what they are—humans are requested to be other than themselves. This is a reinterpretation of Adam's fall, which Twain suggests through the opinions of the derelicts.

In order to have some use in the modern world, myth has to change, to be reinterpreted, to become a dynamic force in people's lives. The monument the derelicts build to Adam is not of marble; it is myth retold in the language of everyday reality. It is no longer the poetic language of its producer; it is not the Biblical language of its original source. It is the spoken language, vernacular language. Through this lowering, from the high genre to lower comedy, myth is preserved. Through spoken language myth regains its original essence of spoken word; it retrieves its original function, through its discussion, and the derelicts' measuring their experience against Adam's. At a level different from reality, myth mirrors the human experience. It solves the problem of man's alienated position in the universe by providing a possible identification that neither scientific evolutionary theory, nor the similarly impersonal laws ruling behavior in society, seems to provide. If myth is the ultimate lie, it is a necessary lie that allows survival and sanity. In order to perform its function, however, myth cannot be officially imposed, lest it become an enslaving lie at the service of power and institutions. It is for this reason that its usefulness can only be ensured through man's sole defense—laughter. From tragic hero, Adam has to become a hapless child and a comic failure.

The closing chapter of "The Refuge of the Derelicts" provides a *mise en abîme* of the thematic development of the story. A lecturing naturalist, who is also a religious preacher trying to reconcile the unreconcilable (the belief in the benevolence of nature and scientific data about the vulturism in nature), indirectly sums up the discussion of myth, and reinforces its role. The lecture works at two levels: It shows vulturism in nature and, by doing so, alludes to the ruthless laws governing society. The derelicts' failure in society is due to their incapacity, or their unwillingness, to live up to these laws and be vultures instead of victims. By showing crude scientific data through unquestionable images, the lecture provides a dismissal of myth; however, the data, being an excess of reality, cannot be absorbed and accepted by human consciousness, which refuses identification with nature. The separation of human consciousness from nature generates an artificial myth of the benevolence of nature that, when uttered, can only be a baffling hypocrisy, a superimposition, and a lie. The sole true possibility of survival for myth in modern times is its lowering to the human level, where it can provide the mirroring and the identification that humans need for their sanity.

The three possible attitudes toward myth Barthes suggests—the producer, the mythologist, and the reader—are contained in "The Refuge of the Derelicts." The poet's idea of a monument to Adam, at the beginning of the story, as well as the lecture on the benevolence of nature in the last chapter, are examples of the attitude of the producer of myths. The skeptical attitude of some derelicts, the free discussions of Adam's character, and, finally, the scientific data provide examples of a mythologist's attitude: the analysis and distancing of myth and its final dismissal. However, the derelicts' identification with Adam portrayed as a hapless child, a victim of the cruel laws of the universe (as they are the victims of the ruthlessness of society) provides an example of "reading into" the myth—a transformation that makes it useful for the modern consciousness.

These three attitudes recur throughout the Papers. Even though we can say that, in "The Refuge of the Derelicts," Twain's intention could not be found in the producer paradigm, in the Papers in general, and even in his works as a whole, this attitude is not alien. In fact, Twain was the producer of the predominant myth of his career—the myth of himself, Mark Twain, the funny fellow, the celebrator of youth and progress. Despite its limiting and self-censoring effect, this literary myth is central to his relationship to his contemporary audience. We have seen, however, how the impossibility of changing this relationship based upon a myth partly caused his withdrawal from publication later in his career. The Papers are the result of this withdrawal, of the shattering of this myth. Yet, in the "The Secret History of Eddypus, the World Empire," Twain produces a myth of himself that transcends any personal myth: In this later dystopian narrative, Twain sees himself as the source of history, the producer of a new interpretation of historical events in purely mythical terms. Through the character of Mark Twain, the Father of History, he indirectly comments on his own literary production, on his own mythmaking.

Among the most powerful myths he produced during his career is that of childhood. There too Twain's position is quite complex. On the one hand he employs a myth already common in the society of his time. On the other hand, he reinterprets it in various ways, either preserving the myth by subjecting it to the test of reality or creating an image of childhood that transcends reality (as in the case of his young Satan character, the protagonist of his last experiment in romance). In the child archetype transpiring through young Satan, Twain sums up many of his attitudes toward myth. While he satirizes the accepted stereotype of the devil archetype, he recovers the child archetype in its original mythical form. In this respect he is both reader of myth and producer of new myths.

Another archetypal image surfaces in the Papers: the trickster. Partly incorporated in the child archetype, the trickster becomes an autonomous character as Superintendent of Dreams in "The Great Dark." There he is in control of an entire world, the world of dreams, into which he tricks his dreaming subjects. Like the previous archetypes, the trickster is a self-reflexive image commenting on the creative activity generating the text. Just as the trickster generates dreams and controls them, so does the author generate and control his text.

The reflexivity of these images—pivotal in the posthumously published Papers and especially in the fantastic stories and *The Mysterious Stranger Manuscripts*—parallels the self-referentiality of the text. The recurring archetypes are metaphors for the creative imagination at work in the text; they allude to writing. Among these archetypal images, the mandala—the archetype of completeness—sums up all the dichotomies of the texts, reconciling their opposed elements. This image, which seeps into the texts either in its circular graphic image or in its aspect of centrality, powerfully metaphorizes the working of the psyche involved in the creation of the text.

Through the recurrent use of these images, Twain places himself in front of myth as a mythologist who dismisses the best-accepted myths of his society; in order to do so, he adopts archetypal images that, because of their depth, obscure the superimposed social myths. By resurrecting the archetypes and using them in an original way in his work, Twain acts as a reader of myth. Moreover, by developing autonomous characters, which stand in the literary world as images capable of generating new images and new meanings, Twain is also a producer. Barthes's three possible ways to myth merge together in Twain's Papers.

The Myth of Adam

The twofold treatment of Twain's most intriguing archetypal image, the child, clearly exemplifies the composite function of mythical characters in the Papers.

The presence of child characters in Twain's works is easily identifiable and clearly predominant. Many major critical works have analyzed that aspect of the writer's work at great length. In his treatment of the child character, Twain was in tune with his time. As Jay Martin points out, Twain, influenced by evolutionary theories, projects his image of Eden through the myth of childhood; in fact Darwinism, following in this respect the Romantic idea, proclaims "the child Father of the man and the savage progenitor of civilization."[7] The child is the only noble savage left; moreover, the child is regarded as a possible model for the study of human beings at a stage in which they are free of materialism.

From the 1870s to the turn of the century, most writers felt a certain nostalgia for their rural pre–Civil War childhood. Aldrich's *Story of a Bad Boy* (1869), Howells's *A Boy's Town* (1890) and *Years of My Young* (1916), Henry A. Shute's *Real Diary of a Real Boy* (1902), and Hamlin Garland's *Boy Life on the Prairie* (1899) were published in this period. The same tendency was also present among the regionalists: Most of them wrote books for children, thus revisiting the past through contact with the infant mind.

Some historical reasons account for the myth of childhood. The deep changes in society after the Civil War pushed writers toward recollection as a form of escape from the present. Obviously the myth of childhood had roots deep in Christianity. It was consolidated by Rousseau's view of the corruption of man's original innocence by the actions of human institutions. It was further developed by the Romantics, who found analogies to their own revolt against society in the child's rebellion against authority. It was in the course of such a literary movement that the child became a subject fit for literary treatment. In dealing with this subject, Leslie Fiedler places special emphasis on the relation between the image of the child and the bourgeois artist. He indicates that the child provided a "safely genteel symbol of protest and impulse, which, however, did not threaten the bourgeois order."[8]

The specific quality of Twain's treatment of the child's image is well explained in Tony Tanner's article "The Literary Children of James and Clemens."[9] Tanner establishes a comparison between Henry James's treatment of the child character and Twain's. While James uses the child's consciousness as a mirror of reality, Twain, through the child, "implies a full moral verdict on the adult world," and therefore the child is for him a lamp rather than a mirror. "He was after something much larger, something as large as a reappraisal of life. He seeks a new viewpoint and a new language in which to transmit this novel vision."[10] Moreover, Tanner indicates, Twain saw in the approximations and omissions of the child's language the possibility of drawing new lyrical intensities. He was especially interested in the functional use of vernacular. This new viewpoint and new language merge in the character of Huck Finn, whose innocence is not based on mere ignorance.

Although Twain's treatment of children evolved and changed greatly during his career, many of Huck's character traits were handed over to the protagonist of the "Colloquy Between a Slum Child and a Moral Mentor." James, the slum child, shares Huck's radical innocence, as indicated by his capacity to view things as they are and voice his opinion through a strong and spicy vernacular. James is very different from the sentimental child characters Twain creates in *The Prince and the Pauper,* who "fit the sentimental view of children held by the genteel section of society."[11] In fact, one can grossly divide Twain's child characters into two main groups: One comprises Huck and all the other rebel children who occasionally seep into the later Papers; the other includes the sentimental children of his most conformist phase.

The Papers contain a twofold evolution of the first group of characters. The burlesque treatment of sentimentality connected with childhood, as in the "Mamie Grant" burlesque, is one aspect. This burlesque treatment is certainly retraceable also to the major works, especially such short stories and sketches as the "Story of a Bad Boy." The other tendency, which is more clearly limited to the later phase and the Papers, consists of the abstraction of the myth of childhood from any contemporary trend. The child becomes an archetypal image, the pure crystallization of Twain's later and complex perceptions. This myth is perfected in the satanic child of *The Mysterious Stranger Manuscripts* who combines child- and devil-archetype in one character, and who is the satirical reversal of the myth of childhood as viewed by Twain's contemporary society and codified by genteel fiction.

Twain follows a literary trend that, although anti-institutional in ideology, was well established and had been practiced by the Romantics from Goethe to Byron. Satan as the voice of the revolution, the voice of enlightenment and progress, was not Twain's innovation. Yet the unification of this literary archetype with the child image is Twain's innovative creation. The iconoclastic character unifies two major deviations from the accepted social order, the rebellious Satan and the rebellious child. We can easily recognize in 44/Philip Traum many of the connotations of his rebellious children from the St. Petersburg world. The symbolically rebellious function of the satanic child is, however, more intensified and more explicit here than in previous creations. Not only is little Satan a child archetype, thus symbolizing an aspect of the human psyche, but he also represents an aspect of Twain's ontological conception. In Twain's view, these two sides—the psyche and man's position in the universe—are parallel and strictly related to each other. The humans' position in the universe is determined by their psychological "constitution." Humans are, indeed, determined and limited mostly by themselves, and therefore can only be liberated and gain power through their own efforts. The satanic aspect is this liberating force, which is the source of artistic creativity, as is shown by Satan's capacity to trigger images and create new worlds.

Satan, however, represents only one side of the child archetype, as well as only one side of the ontological theory. Satan, in Twain's literary creation, would be an empty sign without his counterpart, his disciple and integrating opposite, Adam. While Satan represents the futurity of the child archetype, its thrust toward future and progress, Adam represents its link with a primordial past. While Satan is active, Adam is passive; Satan is a rebel, Adam a victim. This complementary function of Satan stands out clearly in *The Mysterious Stranger Manuscripts*, wherein Adam finds his incarnation in the character/narrator Theodor/August, who impersonates the adamic vision as well as the most extreme elaboration of the adamic character. Through his continuous interaction with the other child, the satanic 44/Traum, and eventually through the final integration of the two into one entity in the final part of the romance, Adam comes to symbolize both everyman in history and the passive side of the psyche. Through the complementary relation to the satanic character, the adamic character acquires a symbolic value in the text. It becomes part of the child archetype.

In this respect, Twain's original innovation is the evolution of the adamic myth. In "The Refuge of the Derelicts," through the discussion of the derelicts, Adam is brought down from the pedestal where a conventional vision fostered by institutions and codified literary genres has placed him and undergoes the test of human experience. Adam then becomes a mirror and acquires meaning and use as a myth. Eventually through this exploration Adam is brought one more step down and reduced to the dimension of a child, unaware, ignorant, and innocent. Through this evolution, not only is myth as a separate entity brought down from a static and elevated position to a mobile and lower state, but what Adam stands for—humanity—is subjected to the same evolution. Humanity is belittled; humanity is reduced to a child's proportions and therefore justified. In *The Mysterious Stranger Manuscripts* this evolution is completed. The mythical Adam is transformed into a character and a narrator. Adam acquires a voice, the voice of "everyman."

The Myth of the Author

The most powerful myth created by Twain during his lifetime is that of himself.[12] It bridges the distance between fiction and reality while it creates a second self for his producer. Through this second self, the writer establishes communication with his audience, yet shields himself against it. He creates a self who, although part of him, is separate and distant enough not to be reached. He creates both a fictional character and a myth.

In "The Secret History of Eddypus," Twain deals with the myth of himself at the triple level that characterizes much of his treatment of myth at large.[13] He is the producer of that myth; he is its mythologist, who deconstructs and analyzes through a burlesque treatment; he is its reader since he uses myth to create a metaphor of his own relationship as an author to his work, and through his work to the world of history. Mark Twain, the Father of History, Bishop of New Jersey, hanged in A.D. 1912 is such a myth.

Amidst the uncertainty of records and the patent falsity of official history (pious romances), the Father of History's papers provide a true and reliable source for the author of the secret and forbidden history of Eddypus. This source, which is kept hidden and untouched, is itself forbidden. The narrator, a devoted historian, is the only person who is able to get hold of the ancient and transgressive manuscript in its pristine form. He has some biographical and bibliographical information concerning his source; Mark Twain was apparently the author of such books as "Old Comrades," "The Gospel of Self," including chapters treating of the "Real Character of Conscience," "Personal Merit," "The Machinery of the Mind," and "The Arbitrary and Irresistible Power of Circumstance and Environment." Mark Twain read such books as "The Innocents Abroad," "Roughing It," "Tramp Abroad," "Pudd'nhead Wilson," "Joan of Arc," "Prince and the Pauper." Records concerning his personal life are a little confused, yet one thing is quite clear: Mark Twain had twenty-six children out of wedlock (he probably had a harem) and, among them, two were particularly dear to his heart— Huck Finn and Tom Sawyer. In describing Mark Twain's personality and mental capacity, the narrator finds one major blemish, his lack of a sense of humor. This causes him to distort reality. Another aspect of his attitude toward his work is his belief that his personal history will reflect the general history of humankind during his lifetime. He also believed that human life is entirely determined by environment and circumstances. On the subject of publication, Mark Twain made it clear that he would not want to publish his papers during his lifetime; at first he thought he would wish to wait one hundred years, but then he changed his mind and decided that one thousand years would be more appropriate. Eventually he realized that in one thousand years language would change so much that readers would no longer be able to decipher his writings; he decided that four hundred and fifty years would be the right length of time. Two fragments of the writings of Mark Twain, as the Father of History, are inserted into the "Secret History." The first is a record of his voice; he addresses his posterity directly from the grave and proposes a toast to several of his contemporaries. The second fragment is an anecdote about a visit to a phrenologist who, not knowing the writer's identity, gives a totally negative evaluation of his personality.

Mark Twain's presence in the "Secret History," like the source he provides, is totally distorted. Yet the deviations, like the deviations of historical data, are meaningful. Not only are they a burlesque of Twain's myth of his own self, they are also evidence of the defeat of the self struggling against annihilation in the mists of time. Twain's attitude as a mythologist seeps into this analytical approach to myth. The self cannot survive history; not only data, but also personality, are erased, leaving only confusion and distortion. These are the only signs that reach posterity. Partly because of the inevitable changes of language at large, the honest struggle for truth carried out by the historian of "The Secret History" is just as meaningless as the willingly fake and manipulative history of the official records. Mark Twain was quite aware that a publication of his hidden papers too long delayed would make them unreadable because of great changes in language and communication. In fact, the narrator's literal reading of his humorous sentences is evidence that a change of code has already occurred, thus preventing a decoding of the signs; only the signifier is perceived by the literal reading of the narrator, while the signified is ignored. The unity of the sign is shattered, and so is its signification. The only thought by Mark Twain recorded without distortions is the one concerning the impact of environment and circumstances on human life. This thought sums up the whole problem of communication to posterity that Mark Twain's presence as a character poses in the text. If individuals are limited in their response by environment and circumstance, a change of context because of the passage of time will determine completely different responses. Because of his need to be truthful and his fear of being repressed, Mark Twain has to delay publication and hide his papers from a contemporary audience who would understand him; however, the delay might cause distortion of the sign or its erasure. Not only does the fear of annihilation and erasure make Mark Twain's presence in this dystopian tale a necessity, it also makes myth the only way of combating oblivion.

However, the distortions are meaningful; they reveal Twain's attitude toward his time and his work. He absorbs the philosophy of his time to the point that he may well be confused with authors of books concerning the mind and the interplay of self and environment. These works are even more truly his than his actual works because they are closer to his true self and his true thoughts. His writings, in turn, can be confused with his readings, because they are the product of his age and society more than of his true self. They are his readings into the social myths of his time. Writing and reading, the two poles of the process of communication, become interchangeable through the distortion. Yet, once more, the distortion is meaningful. Not only is Twain the writer/producer of his stories/myths, but he is also the reader/recipient of myth. As such, he responds to the social myth he himself has created by generating a metaphor of authorship.

Each single attribute related to his fictional self is a paradigm—a set of terms relating metaphorically to each other through potential substitution. So Father relates to source, origin, authorship (thanks to the references to Twain's books), and personal relation; history relates to general and personal history, as well as myth and storytelling; Bishop relates to preserver and divulger of myth, as well as celebrator of rituals, including also social myths and rituals. "Hanged" eventually relates to the death of the author—including his absence from the text—to his censorship and suppression because of having performed some transgressive role.[14] The terms included in each paradigm, besides relating metaphorically to each other, are connected through a syntagmatic relation to the various terms in each paradigm. So source relates to history, to preserver as historian, and to censorship. Origin relates to myth, to its divulgence and celebration, and to its suppression. Authorship finally relates to storytelling, to celebration of social rituals and myths, and to censorship and death of authorship in its various forms. These connections, both in their metaphorical and metonymic relations, illuminate Twain's perception of his own role as a writer and his rapport with his work and his time. They illuminate especially his ambiguous oscillations between celebration and transgression, between the creation of myths and his search for truth. All these terms, instead of opposing each other (as they often do in other instances), merge in the character of Mark Twain, the Father of History, Bishop of New Jersey, "hanged."

Myth reconciles the inherent dichotomies of the writer's position to his work and audience. More specifically, in the text of "The Secret History of Eddypus" the sudden appearance of Mark Twain—somewhat unrelated to the text of the story—provides an alternative to the disappearance of authorship caused through the proliferation of signs. In fact, because of the total uncertainty of the events dealt with, and because of the precarious means of communication (the cipher and the erasable paper), the message itself is jeopardized. The authority of authorship is heavily threatened by the uncertainty of the message. Moreover, in the historical recounting, the identity and voice of the author are smothered by the historical cycles that, because they repeat each other, reinforce the sense of anonymity connected with the authorship. The appearance of the Father of History provides a center to the dispersed narration, a source of authority, a unifying principle. The two fragments, inserted in the narrative with no apparent purpose, function as sudden resurrections of the presence. This presence reflects and reveals Twain's own doubts in the production of the Papers—his own secret history that is meant to reveal the naked truth and to survive censorship through an address to posterity. It reveals Twain's fear of his own practice in the digressive mode of which "The Secret History" is the most extreme example.

There is, however, a dispersion which transcends that of text. History, through the accumulation of events and the flowing of time, removes and erases presence. It destroys authorship by confusing the two extreme poles of the process of communication. It distorts names of people and places. It alters events. The search for a source, the myth of some origin that is always retrievable, compensates for the lack of identity, which the subject experiences when facing the incessant flow of time, the oppressiveness and injustice of power, and the impersonal mechanism of the cosmos. Just as Adam, the child and the victim of a cosmic hoax, provides through myth identification and mirroring for humans in search of a beginning, the Father of History provides the myth of an origin, which must not be located outside of man but rather in humans themselves. Humankind becomes the source of its own knowledge and power. If Adam is the source of human limitations, the Father of History is the source of humans' knowledge about themselves.

If the Father of History alludes to the author's relation to his work (his history, story, myths) while referring to humans' relation to history, the two terms of the metaphor, in their syntagmatic opposition (father being a sign of personal kinship, history of a general relation of human beings), allude to the two poles of personal and general experience. As a unit, the Father of History is the unifying myth summing up personal and general history, internal and external reality. It is strictly related to Twain's own ideal literary form, which he established while working on the autobiography. He claimed then (as the Father of History does while working on his historical paper) that his work aims to be a unification of personal and general history, a mirror both for his life and for that of his contemporaries. In a Whitmanesque mode Twain wants to encompass all. Even more significantly, his literary concept, so astoundingly similar to Jung's own theory of the collective unconscious, echoes the cosmic conception of the psyche as bridging the personal and the collective, absorbing and mirroring the ancestral knowledge in individual consciousness.

The reflexive quality of the text, mirroring and absorbing all, parallels its self-reflexivity by referring to its process of writing, alluding to its origin and development, and describing all. The mythical images surfacing in Twain's later fantastic papers are often oriented toward a self-reflexive function. Another mythical image performing such a self-reflexive role is the Superintendent of Dreams. Just as the Father of History, by providing a source for historical referentiality, creates the reality of history, the Superintendent of Dreams, by inducing the oneiric state, controls imaginative reality. Although apparently opposed, these two realities—the waking world of history and external events, and the dreaming world of imaginary fiction—are in fact the two aspects of the mythical world. History provides the content, the story, the rough draft, the material for myths. Imagination transforms this material into myth by incorporating into it the collective dreams of humankind. The telling, which ensures the survival and divulgence of myth through time, is part of the historical process. It is not based on facts and reality, but on dreams.

The Father of History and the Superintendent of Dreams function in Twain's cosmic concept as complementary characters. An intertextual reading of the Papers allows us to see the relation between them, their points of similarity, and the complementary way in which they interact. Both provide a center and a source in the texts where they surface. The Father of History is the source for historical reference; the Superintendent of Dreams is the originator of the dream he induces his subject into. Both control their fields of action; both function as guides; both work as godlike powers in the texts. Their power is exerted through explicit interventions in the plot. The Father of History, through the fragments inserted in "The Secret History," makes his voice heard from the grave; he then shows himself in action while playing a hoax on some phrenologists. The Superintendent of Dreams addresses the protagonist dreamer, appears to him, and plays tricks on the sailors. The tricks on the phrenologist and on the sailor elucidate one basic similarity in the functions of the two characters. The hoax, by standing to the whole text as a *mise en abîme*, provides an indirect comment on the cosmic conception supported by the text. Both hoaxes are based on a game between appearance and reality. The Superintendent, invisible to the sailor, empties his cup of coffee; the Father of History, not known to the phrenologist, calls for a visit. The invisibility, and the ignorance, implied in these hoaxes allude to two different levels of unknowingness: at work in the cosmos, the invisible forces that constantly baffle the human senses; in the text, the invisible power of the author playing constant tricks on his addressees through artistic illusion. Another aspect of this illusion is a game with proportions: The smallest unit of the text mirrors the text as a whole, and likewise the entire conception of the universe behind it. This is illustrated in the drop of water that is the setting for the journey on the ocean in the dream tale of "The Great Dark"; likewise, the small text of the secret history contains the entire history of humankind. Authorship allows these games, these illusions. The Superintendent of Dreams describes it clearly to his protagonist subject:

> Then the Superintendent of Dreams appeared at my side, and we talked it over. He was willing to provide a ship and crew. . . .
>
> "You and your crew will be much diminished, as to size, but you need not trouble about that, as you will not be aware of it. Your ship itself, stuck upon the point of a needle, would not be discoverable except through a microscope of very high power."
>
> "Are these the fictitious proportions which we and our surroundings and belongings have acquired by being reduced to microscopic objects?"
>
> "They are the proportions, yes—but they are not fictitious. . . ."
>
> "You came from a small and very insignificant world. The one you are in now is proportioned according to microscopic standards—that is to say, it is inconceivably stupendous and imposing."[15]

This "stupendous world," which is "imposing" although miniaturized, is the world of both imagination and fiction. Fiction expands the human through imagination, and, at the same time, encompasses and reduces it to the miniature proportions of the text.

Through these mythical images, Twain crystallizes his concept of art. Through them, he explores the relation between text and author, between text and ontology. They illustrate Twain's digressive and all-inclusive principle of composition whereby the text includes and alludes constantly to other texts, responding without restraint to any stimulation from the extratextual world. While they unify the diffuse material of the Papers by pointing out the recurrences, they also create a nexus between the world of the text and the external world of events and discourse; even more significantly, they allude to the collective consciousness, which they express through crystallization into archetypal images.

Another related aspect of these crystallizing mythical images is their similarity to folk-images, whose recurrence in various cultures and literary products has attracted the interest of anthropology and psychology. In particular, the Superintendent of Dreams's playful attitude reminds one of the well-known trickster image, a folk motif dealt with in a study by Radin, Kerényi, and Jung.[16] According to Jung's psychological interpretation, the trickster image, frequently emerging in the Winnebago Indian culture, should be related to the concept of the shadow and, in turn, to the anima—the feminine side of the psyche deeply responsible for artistic creation. Both the Superintendent of Dreams and the Father of History are also related to another archetypal image frequently recurring in fairy tales—the spirit. Jung observes that the spirit, often impersonated by a wise old man, "takes the form of urging people to 'sleep on it.' "[17] He also provides a source of knowledge, reflection, and insight.

These notations on the archetypal aspect of the mythic images are meant to emphasize the relation between Twain's work and folklore, and thereby his connection with a vaster context of collective imagination. The images are also evidence of the relation between Twain's explorations of the oneiric world and his experimental literary activity. Exploration of the powers of the psyche and of the possibilities of writing become unified in archetypal images alluding and referring, at the same time, to the subconscious and the text. The mandala image, in particular, suggests a merging of the working of the psyche with writing. While it describes the unification of opposites and the attraction to the center in the human psyche, it also alludes to the text as a unit, as the circularity of recurring motifs, and as a creative process. The center of the mandala is always the sought after and unreachable source, the origin, "the thing."

One problem in the interpretation of these figures, as was pointed out at the beginning of this discussion, surfaces again as soon as we move from Twain's burlesque of myth to his metaphoric use of myth in his stories. The archetypal images do not exclude the satire of myth and its social function, the exploration of its meaning and usefulness. If the Father of History is similar to the representation of the spirit in its archetypal form—a wise old man providing knowledge—he is also the representation of absence and of the useless struggle to preserve identity through the passing of time. His wisdom is a sign, but an empty one because its meaning is unintelligible. The Superintendent of Dreams, on the other hand, while impersonating the creative spirit in the text, also indicates that the spirit can survive only through the incessant creation of illusion, because no reality can ever be reached. In fact, fiction is the only reality, and myth making is part of its process of creation. For this reason both the humorous and the straightforward treatment of myth point ultimately in the same direction: the creation of old/new myths.

Conclusion
The Duplicating Imagination

If a metaphorical image could sum up Twain's later and posthumously published production it should be that of the duplicating process in "No. 44." Dual images recur indeed throughout Twain's works at large, both in his better-known works and in other pieces that have not been dealt with in this study. For example, in a newly found later story, "How Nancy Jackson Married Kate Wilson," the young female protagonist is compelled to perform a male role, thus doubling herself through travesty. However, duplication, as a metaphor surfacing in "No. 44" and as used here in reference to the Papers, is a special kind of doubling that implies both the unlimited expansion of the imaginative process and the self-reflexivity of the text.

Twain's interest in dreams, the duplicates of waking reality, reveals a facet of both his life and literary career. More biographically oriented studies might point out the healing function that Twain's annotations of his own dreams and the associative method of his later writing performed during the last decades of his life. Here, instead, emphasis is placed on the connection between Twain's attitude toward the oneiric experience and the fantastic imagination at work in the later fantasies. Twain thinks of the oneiric experience as an expansion of the powers of the mind; his fantastic stories reflect this belief through the violation of the borders of reality. The fantastic experience duplicates reality and, through its hidden essence, fantasy becomes reality. Similarly, in Twain's annotations on dreams, dream becomes reality.

Not only is there a connection between personal dreams and literary fantasies but also between Twain's "fantastic" attitude and his attitude toward writing. He sees the link between the unconscious working of the psyche and literary creativity. He traces the source of creativity in the psyche (the dream artist). If dream and fantasy are the only reality, writing is part of that truer alternate reality, that "other" world that contains the essence and the core of experience. The style of his later and posthumously published works and the method of writing that Twain describes reflect these convictions. The free-associative method, the blending of styles and genres, and the estrangement procedure are facets of Twain's duplicating imagination.

Throughout this study, while I point out Twain's link with his time, I also argue that he anticipates both our contemporary awareness of the fragmentation of experience and some modern and postmodern literary procedures. The fragmentation of the text, the self-referential quality of many passages of the Papers, and the allusions to the writing process reveal the writer's concern with issues that are very real to us. Twain's concept of the ideal writing allies him with some of the structuralist and poststructuralist theoreticians; this is particularly true of his striving for a written text capable of overcoming the separation between written and oral performances—the Barthesian zero degree of writing. His parody of the higher genres, through the estrangement procedure and heteroglossia, aims at obliterating the distance between the written and the oral. Twain conceives the ideal text as the perfect duplication of the human voice. It must reach the essence of reality.

Myth is still another aspect of duplication. At a level different from reality, it duplicates and reconciles the conflicts of the real world. Through mordant satire of the myths of his time and society and the use of folkloric and mythic motifs in an unusual context, Twain tries to retrieve the very essence of myth and foster its innovation.

Because of his concern with the problems of verbal communication, his concept of the literary text, and his transgressive experimental attitude, Twain, a writer rooted in his time and culture, also becomes our contemporary, and a citizen of the world. Through text-centered interpretive strategies linked to contemporary literary discourse, my work has meant to suggest such directions of study.

ℐotes

Introduction

1. Among recent works dealing with the Mark Twain Papers, see William
M. Gibson, *The Art of Mark Twain* (New York: Oxford University Press, 1976);
William R. Mcnaughton, *Mark Twain's Last Years as a Writer* (Columbia and
London: University of Missouri Press, 1979); Sholom J. Kahn, *Mark Twain's
Mysterious Stranger: A Study of the Manuscript* (Columbia and London:
University of Missouri Press, 1978); Susan K. Harris, *Mark Twain's Escape
from Time* (Columbia and London: University of Missouri Press, 1982); Louis
J. Budd, *Our Mark Twain* (Philadelphia: University of Pennsylvania Press,
1983); Sara de Saussure Davis and Philip D. Beidler, eds., *The Mythologizing
of Mark Twain* (Tuscaloosa: University of Alabama Press, 1984); Everett
Emerson, *The Authentic Mark Twain* (Philadelphia: University of Pennsylvania Press, 1984); Robert Sewell, *Mark Twain's Languages: Discourse, Dialogue, and Linguistic Variety* (Berkeley: University of California Press, 1987);
Randy Nelson, "Probing the Great Dark: Dream Features of Mark Twain's Late
Works," Diss. Princeton University, 1976; Mary Holland McGraw, "The Dream
and the Creative Imagination in Mark Twain's *The Mysterious Stranger Manu-
scripts*," Diss. Oklahoma State University, 1979; Drue Annelle Porter, "The
Dream Motif in Mark Twain's *Mysterious Stranger Manuscripts*," Diss. East
Texas State University, 1981; David Ketterer, "Power Fantasy in the 'Science
Fiction' of Mark Twain," *Bridges to Fantasy*, G. Slusser, E. Rabkin, and R.
Scholes, eds. (Carbondale and Edwardsville: Southern Illinois University Press,
1982), pp. 130–41, and his introduction to *The Science Fiction of Mark Twain*
(Hamden, Conn.: Archon Books, 1984).

2. *Mark Twain's Autobiography,* ed. Albert Bigelow Paine (New York and London: Harper & Bros., 1924), 1:193, 326–27.

3. For a definition of the zero degree in writing, see Roland Barthes, *Writing Degree Zero,* trans. Annette Lavers (Boston: Beacon Press, 1967).

4. *Mark Twain–Howells Letters,* ed. Henry Nash Smith and William M. Gibson (Cambridge, Mass.: Harvard University Press, Belknap Press, 1960), p. 698. Twain had already expressed the same intention in a letter to Mr. Skrine, dated 22 August 1897, in which he mentioned that two of the five books he was at work on were not for publication in his lifetime (SLC to Mr. Skrine, TS MTP). In another letter to Mr. Mac Veagh, dated the same day, Twain expressed the wish to use his writings for personal recreational purposes (SLC to Mr. Mac Veagh, TS MTP). Again, on 10 December 1898, in a letter to Frank Bliss, he stated that he was not going to finish any of the books he was working on, at least not for a while (SLC to Frank Bliss, TS MTP). As late as 1904, in a letter to Muriel Pearls, he revealed that he did not intend to publish the book he was working on. He was then writing "No. 44" (SLC to Muriel Pearls, TS MTP). Finally, in a London interview with the *Daily Chronicle,* dated 3 June 1899, he declared that he was planning to stop writing for publication and that one of the two books he was writing should never be published, while the other was meant for a "remote posterity" (Clippings file, MTP).

5. In a letter to Duneka, dated 5 January 1904 (SLC to Duneka, TS MTP), and in two letters to his daughter Clara, dated respectively 29 June and 16 July 1905 (SLC to Clara Clemens, TS MTP), Twain expressed the intention of completing the revision of some of his unfinished works. Isabel Lyon's (Twain's secretary's) diary also provides evidence that Twain expressed verbally the intention of revising "No. 44" for future publication, even though his initial intention had been not ever to publish *The Mysterious Stranger Manuscripts* (Isabel Lyon's Diary, 3 July 1905, TS MTP).

6. Charles Neider, *Mark Twain* (New York: Horizon Press, 1967), pp. 110–32.

7. Neider, p. 117.

8. Neider, p. 120.

9. Neider had mentioned this fact in the introduction to his edition of the *Autobiography* and later expanded on it in his book on Twain. There he revealed the censoring role played by Clara Clemens: namely, her suppression of *Letters from the Earth,* an anthology of Mark Twain's short stories, edited by De Voto in 1939 and finally published in 1962; her request that De Voto omit the chapters on religion from *Mark Twain in Eruption;* and the application of the same restrictions to Neider's edition of the *Autobiography.* It appears from her correspondence with Neider that she was afraid "the Communists would make *generous* use of such a weapon as Mark Twain's attack on God. . . . We certainly are not going to place my blessed father and superior character on the side of the all-good-destroying Communists," she added. Quoted in Neider, pp. 144–45.

10. *Mark Twain–Howells Letters,* p. 811.

11. "United States of Lyncherdom" was published posthumously in 1923 in the collection edited by Paine, *Europe and Elsewhere*.

12. As W. M. Gibson shows in "Mark Twain and Howells: Anti-Imperialists," *New England Quarterly* 20 (1947), 443, Howells and other Boston intellectuals were just as involved as Twain in anti-imperialist issues.

13. In 1897 Brander Matthews stated that Twain was viewed by the public as "a writer whose sole duty it was to make us laugh, and to whom therefore we need never give a second thought after the smile had faded from our faces." "Mark Twain—His Work," *Book-Buyer* (13 January 1897):977. Quoted by Henry Nash Smith, "Mark Twain, 'The Funniest Man in the World,'" *The Mythologizing of Mark Twain,* p. 59.

14. In *Mark Twain: The Fate of Humor* (Princeton, N.J.: Princeton University Press, 1966), James M. Cox suggests the essentially Freudian hypothesis of humor as a result of suppression, while he discusses the role played in Twain's literary career by his wife, Olivia Langdon. Van Wyck Brooks's earlier description of Twain's wife as a purely negative, repressive, and authoritarian influence blocking the free evolution of the artist is thus reversed by Cox's study. Cox maintains that Twain chose Olivia's censorship as a needed disciplining force to channel his creative energy and make his work acceptable to the genteel society to which part of him aspired. She represented, in the role playing of their personal and literary relationship, the principle of suppression against which his coarse, rebellious side fought (and won) by emerging to the surface of literary creation through an acceptable form of humor. At her death, Twain sought to replace her censorship with others'—namely that of his old friend Howells, who already had played the role when Olivia was still alive, and later with that of Albert Bigelow Paine. Before meeting Olivia, Twain had adopted other censoring figures, such as Mrs. Fairbanks. When this role was not provided by others, he censored himself.

15. Alan Gribben gives a more detailed account of the history of the Mark Twain Papers in "Removing Mark Twain's Mask: A Decade of Criticism and Scholarship, Part 1," *ESQ* 26, no. 99 (1980): 101–5.

16. Franklin R. Rogers, ed. and introd., *Mark Twain's Satires and Burlesques* (Berkeley and Los Angeles: University of California Press, 1967).

17. John S. Tuckey, ed. and introd., *Mark Twain's Which Was the Dream? and Other Symbolic Writings of the Later Years* (Berkeley and Los Angeles: University of California Press, 1967).

18. Walter Blair, ed. and introd., *Mark Twain's Hannibal, Huck and Tom* (Berkeley and Los Angeles: University of California Press, 1969).

19. The Paine-Duneka edition had been accepted for almost fifty years as the only finished version of *The Mysterious Stranger*. Clearly, Paine had manipulated the manuscripts and attached a final chapter that he had partly altered to fit the first version of the story. The first manuscript itself underwent cuttings and censoring: The character of an astrologer was borrowed from the third manuscript and given the speech of a priest; the final chapter of the third manuscript was grafted to the broken-off first manuscript version; a bridging paragraph was composed; and the names of characters were altered. Gibson

points out that Paine perpetrated his fraud willingly and lied when he said, "Happily, it was the ending of the story in its first form" when referring to what he described as the sudden discovery of the final chapter. In fact he changed the names of the characters, and this proves his awareness of committing a fraud. William M. Gibson, ed. and introd., *Mark Twain's Mysterious Stranger Manuscripts* (Berkeley and Los Angeles: University of California Press, 1969), pp. i–xxxiv.

20. John S. Tuckey, ed. and introd., *Mark Twain's Fables of Man* (Berkeley, Los Angeles, London: University of California Press, 1972), pp. i–iv. Tuckey arranges these mostly satirical pieces into a thematic order. As he points out, Twain had tried unsuccessfully to have some of them published during his lifetime. What might have prevented the publication of most of the pieces dealing with religion is that they were too outspoken or profane for the times. Twain himself was aware of this, and that is why he performed a self-censorship on the works by forbidding their publication for five hundred years after his death. Even though some of the pieces might have been considered below Twain's standards, and flawed in various ways, the reason behind the delayed publication might be ascribed mainly to their content.

21. Cox, pp. 271–72.

22. John R. May, "The Gospel According to Philip Traum: Structural Unity in the *Mysterious Stranger*," *Studies in Short Fiction* 8 (1971): 411–22.

23. Van Wyck Brooks, *The Ordeal of Mark Twain* (New York: E. P. Dutton, 1920), p. 13.

24. Bernard De Voto, *Mark Twain's America* (Boston: Little, Brown, 1932).

25. Bernard De Voto, *Mark Twain at Work* (Cambridge, Mass.: Harvard University Press, 1942), pp. 105–30.

26. Kenneth S. Lynn, *Mark Twain and Southwestern Humor* (Boston: Little, Brown, 1959).

27. Tony Tanner, "The Lost America—The Despair of Henry Adams and Mark Twain," *Modern Age* 5 (Summer, 1961): 299–310.

28. John S. Tuckey, "Introduction," *Mark Twain's Which Was the Dream? and Other Symbolic Writings of the Later Years* (Berkeley and Los Angeles: University of California Press, 1967).

29. Henry Nash Smith, *Mark Twain: The Development of a Writer* (Cambridge, Mass.: Harvard University Press, Belknap Press, 1962), p. 186.

30. Lynn, p. 276.

31. Lynn, p. 278.

32. Albert E. Stone, Jr., *The Innocent Eye: Childhood in Mark Twain's Imagination* (New Haven, Conn.: Yale University Press, 1961), p. 260.

33. Roger B. Salomon, *Twain and the Image of History* (New Haven, Conn.: Yale University Press, 1961), p. 126.

34. Hamlin Hill, *Mark Twain: God's Fool* (New York: Harper & Row, 1973).

35. Ellwood Johnson, "Mark Twain's Dream Self in the Nightmare of History," *Mark Twain Journal* 15, no. 13 (1970): 7–9.

36. Stanley Brodwin, "Mark Twain's Masks of Satan: The Final Phase," *American Literature* 45 (1973): 206–24.

37. Paul Delaney, "The Dissolving Self: The Narrators of the Mysterious Stranger Fragments," *Journal of Narrative Technique* 6 (1976): 53–62.

38. Richard Tuerk, "Appearance and Reality in Mark Twain's 'Which Was the Dream,' 'The Great Dark' and 'Which Was It,' " *Illinois Quarterly* 40 (1978): 25–28.

39. See Gribben, Part 1, 107, and Part 2, 151.

40. For a definition of the concept of "implied reader," see Wolfgang Iser, *The Implied Reader: Patterns of Communication in Prose Fiction from Bunyan to Beckett* (Baltimore, Md.: The Johns Hopkins University Press, 1974); Susan Suleiman, ed., *The Reader in the Text* (Princeton, N.J.: Princeton University Press, 1980); and Umberto Eco, *The Role of the Reader* (Bloomington: Indiana University Press, 1979).

41. According to Ferdinand de Saussure's definition in *Course in General Linguistics,* trans. Wade Baskin (New York: McGraw-Hill, 1966), 'signified' means concept, while 'signifier' means the acoustic image that, matched to a 'signified', forms the sign.

42. See Roman Jakobson, *Essais de linguistique générale,* trans. and preface Nicolas Ruwet (Paris: Les Editions de Minuit, 1963), pp. 209–48.

43. Function is the relation of a part to the whole. More specifically, in Jakobson's linguistics, function is the specific use of language in relation to the various components of the process of communication.

44. Examples of works centered on the message are provided both by Kahn's study of the *Mysterious Stranger Manuscripts* and Susan K. Harris's *Mark Twain's Escape from Time: A Study of Patterns and Images.* Such biographies as Wagenknecht's, Kaplan's, Hill's, and Emerson's, as well as books probing the writer's intentions, such as Mcnaughton's *Mark Twain's Last Years as a Writer,* Tuckey's *Mark Twain and Little Satan,* and Gibson's *The Art of Mark Twain,* are studies of the addresser. One should also include in this group such psychologically oriented interpretations as Brooks's *The Ordeal of Mark Twain.* Because the publication of the Papers is quite recent, a study of the addressee can only be rather limited; however, many works of criticism centered upon Twain's major works contain information related to the history of their reception. A contextual method has been used, to greater or lesser extent, by a variety of critics of Twain, such as Gibson, Mcnaughton, and Tuckey. The only work on the Mark Twain Papers that bears directly on a generic discourse is Franklin Rogers's "Introduction" to *Satires and Burlesques.* However, some of the best critical works on Twain's major writings are focused at least partly on the code. Finally, the various scholars involved in the publication of the Papers by the University of California Press provide an example of philological work.

45. Henry Nash Smith, *Democracy and the Novel: Popular Resistance to Classic American Writers* (New York: Oxford University Press, 1978).

46. Smith, p. 107.

47. Cox, pp. 305–6, 309.

48. See Francesco Orlando, *Toward a Freudian Theory of Literature: With an Analysis of Racine's "Phèdre",* trans. Charmaine Lee (Baltimore, Md.: The Johns Hopkins University Press, 1978).

49. Cox, p. 304.

50. *Mark Twain–Howells Letters*, 2, 782.

51. See Jacques Lacan, *Ecrits* (Paris: Editions du Seuil, 1966).

52. See Jacques Derrida, *Writing and Difference*, trans. Alan Bass (Chicago: University of Chicago Press, 1978).

53. Gérard Genette, *Figures III* (Paris: Editions du Seuil, 1976); Genette, *Narrative Discourse: An Essay in Method*, trans. Jane E. Lewin (Ithaca, N.Y.: Cornell University Press, 1980). Based on three basic elements—the "fabula" (the narrative content), the narration (the story shaped by the narrator), and the discourse (the narrative act, the narrator's voice)—Genette's analysis deals also with three related aspects: the temporal relations between narration and story; the moods of narration; and the narrative voice and its relation to both story and narration. One should also note that Genette's concepts of story and narration are an elaboration of the Russian formalists' pioneer work. See especially the essays by Juri Tynianov and Boris Tomasevskij in *Théorie de la littérature: Textes des formalistes russes*, ed. and trans. T. Todorov (Paris: Editions du Seuil, 1965), pp. 114–19, 263–308.

54. See Tzvetan Todorov, *The Fantastic: A Structural Approach to a Literary Genre*, trans. Richard Howard (Cleveland, Ohio: Press of Case Western Reserve University, 1973).

55. Propp defines the function of a character as the action of a given character in relation to its meaning for the development of the narration. See Vladimir Propp, *Morphology of the Folktale*, trans. Laurence Scott (Austin: University of Texas Press, 1968).

56. Greimas's typology of actions derives from Propp's pioneer study of the structure of Russian fairy tales. In *Morphology of the Folktale*, Propp discovers thirty-two functions; Greimas simplifies that model by reducing it to six basic categories. See Greimas, *Sémantique Structurale* (Paris: Larousse, 1966).

57. See Juri Lotman, *Theses on the Semiotic Study of Culture (as Applied to Slavic Texts)* (Lisse, Netherlands: Peter de Ridder Press, 1975); and *Antropologia della Cultura* (Milano: Bompiani, 1974), not yet available in English translation.

58. Obviously the scheme can always be reversed because, to the cultures living outside, the internal cultures appear uncivilized.

59. See Mikhail Bakhtin, *The Dialogic Imagination: Four Essays*, trans. Caryl Emerson and Michael Holquist (Austin: University of Texas Press, 1981).

60. According to Ferdinand de Saussure, *langue* is the language of a given community, while *parole* is the individual expression. Often in the text, references will be made to the opposition to allude to the difference between the mainstream codes, languages, and conventions and Mark Twain's reinterpretation of them.

61. H. N. Smith, *Mark Twain: The Development of a Writer*, pp. 1–21.

62. Tuckey, p. xvii, and "Mark Twain's Later Dialogue: The 'Me' and the Machine," *American Literature* 41, no. 4 (1969), 532–42.

63. See Northrop Frye, *The Secular Scripture: A Study of the Structure of Romance* (Cambridge, Mass.: Harvard University Press, 1976).

64. See Carl Gustav Jung, *The Archetypes and the Collective Unconscious,* vol. 9, part 1, in *The Collected Works,* trans. R. F. C. Hull (London: Routledge and Kegan Paul, 1975), and *Essays on a Science of Mythology: The Myths of the Divine Child and the Mysteries of Eleusis* (with Karl Kerényi), trans. R. F. C. Hull (Princeton, N. J.: Princeton University Press, 1969).

Chapter 1

1. W. D. Howells writes: "In fact, the American who chooses to enjoy his birth right to the full, lives in a world wholly different from the Englishman's, and speaks (too often through his nose) another language: he breathes a rarefied and nimble air full of shining possibilities and radiant promises which the fog-and-soot-clogged lungs of those less favored islanders struggle in vain to fill themselves with." *Criticism and Fiction and Other Essays* (New York: New York University Press, 1959), p. 61. He continues: "Our novelists therefore concern themselves with the more smiling aspects of life, which are the more American, and seek the universal in the individual rather than the social interests. It is worthwhile, even at the risk of being called commonplace, to be true to our well-to-do actualities; the very passions themselves seem to be softened and modified by conditions which formerly at least could not be said to wrong any one, to cramp endeavor, or to cross lawful desire. . . . We have death in America . . . but this is tragedy that comes in the very nature of things, and is not peculiarly American, as the large, cheerful average of health and success and happy life is" (p. 62).

2. It is necessary here to stress again that, despite contradictions and ambivalent feelings about the publication of his later works, Twain expressed quite eloquently his perception of a close link between experimentation and private writing. See, in particular, a letter to Howells dated 12 May 1899, already quoted in the introduction (p. 4), as well as other letters referred to in note 4 to the introduction. *Mark Twain–Howells Letters,* ed. Henry Nash Smith and William M. Gibson (Cambridge, Mass.: Harvard University Press, Belknap Press, 1960), p. 698.

3. Mikhail Bakhtin, *The Dialogic Imagination: Four Essays,* trans. Caryl Emerson and Michael Holquist (Austin: University of Texas Press, 1981), p. 67.

4. Franklin R. Rogers, *Mark Twain's Burlesque Patterns* (Dallas, Tex.: Southern Methodist University Press, 1960), pp. 3–13. As Rogers points out, Paine called Twain's burlesque tendency an imp. Brooks alters the meaning of this appellation and declares that the imp of the burlesque is Twain's repressed artistic spirit. However, elsewhere Brooks sees Twain's burlesque as both a compromise with the western environment and a compromise between rebellion and conformity. Gladys Bellamy considers it a form of social reform. De

Voto and Parrington, on the other hand, relate burlesque and realism. They approach burlesque merely as a way of ridiculing people and situations, rather than as a literary genre. Branch views it as a corrective of insincerity in art, a criticism and a refutation of the work or genre burlesqued.

5. Rogers, p. 10. Burlesque, thus defined, played an important role in the apprenticeship of many British writers, such as Fielding, Austen, and Thackeray. Rogers points out that these writers learned literary devices used in their later works from the early practice of burlesque.

6. See Shelley Fisher Fishkin, *From Fact to Fiction: Journalism and Imaginative Writing in America* (Baltimore, Md.: The Johns Hopkins University Press, 1985), pp. 55–84.

7. F. R. Rogers, ed. and introd., *Mark Twain's Satires and Burlesques* (Berkeley and Los Angeles: University of California Press, 1967). Hereafter, page numbers referring to this book will be cited parenthetically in the text of the chapter. In the editorial introduction Rogers traces the formal evolution of Twain's burlesque patterns from earlier to later narrative, showing their persistence throughout his career. The importance of this volume lies mainly in the opportunity it creates to explore Twain's experimentalism and to study and understand the creative process.

8. Among the Russian formalists, Viktor Sklovskij dealt in particular with the estrangement procedure. See *O teorii prozy*, "Iskusstvo kak priem" and "Stroenie rasskaza i romana" (Moscow, 1929), pp. 7–23, 68–86.

9. It is certainly a pure coincidence; yet this burlesque does resemble the Russian bumpkin's description of Wagner in Tolstoy's *What Is Art?*

10. In fact, the similarity with Brecht's concept of alienation is suggested by the peculiarly theatrical form of this burlesque. The characters' stepping out of the fiction, as the actors would in a Brechtian play, prevents empathy. On this subject Brecht wrote: "A representation that alienates is one which allows us to recognize its subject, but at the same time makes it seem unfamiliar." Bertolt Brecht, *Brecht on Theatre: The Development of an Aesthetic,* ed. and trans. John Willett (London: Methuen, 1964), p. 191.

11. *Mark Twain's Fables of Man,* ed. and introd. John S. Tuckey (Berkeley, Los Angeles, and London: University of California Press, 1972), p. 107.

12. See Sigmund Freud, *Das Unheimliche: Aufsatze zur literatur* (Frankfurt am Main: S. Fischer, 1963).

13. *Mark Twain–Howells Letters,* 1:369. This passage is quoted also by Rogers, introd., *Satires and Burlesques,* p. 49.

14. Most of the narratological jargon used in this and subsequent chapters derives from Gérard Genette's theoretical work *Figures III.* Genette's study of the relation between story and narration is particularly helpful here. For the sake of clarity, narratological terms will be indicated in parentheses throughout the chapter. By 'diegesis' or 'intradiegesis' Genette means the main or introductory story in a narration, whereas 'metadiegesis' is the story in the story; 'metalanguage' is the discourse about language, the critical activity. Genette's use of the term 'diegesis' is also roughly equivalent to 'telling,' a more common term in Anglo-Saxon criticism.

15. See Roland Barthes, *Writing Degree Zero*, trans. Annette Lavers (Boston: Beacon Press, 1967).

16. For a codification of the autobiographical genre, see Philippe Lejeune, *Le pacte autobiographique* (Paris: Editions du Seuil, 1975).

17. Mark Twain, *Burlesque Autobiography and First Romance* (New York: Haskell House, 1970), p. 18.

18. "The Secret History of Eddypus, the World Empire," *Fables of Man*, 315–82.

19. Among utopian novels written during the last decades of the nineteenth century, worth remembering are Edward Bellamy's *Looking Backward, 2000–1887* (1888) and William Morris's *News from Nowhere* (1890).

20. Although "The Secret History of Eddypus, the World Empire" can easily be recognized as a dystopia, I refer to it as a burlesque utopia because I want to emphasize, in this chapter, its parodic quality. David Ketterer also includes the tale in his collection *The Science Fiction of Mark Twain* (Hamden, Conn.: Archon Books, 1984); the futuristic theme in the tale allies it to science fiction as well.

21. In *The Education of Henry Adams*, Adams creates a similarly prismatic figure of himself; from his personal experience he deducts general rules and ways of interpreting the larger experience of history.

22. *Fables of Man*, pp. 33–44.

23. Biographers often relate Twain's friendships with young girls during the last years of his life. Joyce W. Warren, *The American Narcissus: Individualism and Women in Nineteenth-Century American Fiction* (New Brunswick, N.J.: Rutgers University Press, 1984), deals with this aspect of the writer's life: "With his wife and daughters no longer around him, he sought friendship (apparently platonic) with very young girls, whom he called his 'Angel Fish. . . .' They represented no threat to the self. He insisted that they must remain young and unspoiled—the symbol of pretty innocence and girlish selflessness that had always characterized his view of women" (p. 185). Such a view contrasts, however, with that expressed by the story "Little Bessie."

24. *Fables of Man*, pp. 133–40.

25. *Fables of Man*, pp. 149–51.

26. *Fables of Man*, pp. 425–29.

27. See Vladimir Propp, *Morphology of the Folktale*, trans. Laurence Scott, introd. Svatava Pirkova-Jakobson, pref. Louis A. Wagner, new introd. Alan Dundes (Austin: University of Texas Press, 1968).

28. See David E. Sloane, *Mark Twain as a Literary Comedian* (Baton Rouge and London: Louisiana State University Press, 1979).

29. Pascal Covici, Jr., *Mark Twain's Humor: The Image of a World* (Dallas, Tex.: Southern Methodist University Press, 1962).

30. Kenneth S. Lynn, *Mark Twain and Southwestern Humor* (Boston: Little, Brown, 1959), p. 17.

31. Lynn calls the frame a *cordon sanitaire*.

32. However, in such early works as Augustus Baldwin Longstreet's *Georgia Scenes* the backwoodsman is mostly described and quite rarely allowed to

speak. Later on, both Johnson J. Hooper's *Some Adventures of Captain Simon Suggs* and Thomas Bangs Thorpe's "The Big Bear of Arkansas" show a predominance of vernacular speech that undermines considerably the utterance of the genteel narrator. *Sut Lovingood's Yarns* marks a further step in the same direction, while the gentleman's role is repressed in *Georgia Sketches* by Richard Malcolm Johnston. Yet Joseph G. Baldwin's *Flush Times in Alabama* carries out another reversal of tendency: The vernacular is kept under restraint by the narrator's overliterary utterance. Lynn, pp. 132–39.

33. On this subject, Bakhtin writes: "One of the most ancient and widespread forms for representing the direct word of another is parody" (p. 51). He adds: "Thus it is that in parody two languages are crossed with each other, as well as two styles, two linguistic points of view, and in the final analysis two speaking subjects. It is true that only one of these languages (the one that is parodied) is present in its own right; the other is present invisibly, as an actualizing background for creating and perceiving" (p. 76).

34. See Henry Nash Smith, *Democracy and the Novel: Popular Resistance to Classic American Writers* (New York: Oxford University Press, 1978), pp. 110–11.

35. "3000 Years Among the Microbes," *Mark Twain's Which Was the Dream? and Other Symbolic Writings of the Later Years*, p. 434.

36. "The Enchanted Sea-Wilderness," *Which Was the Dream?*, p. 77.

37. *Fables of Man*, p. 345.

38. *Mark Twain's Hannibal, Huck and Tom*, ed. and introd. Walter Blair (Berkeley and Los Angeles: University of California Press, 1969), pp. 23–66. In his introduction Blair points out that the pieces composed during the earlier period (1876–84) were prompted by both financial needs and the desire to escape into a world of boyhood, while the later pieces of the collection (1897–99) provided Twain with some sort of therapy in the face of financial and personal disasters.

39. In this respect, one should also consider that Twain's idea of the small community is not always idyllic. For example, Hadleyburg in "The Man That Corrupted Hadleyburg" and Dawson Landing in *Pudd'nhead Wilson* display gloomy features.

40. Henry Nash Smith deals with this topic in *Mark Twain: The Development of a Writer* (Cambridge, Mass.: Harvard University Press, Belknap Press, 1962). Tony Tanner, in *The Reign of Wonder* (Cambridge: Cambridge University Press, 1965), also discusses Twain's linguistic duality. Tanner traces Twain's oscillation between the language of the official culture and the vernacular of the lower strata of society. A very extensive and thorough study of Twain's languages and linguistic theory is Robert Sewell's *Mark Twain's Languages* (Berkeley: University of California Press, 1987). As I do in the present study, Sewell relies on the Bakhtinian concept of heteroglossia.

41. See Bakhtin, pp. 60–61.

42. Bakhtin writes: "Closely connected with the problem of polyglossia and inseparable from it is the problem of heteroglossia *within* a language, that is,

the problem of internal differentiation, the stratification characteristic of any national language" (p. 67).

43. David Carkeets's novel *I Been There Before* (New York: Harper & Row, 1985) could be regarded as a reinterpretation of this aspect of the Papers. Carkeets creates a metafictional fantasy featuring Twain's return from the grave and subsequent visit to the various shrines of his own myth, including the Mark Twain Project at Berkeley. In this postmodern novel Carkeets uses many of the literary devices that we observe in the fictional pieces of the Papers.

Chapter 2

1. David Ketterer, "Power Fantasy in the 'Science Fiction' of Mark Twain," *Bridges to Fantasy*, ed. G. Slusser, E. Rabkin, and R. Scholes (Carbondale and Edwardsville: Southern Illinois University Press, 1982), pp. 130–41. Ketterer expands on this concept also in the introduction to *The Science Fiction of Mark Twain*, D. Ketterer ed. and introd. (Hamden, Conn.: Archon Books, 1984), p. xiv. In that volume he has included pieces that bear some science-fictional traits even though they are not strictly science fiction. Ketterer also points out that "Mark Twain's importance in the history of science fiction rests partly on the fact that he was the first American writer to exploit fully the possibilities for humor in science fiction" (p. xiv).

2. Eric Rabkin, *The Fantastic in Literature* (Princeton, N.J.: Princeton University Press, 1976), pp. 3–41. Rabkin writes: "One of the key distinguishing marks of the fantastic is that the perspectives enforced by the ground rules of the narrative world must be diametrically contradicted" (p. 8); and also: "many works which we would not call Fantasies (satires, for example) make important use of the fantastic; however, the fantastic is clearly the central quality in works we would unequivocally call Fantasies" (p. 28).

3. Tzvetan Todorov, *The Fantastic: A Structural Approach to a Literary Genre*, trans. Richard Howard (Cleveland, Ohio: Press of Case Western Reserve University, 1973). Todorov delimits the genre of the fantastic as based upon a moment of hesitation on the reader's part when facing events that he or she cannot decide whether to interpret as supernatural or actual. When this hesitation is not possible (because already at the beginning of the narration all the rules of reality are clearly subverted) we are in the presence of the marvelous. A lack of hesitation between reality and unreality also characterizes the uncanny, where it is clear that the reader is facing some unusual event—such as a dream—which, however, will not subvert the rules of reality.

4. Adverse criticism of both Rabkin's and Todorov's approach to the fantastic has been made by David Clayton, "On Realistic and Fantastic Discourse," *Bridges to Fantasy*, ed. G. Slusser, E. Rabkin, and R. Scholes (Carbondale and

Edwardsville: Southern Illinois University Press, 1982), pp. 59–77. Clayton finds Todorov's view too narrow and Rabkin's theory of fantasy too general. In particular he opposes Rabkin's concept that the fantastic implies the reversal of ground rules. In Clayton's opinion "the most compelling examples of fantastic literature . . . are all works which build up a convincing realistic facade in contrast with which the unforeseen intrusion of the fantastic seems far more disturbing than it would in a world governed entirely by fantasy" (p. 66). Harold Bloom, on the other hand, dismisses Todorov in "Clinamen: Towards a Theory of Fantasy," *Bridges to Fantasy*, p. 5: "and I pause here to cast off, with amiable simplicity, the theory of fantasy set forth by Todorov. We do *not* hesitate between trope and the uncanny in reading Hoffmann . . . the reader who hesitates *is* lost and *has* lost that moment which is the agonistic encounter of deep, strong reading. Where literary fantasy is strong, the trope itself introjects the uncanny."

5. I am referring here in particular to the research developed by Laing, Lacan, and Cooper.

6. John S. Tuckey, introd., *Mark Twain's Which Was the Dream? and Other Symbolic Writings of the Later Years* (Berkeley and Los Angeles: University of California Press, 1967), pp. 1–32.

7. Ketterer, pp. 139–40.

8. John S. Tuckey, "Mark Twain's Later Dialogue: The 'Me' and the Machine," *American Literature* 41, no. 4 (1969): 532–42.

9. Maria Ornella Marotti, "Mark Twain alle soglie della fantascienza," *Studi Americani* 23–25 (1979): 177–212.

10. According to Gérard Genette, *Figures III* (Paris: Editions du Seuil, 1976), intradiegesis or diegesis is the first tale, or the frame, whereas metadiegesis is the second tale, or enframed narration.

11. Max Milner, *La Fantasmagorie* (Paris: Presses Universitaires de France, 1982), stresses the role of the optical metaphor in fantastic literature.

12. As indicated in the introduction, I am indebted to Francesco Orlando's neo-Freudian theory of literature. See Francesco Orlando, *Toward a Freudian Theory of Literature: With an Analysis of Racine's "Phèdre,"* trans. Charmaine Lee (Baltimore, Md.: The Johns Hopkins University Press, 1978). According to Orlando's theory, the literary text plays a role in social life comparable to that of the joke: It allows the resurfacing of drives whose expression has been censored by society and/or by the superego in a form acceptable to the suppressing agents. In the light of this interpretation, the symbolic relations in the literary text, as well as any rhetorical figure, display the signs of both the suppression and the resurfacing of the suppressed drive.

13. See Louis Vax, *Les Chefs-d'oeuvre de la littérature fantastique* (Paris: Presses Universitaires de France, 1979).

14. Twain's earliest successful experiment with a framed narration in the mode of the western tall tale is "The Celebrated Jumping Frog of Calaveras County" (1865). Another interesting framed narration is "A True Story Repeated Word for Word as I Heard It," which he published in 1874 in the

Atlantic. After a short introduction by an educated narrator, a former slave recounts her life story in her own words. Twain reproduces powerfully the woman's original speech. It must be noted, however, that in "A True Story" there is no juxtaposition between vernacular and genteel worldviews.

15. This is partly inspired by Jacques Lacan's concept of the "mirror stage" in the development of the individual. See Jacques Lacan, "Le stade du miroir comme formateur de la fonction du Je," *Ecrits* (Paris: Editions du Seuil, 1966), pp. 93–100.

16. To be found in the still unpublished Mark Twain's Notebooks and Journals 37, the typescript of which is part of the Mark Twain Papers. All previously unpublished words by Mark Twain quoted in this book are © 1982 by Edward J. Willi and Manufacturers Hanover Trust company as Trustees of the Mark Twain Foundation, which reserves all reproduction or dramatization rights in every medium. They are published here with the permission of the University of California Press and Robert H. Hirst, General Editor of the Mark Twain Project at Berkeley. All citations of such material are identified by the symbol †. Hereafter, when referring to this unpublished material I will use the abbreviation N & J, TS MTP; page numbers and other references will be cited parenthetically in the text. The same quotation is contained in *Mark Twain's Notebooks*, ed. A. B. Paine (New York: Harper and Brothers, 1935), p. 266. Paine edited the passage, putting a period after "away."

17. Paine edited this passage as follows: "I was actually there in person—in my spiritualized condition. My, how vivid it all was! Even to the texture of her shirt, its dull white color, and the pale brown tint of a stain on the shoulder of it. I had never seen that girl; I was not acquainted with her—but dead or alive she is a reality; she exists and she was there. Her pie was a spiritualized pie, no doubt, and also her shirt and the bench and the shed—but their actualities were at that moment in existence somewhere in the world." Joyce W. Warren, *The American Narcissus* (New Brunswick, N.J.: Rutgers University Press, 1984), uses this dream as an example of Twain's prudery and double standards concerning women's sexual behavior. The "Negro wench" is the prototype of "the lower-class or impure 'gal,'" whom Twain does not regard as a marriage partner," and who "is associated with sex and other ungenteel aspects of femaleness" (p. 171).

18. *Lichtenberg: A Doctrine of Scattered Occasions: Reconstructed from His Aphorisms and Reflections,* ed. Joseph Peter Stern (Bloomington: Indiana University Press, 1959), p. 232.

19. On this subject James writes: "The world of dreams is our real world whilst we are sleeping, because our attention then lapses from the sensible world. Conversely, when we wake the attention usually lapses from the dream-world and that becomes unreal. But if a dream haunts us and compels our attention during the day it is very apt to remain figuring in our consciousness as a sort of sub-universe alongside of the waking world. Most people have probably had dreams which it is hard to imagine not to have been glimpses into an actually existing region of being, perhaps a corner of the 'spiritual

world' " (*Principles of Psychology,* 2, 294). There is some evidence, as Alan Gribben suggests, that Twain was aware of William James's research; he mentioned some of James's theories in a letter to Livy in 1894, and entered James's book in a list of books that he intended to read. See Alan Gribben, *Mark Twain's Library: A Reconstruction* (Boston: G.K. Hall, 1980), p. 351. Gribben deals also with Twain's interest in phrenology in "Mark Twain, Phrenology and the 'Temperaments': A Study in Pseudoscientific Influence," *American Quarterly* 24 (March 1972): 45–68. Howard Kerr, *Mediums, and Spirit-Rappers, and Roaring Radicals: Spiritualism in American Literature, 1850–1900* (Urbana: University of Illinois Press, 1972) traces Twain's interest in spiritualism, while Martin Ebon, *They Knew the Unknown* (New York: World, 1971) deals with his belief in mental telepathy.

20. Mark Twain, "My Platonic Sweetheart," holograph, TS MTP, Box 16, No. 3a.

21. I am using here a term suggested by the Russian formalist Boris Tomasevskij in "Thèmatique," *Théorie de la littérature,* Tzvetan Todorov ed. and trans., Roman Jakobson Introd. (Paris: Editions du Seuil, 1965), pp. 263–308. Fable is the nucleus of a literary fictional work that is a set of events mutually relating to each other. Fable is a basic situation devoid of the organization and development of characters' relations given by the literary construction.

22. "The Enchanted Sea-Wilderness," *Mark Twain's Which Was the Dream? and Other Symbolic Writings,* p. 77. Hereafter, page numbers referring to this book will be cited parenthetically in the text of the chapter.

23. The textual strategies applied to the texts in this chapter are inspired by Gérard Genette's study of narratology in *Figures III.* As indicated in the introduction to this book, Genette's analysis of the text is centered around three elements: the "fabula," or story (the narrative content); the narration (the story shaped by the narrator); and the discourse (the narrative act, the narrator's voice). Based on these elements, the analysis deals with three related aspects: the temporal relations between narration and story; the moods of narration; and the narrative voice and its relation to both story and narration. The text is thus defined and explored through its narrative structures. This approach is helpful for a study of Twain's literary devices in the fantastic tales in which the mixed status of the narrators/characters increases the uncertainty that is part of the conventions of the fantastic genre. Genette uses some technical jargon in his analysis that, for the sake of clarity, is indicated parenthetically throughout the chapter.

24. See Carl Gustav Jung, "Concerning Mandala Symbolism," *The Archetypes and the Collective Unconscious,* vol. 9, part 1, in *The Collected Works,* trans. R. F. C. Hull (London: Routledge and Kegan Paul, 1975), pp. 355–86.

25. *Mark Twain–Howells Letters,* ed. H. N. Smith and W. Gibson (Cambridge, Mass.: Harvard University Press, Belknap Press, 1960), pp. 675–76. Twain's intention to write a comic story is proven also by the parody of navy language, a burlesque of W. Clark Russel's works, and the episode in which

the Superintendent of Dreams plays a trick on a sailor by taking away his cup of coffee while remaining invisible to him.

26. Daryl E. Jones, "The *Hornet* Disaster: Twain's Adaptation in 'The Great Dark,' " *American Literary Realism* 9 (Summer 1976), 243–48, maintains that the episode of the *Hornet* disaster is the source for "The Great Dark." This episode was the subject of another article by Twain, "My Debut as a Literary Person," published by *Century* in November 1899.

27. N & J 40, TS MTP, p. 46.† However, De Voto published the following holograph note: "It is midnight. Alice and the children come to say goodnight. I think them dreams. Think I am back home in a dream." *Letters from the Earth,* ed. Bernard De Voto (Greenwich, Conn.: Fawcett, 1963), p. 277. A later notebook entry suggests a slightly different ending: "I sat for 3 hours where I could see him writing. Then the nurse brought the children to say good night—we entered & he said 'O my God, who are you?' " N & J 41, TS MTP, p. 26.†

28. Tuckey, Introduction, *Which Was the Dream?*, p. 18.

29. "The Great Dark," in *Which Was the Dream?*, p. 102. Hereafter, page numbers referring to this book will be cited parenthetically in the text of the chapter.

30. John H. Davis maintains that Twain creates a series of dissolving frameworks in this story that heightens the uncertainty of the reader deciding between dream and reality. "The Dream as Reality: Structure and Meaning in Mark Twain's 'The Great Dark,' " *Mississippi Quarterly* 35, no. 4 (Fall 1982), 407–26.

31. Some of these considerations are inspired by a study by Gerhard Hoffman, "The Fantastic in Fiction: Its 'Reality' Status, Its Historical Development and Its Transformation in Postmodern Narration," *REAL;* 1982, pp. 267–365.

32. For an extensive analysis of Twain's female characters, see Joyce W. Warren.

33. See Carl Gustav Jung, "The Phenomenology of the Spirit in Fairytales," in *The Archetypes and the Collective Unconscious,* pp. 207–55.

34. Samuel Clemens, *The Autobiography of Mark Twain,* ed. and introd. Charles Neider (New York: Harper, 1959), p. xi.

35. Max Milner argues that optical perception has affected the imagination by providing writers with material and procedures. It is also a metaphor for literature as a machine to show things, a machine of perception and exploration. Milner, p. 7.

36. These tales have been defined by Tanner as signs of Twain's alienation from his epoch, of his fear of emerging technology and mass immigration. See Tony Tanner, "The Lost America—The Despair of Henry Adams and Mark Twain," *Modern Age* 5 (Summer 1961): 299–310. I do not agree completely with Tanner's interpretation. Although Twain went from enthusiastic acceptance of technology to a more cautious attitude with responsible awareness of dangers implied in its use, he always gave technology an important symbolic role in his fiction. An example of Twain's fascination with technology is his

use of fingerprints in *Pudd'nhead Wilson;* he conceived their use in criminal justice, whereas, at the time, they were only a parlor game. Moreover, the writer's political interests did not fade away. Especially from 1898 on, he was very involved with the events of his time.

Chapter 3

1. *The Mysterious Stranger Manuscripts* collect the three versions of Twain's original texts. As already indicated in the introduction (see note 19), they provide evidence of what John S. Tuckey had found out and denounced in his book *Mark Twain and Little Satan:* The Paine-Duneka edition was a fraud. In the introduction to *The Mysterious Stranger Manuscripts*, Gibson shows that Paine had perpetrated his fraud willingly, changing the names of characters (Gibson, x). In *Mark Twain's Mysterious Stranger*, Sholom Kahn reveals the thematic inconsistencies that resulted from the matching of "Chronicle of Young Satan" to the ending of "No. 44." For example, the choice by Paine and Duneka of 1590 as the date for the setting of the *Stranger* is an anachronism. The Turks brought coffee to Vienna during the 1683 siege; yet in chapter 2 a castle servant offers coffee to the boys. Kahn, p. 20.

2. John S. Tuckey, *Mark Twain and Little Satan* (Westport, Conn.: Greenwood Press, 1963), argues that Twain worked on "Chronicle of Young Satan" from October 1897 to January 1898, from May to October 1899, and from June to August 1900. Meanwhile, he had worked at "Schoolhouse Hill" from November to December 1898. He was occupied with "No. 44, the Mysterious Stranger" from November 1902 to October 1903 and from January to June 1904. From February to June 1904 he worked at the conclusion and, from June to July 1905, at a different part of the work; he added another chapter in 1908.

3. Mark Twain, *Adventures of Huckleberry Finn* (New York: Harper & Row, 1987), p. 17.

4. In this respect, Shelley Fisher Fishkin remarks: "By making his book a chaotic melange of fictive forms, Twain prevents any one form from exercising authority or manifesting autonomy and makes his reader conscious of the ultimately fictive and arbitrary nature of all texts, including the one at hand." *From Fact to Fiction: Journalism and Imaginative Writing in America* (Baltimore, Md.: The Johns Hopkins University Press, 1985), p. 81.

5. Throughout her study of "No. 44" Susan K. Harris points out Twain's quest for freedom from the human condition. *Mark Twain's Escape from Time* (Columbia and London: University of Missouri Press, 1982); see especially p. 36.

6. *Mark Twain's Mysterious Stranger Manuscripts*, ed. and introd. William M. Gibson (Berkeley and Los Angeles: University of California Press, 1969),

pp. 35, 221. All page numbers referring to this book will be cited parenthetically in the text of the chapter.

7. See Wayne C. Booth, *The Rhetoric of Fiction* (Chicago and London: The University of Chicago Press, 1961) pp. 71–76, 211–21, 395–99.

8. Susan K. Harris argues: "Through 44, August achieves what the alienated writer, in his role as creator of fictional worlds, would like to achieve: he has destroyed human history and the created universe, and put the teller of the story in God's place." Harris, p. 156.

9. See Robert Scholes, "The Roots of Science Fiction," in *Science Fiction,* ed. Mark Rose (Englewood Cliffs, N.J.: Prentice-Hall, 1976), pp. 46–56, and also *Structural Fabulations* (Notre Dame and London: University of Notre Dame Press, 1975), pp. 27–44. Moreover, in the introduction to *The Science Fiction of Mark Twain* David Ketterer remarks: "The label 'fantasy' tells the reader that the universe of the novel is self-contained, realistic on its own terms but discontinuous . . . with the known world." He also adds: "The intrusion of the fantastic into what appears to be a science-fiction or a naturalistic text often simply alters the function of the fantasy material. Instead of being encouraged to think about psychology and morality, the reader must consider matters of epistemology." Ketterer ed. (Hamden, Conn.: Archon Books, 1984), p. xiv. Even though he does not classify *The Mysterious Stranger Manuscripts* as science fiction and does not include them in the collection, Ketterer points out their science-fictional aspects.

10. See note 3 to chapter 2 of this study on Todorov's "marvelous."

11. Kahn, p. 185.

12. See Northrop Frye, *The Secular Scripture: A Study of the Structure of Romance* (Cambridge, Mass.: Harvard University Press, 1976).

13. Frye calls this kind of episodic structure in romance the "and then" narration. Erich Auerbach, *Mimesis,* trans. Willard Trask (Garden City, N.Y.: Doubleday, 1957), p. 5, points out the use of similarly digressive syntactical strategies in Homer's *Odyssey.* Susan K. Harris, on the other hand, interprets the discontinuity in the narration as a "reflection of Twain's concern with the abolition of time." Harris, p. 37.

14. The lack of causality is, in Frye's opinion, the difference between realism and romance: While the former follows a horizontal sequence of events connected by a causal factor, the latter unfolds on two vertical levels.

15. Kahn explores the sources for the cheating of the devil and finds them in both folklore and history. Kahn, pp. 200–201.

16. See Carl Gustav Jung, "The Psychology of the Child Archetype," *The Archetypes and the Collective Unconscious,* vol. 9, part 1, in *The Collected Works,* trans. R. F. C. Hull (London: Routledge and Kegan Paul, 1975), pp. 151–82.

17. See "The Holy Children" and "The Second Advent," *Mark Twain's Fables of Man,* ed. and introd. John S. Tuckey (Berkeley, Los Angeles, London: University of California Press, 1972) pp. 69–77, 50–68.

18. Both Kahn and Tuckey stress that the three versions "are not so much different drafts of one story as three different stories," while Gibson stresses

the continuities among the versions. Tuckey, *Mark Twain's The Mysterious Stranger and the Critics* (Belmont, Calif.: Wadsworth, 1968), p. 86, and William M. Gibson, *The Art of Mark Twain* (New York: Oxford University Press, 1976).

19. The characters of *The Mysterious Stranger Manuscripts* can be described better by their functions than by their psychological connotations, because these characters tend to respond more and more to mythical models than to conform to the conventions of fictional realism. Vladimir Propp, *Morphology of the Folktale*, trans. Laurence Scott (Austin: University of Texas Press, 1968), defines the function of a character as the action of a given character in relation to its meaning for the development of the narration. Propp discovers thirty-two functions in Russian fairy tales; in *Sémantique Structurale* (Paris: Larousse, 1966), J. G. Greimas simplifies that model and reduces it to six basic categories. The analysis of the functions of characters in the present chapter is inspired by the typology traced by both Greimas and Propp.

20. This is a point on which my interpretation and Kahn's diverge significantly. Although I too find "No. 44" more interesting than the three previous versions, I notice a similarity in the roles and functions of characters. Our difference derives from different theoretical perspectives and textual strategies.

21. There have been various suggestions about the origin of the name "44." See Kahn, pp. 205–6.

22. In my view of the role of space in the text I am particularly indebted to Juri Lotman's anthropological study of culture, in which the Russian semiotician deals with the cultural concept of space. See Juri Lotman, *Antropologia della Cultura* (Milano: Bompiani, 1974). This text has not been translated into English; for my study I have used the Italian translation from the Russian. Some of Lotman's essays on culture are included, however, in *Soviet Semiotics*, ed., trans., and introd. by Daniel P. Lucid (Baltimore, Md.: The Johns Hopkins University Press, 1977). Of particular interest for the purpose of this study are the following essays by Lotman in *Soviet Semiotics*: "Primary and Secondary Communication-Modeling Systems," pp. 95–98; "Two Models of Communication," pp. 99–102; "Problems in the Typology of Texts," pp. 119–24; "Problems in the Typology of Culture," pp. 213–22; "Numerical Semantics and Cultural Types," pp. 227–32; and "Myth-Name-Culture" (written in collaboration with B. A. Uspenskij), pp. 233–52.

23. Lotman describes this particular type of doubling in "Numerical Semantics and Cultural Types": "The general structure of the system of levels is based on the principle of the 'Matreieska' [a wooden doll in peasant dress with successively smaller dolls fitted into it—trans.]: each level has an external layer, for which it functions as the content, and an internal layer, in relation to which it acquires the features of expression." Lotman, pp. 227–8. Gilbert Durand, *Les structures anthropologiques de l'imaginaire* (Paris: Bordas, 1969), pp. 233–47, deals in great detail with this kind of doubling and its recurrence in the collective imagination. Taking a rather different approach, Susan K. Harris argues that Twain thought of his writing as a mediation between his dream self, or dream artist, and his waking self, as well as between his inner

self and the outer world of history. Harris, p. 146. Sholom Kahn, on the other hand, interprets the relationship between August and his Duplicate as the theme of the brotherhood of humankind. Kahn, p. 164.

24. Durand deals with different interpretations of the circular image of centrality. While Jung insists on interpreting the mandala as the symbol of totality, Rank sees the image of the center as the maternal womb, and both Bachelard and Durand emphasize the quality of a mysterious center of intimacy connected with the central and circular image. Durand also connects the image of the center to the idea of repetition and doubling. Durand, pp. 280–93. Georges Poulet, *Les métamorphoses du cercle* (Paris: Plon, 1961) deals with the transformations of the meaning of the circular image throughout the development of literary history.

25. Kahn emphasizes the role of the microcosmos that the castle plays. Kahn, pp. 103–6.

26. Paul Delaney, "The Dissolving Self: The Narrator of Mark Twain's *Mysterious Stranger* Fragments," *Journal of Narrative Technique* 6 (1976): 53–62, suggests that the expression "mental and spiritual clock," referring to the Austrian setting, reveals "ways—other than chronological—to measure time, ways which become in the context of all three manuscripts the only meaningful measure of time's passage" (p. 59). Delaney relates this time perspective to the development of the point of view of the protagonist, which seems to be, at the same time, both rooted in time and atemporal. Susan K. Harris argues, instead, that 44's overcoming of chronological time allows the breaking up of automatic natural laws that make the consequence of acts inevitable. This causes a breakthrough in Twain's deterministic vision. Harris, p. 146.

27. Kahn, p. 159.

28. Kahn also points out the consistency of these final chapters, which "pay careful attention to the overall scheme and purposes that had governed the earlier writing." Kahn, p. 161. Gibson, on the other hand, gives a negative evaluation of chapter 33: "He wrote the pageant chapter as part of an effort—never fulfilled—to link the body of his story to the 'Conclusion of the book.' " Gibson, *The Art of Mark Twain,* p. 11.

29. Frye indicates how the vision of freedom expressed by some characters, as well as the structural freedom of romance, reflect the need for freedom that "romancer" and character experience. Susan K. Harris argues, instead, that the liberation from the flesh is another aspect of Twain's escape from time; the decay of the flesh represents the passing of chronological time. Harris, p. 37. Kahn also points out that "Twain associated the body with limitation, necessity, mechanistic laws, and even 'slavery.' " Kahn, p. 155.

30. See "The Stupendous Procession," *Mark Twain's Fables of Man,* John S. Tuckey ed. and introd. (Berkeley, Los Angeles, London: University of California Press, 1972), pp. 403–19.

31. Harris argues that the ending of "No. 44" is a philosophical dead end. Harris, p. 39. Kahn instead sees "Nothing exists but You" as "a remote American echo of the Cartesian cogito." Kahn, p. 197.

32. Jacques Lacan, *Ecrits* (Paris: Editions du Seuil, 1966).

Chapter 4

1. As Mircea Eliade indicates, myth up to the 1900s meant a "fable"—a corpus of legends—which was considered the opposite of reality. This attitude toward myth was prompted by rationalist thought, deriving from the Enlightenment and positivism, and by Christianity. Ethnological studies during this century have gradually modified the attitude: We have come to understand the value of myth in archaic societies as the foundation of all social and cultural life. Moreover, under the impact of anthropology and psychoanalysis, we have come to regard myth as a way of thinking different from ours and, more recently, as a component of the history of thought. We view myth as "collective thought," while we notice also a continuity between archaic and modern worlds. Mircea Eliade, *Myths, Dreams and Mysteries: The Encounter Between Contemporary Faith and Archaic Realities,* trans. Philip Mairet (London: Harvill Press, 1960), pp. 23–37.

2. See Joseph Campbell, *The Mythic Image* (Princeton, N.J.: Princeton University Press, 1974).

3. In his interpretation of myth Lévi-Strauss separates myths into various segments and examines their mutual relation. See Claude Lévi-Strauss, *Structural Anthropology,* trans. Claire Jacobson and Brooke Grundfest Schoepf (New York: Basic Books, 1963), pp. 206–32.

4. Roland Barthes, *Mythologies,* trans. Annette Lavers (New York: Hill & Wang, 1957), p. 109.

5. Barthes argues that the producer of myths focuses on the "empty signifier, and let[s] the concept fill the form of the myth without ambiguity, and . . . find[s] . . . himself before a simple system, where the signification becomes literal again"; the mythologist, on the other hand, "focus[es] on a full signifier [which] clearly distinguish[es] the meaning and form, and consequently the distortion which the one imposes on the other, . . . he undo[es] the signification of the myth, and . . . receive[s] the latter as an imposture"; finally, the reader of myths "focus[es] on the mythical signifier as on an inextricable whole made of meaning and form, . . . [and] receive[s] an ambiguous signification: [he] respond[s] to the constituting mechanism of myth, to its own dynamics" (p. 320).

6. "The Refuge of the Derelicts," *Mark Twain's Fables of Man,* John S. Tuckey, ed. and introd. (Berkeley, Los Angeles, London: University of California Press, 1972), pp. 157–248. Hereafter, page numbers referring to this book will be cited parenthetically in the text of the chapter.

7. Jay Martin, "Twain and the Image of the Child," *Harvests of Change: American Literature, 1865–1914* (Englewood Cliffs, N.J.: Prentice-Hall, 1967), pp. 184–93.

8. Leslie Fiedler, *No! in Thunder: Essays on Myth and Literature* (London: Eyre and Spottiswoode, 1963), p. 256.

9. Tony Tanner, "The Literary Children of James and Clemens," *Nineteenth Century Fiction* 16 (December 1961): 205–18.

10. Tanner, 207.

11. Tanner, 211.

12. Louis J. Budd thoroughly explores the aspect of Twain's mythmaking in *Our Mark Twain: The Making of His Public Personality* (Philadelphia: University of Pennsylvania Press, 1983) and in "A 'Talent for Posturing': The Achievement of Mark Twain's Public Personality," *The Mythologizing of Mark Twain,* ed. Sara de Saussure Davis and Philip D. Beidler, introd. Davis (Tuscaloosa: The University of Alabama Press, 1984), pp. 77–98. Two more articles in the book deal with related aspects of Twain's personal myth making: Alan Gribben, "Autobiography as Property: Mark Twain and His Legend," pp. 39–55, and Henry Nash Smith, "Mark Twain, 'Funniest Man in the World,' " pp. 56–76.

13. "The Secret History of Eddypus," *Mark Twain's Fables of Man,* John S. Tuckey, ed. and introd. (Berkeley, Los Angeles, London: University of California Press, 1972), pp. 315–82.

14. See Michel Foucault, "What Is an Author?" *Language, Counter-Memory, Practice,* trans. Donald Bouchard and Sherry Simon (Ithaca, N.Y.: Cornell University Press, 1977), p. 125. Foucault's exploration of the cultural concept and role of authorship has inspired some of the ideas expressed in this chapter concerning Twain's myth of the author.

15. "The Great Dark," *Mark Twain's Which Was the Dream? and Other Symbolic Writings of the Later Years,* John S. Tuckey, ed. and introd. (Berkeley and Los Angeles: University of California Press, 1967), pp. 104 and 123.

16. Carl Gustav Jung, "On the Psychology of the Trickster Figure," in Paul Radin, ed., *The Trickster: A Study in American Indian Mythology* (New York: Philosophical Library, 1956) pp. 195–211.

17. Carl Gustav Jung, "The Spirit in Fairy Tales," *The Archetypes and the Collective Unconscious,* vol. 9, part 1, in *The Collected Works,* trans. R. F. C. Hull (London: Routledge and Kegan Paul, 1975), p. 220.

$\mathcal{B}$ibliography

Works by Mark Twain

MANUSCRIPTS

"Adam's Diary," additions to, Box 15, no. 5.
"Adam's Diary," unpublished fragment of, Box 15, no. 6.
Letters, typescript of unpublished, MTP.
"My Platonic Sweetheart," Box 16, no. 3a.
Notebooks, typescript of unpublished, MTP.

PUBLISHED WORKS

Adventures of Huckleberry Finn. New York: Harper & Row, 1987.
Autobiographical Sketch. Written for Samuel Moffett. Worcester, Mass.: Privately printed, 1918.
The Autobiography of Mark Twain. Edited with an Introduction by Charles Neider. New York: Harper, 1959.
The Complete Essays. Introduction by Charles Neider. Garden City, N.Y.: Doubleday, 1963.
The Complete Short Stories. Introduction by Charles Neider. Garden City, N.Y.: Doubleday, 1957.
The Complete Works of Mark Twain. Authorized edition. 24 volumes. New York: Harper, 1922.
The Curious Republic of Gondour and Other Whimsical Sketches. Folcroft, Pa.: Folcroft Press, 1969.

The Diaries of Adam and Eve by Mark Twain. Foreword by J. V. Ridgely. New York: American Heritage Press, 1971.

Early Tales & Sketches. Vols. 1 (1851–64) and 2 (1864–65). Edited by Edgar Marquess Branch and Robert H. Hirst. Berkeley, Los Angeles, London: Iowa Center of Textual Studies, University of California Press, 1979.

Letters from the Earth. Edited by Bernard De Voto. Greenwich, Conn.: Fawcett, 1962.

Life as I Find It. Edited with an Introduction by Charles Neider. Garden City, N.Y.: Hanover House, 1961.

Mark Twain's Autobiography. Edited by Albert B. Paine. New York and London: Harper & Bros., 1924.

Mark Twain's Burlesque Autobiography and First Romance. New York: Haskell House, 1970.

Mark Twain's Correspondence With Henry Huttleston Rogers, 1893–1909. Edited with an Introduction by Lewis Leary. Berkeley: University of California Press, 1969.

Mark Twain in Eruption: Hitherto Unpublished Pages about Men and Events by Mark Twain. Edited with an Introduction by Bernard De Voto. New York: Grosset & Dunlap, 1940.

Mark Twain's Fables of Man. Edited with an Introduction by John S. Tuckey. Berkeley, Los Angeles, London: University of California Press, 1972.

Mark Twain's Letters. Edited by Edgar Marquess Branch, Michael B. Frank, Kenneth M. Sanderson, Harriet Elinor Smith, Lin Salamo, and Richard Bucci. Berkeley: University of California Press, 1988.

Mark Twain's Hannibal, Huck and Tom. Edited with an Introduction by Walter Blair. Berkeley and Los Angeles: University of California Press, 1969.

Mark Twain–Howells Letters. Edited by Henry Nash Smith and William M. Gibson. Cambridge, Mass.: Harvard University Press, Belknap Press, 1960.

Mark Twain's Letters to His Publishers, 1867–1894. Edited with an Introduction by Hamlin Hill. Berkeley: University of California Press, 1967.

Mark Twain's Mysterious Stranger Manuscripts. Edited with an Introduction by William M. Gibson. Berkeley and Los Angeles: University of California Press, 1969.   ·

Mark Twain's Notebooks. Edited by Albert B. Paine. New York: Harper and Brothers, 1935.

Mark Twain's Notebooks and Journals. Vol. 1. Edited by Frederick Anderson, Michael B. Frank, and Kenneth M. Sanderson. Berkeley: University of California Press, 1975.

———. Vol. 2. Edited by F. Anderson, L. Salamo, and B. L. Stein. Berkeley: University of California Press, 1975.

———. Vol. 3. Edited by R. P. Browning, M. B. Frank, and L. Salamo. Berkeley: University of California Press, 1979.

Mark Twain's Roughing It. Berkeley, Los Angeles, London: University of California Press, 1973.

Mark Twain's Satires and Burlesques. Edited with an Introduction by Franklin
    R. Rogers. Berkeley and Los Angeles: University of California Press, 1967.
Mark Twain's What Is Man? and Other Philosophical Writings. Berkeley,
    Los Angeles, London: Iowa Center of Textual Studies, University of
    California Press, 1973.
Mark Twain's Which Was the Dream? and Other Symbolic Writings of the
    Later Years. Edited with an Introduction by John S. Tuckey. Berkeley
    and Los Angeles: University of California Press, 1967.
The Science Fiction of Mark Twain. Edited with an Introduction by David
    Ketterer. Hamden, Conn.: Archon Books, 1984.
1601, or A Fireside Conversation in ye Time of Queene Elizabeth by Mark
    Twain. Privately printed, 1929.
The War Prayer by Mark Twain. New York: Harper & Row, 1968.

Selected Bibliography
of Critical Works about Mark Twain

BOOKS AND DISSERTATIONS

Blair, Walter. *Mark Twain and Huck Finn*. Berkeley: University of California
    Press, 1960.
————. "Introduction." In *Mark Twain's Hannibal, Huck and Tom*. Berkeley:
    University of California Press, 1969.
————. *Native American Humor*. San Francisco: Chandler, 1960.
Branch, Edgar, ed. *Clemens of the Call: Mark Twain in San Francisco*. Berkeley
    and Los Angeles: University of California Press, 1969.
Brashear, Minnie. *Mark Twain, Son of Missouri*. Chapel Hill: The University
    of North Carolina Press, 1934.
Brooks, Van Wyck. *The Ordeal of Mark Twain*. New York: E. P. Dutton, 1920.
Budd, Louis J. *Mark Twain—Social Philosopher*. Bloomington: Indiana Uni-
    versity Press, 1962.
————. *Our Mark Twain: The Making of His Public Personality*. Philadelphia:
    University of Pennsylvania Press, 1983.
Burrison, J. A. *The Golden Era: The Folk-Tale and Its Literary Use by Mark*
    Twain and Joel C. Harris. Atlanta: Georgia State University Press, 1968.
Covici, Pascal, Jr. *Mark Twain's Humor: The Image of a World*. Dallas, Tex.:
    Southern Methodist University Press, 1962.
Cox, James M. *Mark Twain: The Fate of Humor*. Princeton, N.J.: Princeton
    University Press, 1966.
De Voto, Bernard. *Mark Twain's America*. Boston: Little, Brown, 1932.

———. *Mark Twain at Work*. Cambridge, Mass.: Harvard University Press, 1942.

Ebon, Martin. *They Knew the Unknown*. New York: World, 1971.

Emerson, Everett. *The Authentic Mark Twain: A Literary Biography of Samuel L. Clemens*. Philadelphia: University of Pennsylvania Press, 1984.

Fiedler, Leslie. *Love and Death in the American Novel*. New York: Criterion Books, 1960.

———. *No! in Thunder: Essays on Myth and Literature*. London: Eyre and Spottiswoode, 1963.

Fishkin, Shelley Fisher. *From Fact to Fiction: Journalism and Imaginative Writing in America*. Baltimore, Md.: The Johns Hopkins University Press, 1985.

Foner, Philip S. *Mark Twain Social Critic. (His Thinking on Politics, Religion, Capital)*. New York: International, 1958.

Geismar, Maxwell. *Mark Twain, an American Prophet*. Boston: Houghton Mifflin, 1970.

Gibson, William M. *The Art of Mark Twain*. New York: Oxford University Press, 1976.

———. "Introduction." In *The Mysterious Stranger Manuscripts*. Berkeley and Los Angeles: University of California Press, 1969.

Gribben, Alan. *Mark Twain's Library: A Reconstruction*. Boston: G. K. Hall, 1980.

Harris, Susan K. *Mark Twain's Escape from Time: A Study of Patterns and Images*. Columbia and London: University of Missouri Press, 1982.

Hill, Hamlin. *Mark Twain: God's Fool*. New York: Harper & Row, 1973.

Hoffman, Daniel. *Form and Fable in American Fiction: Folk Elements in Clemens and Others*. New York: Oxford University Press, 1961.

Howells, William D. *My Mark Twain: Reminiscence and Criticism*. New York: Harper and Brothers, 1910.

Kahn, Sholom, Jr. *Mark Twain's Mysterious Stranger: A Study of the Manuscript Texts*. Columbia and London: University of Missouri Press, 1978.

Kaplan, Justin. *Mr. Clemens and Mark Twain: A Biography*. New York: Simon and Schuster, 1966.

Kerr, Howard. *Mediums, and Spirit-Rappers, and Roaring Radicals: Spiritualism in American Literature, 1850–1900*. Urbana: University of Illinois Press, 1972.

Krause, Sydney J. *Mark Twain as Critic*. Baltimore, Md.: The Johns Hopkins University Press, 1967.

Lorch, Fred W. *The Trouble Begins at 8: Mark Twain's Lecture Tours*. Ames: Iowa State University Press, 1968.

Lynn, Kenneth S. *Mark Twain and Southwestern Humor*. Boston: Little, Brown, 1959.

McGraw, Mary Holland. "The Dream and the Creative Imagination in Mark

Twain's *The Mysterious Stranger Manuscripts.*" Diss. Oklahoma State University, 1979.

Mcnaughton, William R. *Mark Twain's Last Years as a Writer.* Columbia and London: University of Missouri Press, 1979.

Neider, Charles. *Mark Twain.* New York: Horizon Press, 1967.

Nelson, Randy. "Probing the Great Dark: Dream Features of Mark Twain's Late Works." Diss. Princeton University, 1976.

Paine, Albert Bigelow. *Mark Twain: A Biography.* New York and London: Harper and Bros., 1912.

Porter, Drue Annelle. "The Dream Motif in Mark Twain's *Mysterious Stranger Manuscripts.*" Diss. East Texas State University, 1981.

Rogers, Franklin R. *Mark Twain's Burlesque Patterns, as Seen in the Novels and Narratives, 1855–1885.* Dallas, Tex.: Southern Methodist University Press, 1960.

———. "Introduction." In *Mark Twain's Satires and Burlesques.* Berkeley and Los Angeles: University of California Press, 1967.

Salomon, Roger B. *Twain and the Image of History.* New Haven, Conn.: Yale University Press, 1961.

Sewell, Robert. *Mark Twain's Languages: Discourse, Dialogue, and Linguistic Variety.* Berkeley: University of California Press, 1987.

Sloane, David E. *Mark Twain as a Literary Comedian.* Baton Rouge and London: Louisiana State University Press, 1979.

Smith, Henry Nash. *Democracy and the Novel: Popular Resistance to Classic American Writers.* New York: Oxford University Press, 1978.

———. *Mark Twain: The Development of a Writer.* Cambridge, Mass.: Harvard University Press, Belknap Press, 1962.

———. *Mark Twain's Fable of Progress: Political and Economic Ideas in "A Connecticut Yankee in King Arthur's Court."* New Brunswick, N.J.: Rutgers University Press, 1964.

Spengemann, William C. *Mark Twain and the Backwood Angels: The Matter of Innocence in the Works of Samuel L. Clemens.* Kent, Ohio: Kent State University Press, 1966.

Stone, Albert E., Jr. *The Innocent Eye: Childhood in Mark Twain's Imagination.* New Haven, Conn.: Yale University Press, 1961.

Tuckey, John S. *Mark Twain and Little Satan: The Writing of the 'Mysterious Stranger.'* Westport, Conn.: Greenwood Press, 1963.

———. *Mark Twain's The Mysterious Stranger and the Critics.* Belmont, Calif.: Wadsworth, 1968.

———. "Introduction." In *Mark Twain's Fables of Man.* Berkeley, Los Angeles, London: University of California Press, 1972.

———. "Introduction." In *Mark Twain's Which Was the Dream? and Other Symbolic Writings of the Later Years.* Berkeley and Los Angeles: University of California Press, 1967.

Warren, Joyce W. *The American Narcissus: Individualism and Women in*

Nineteenth-Century American Fiction. New Brunswick, N.J.: Rutgers University Press, 1984.

Wiggins, Robert. *Mark Twain—Jackleg Novelist.* Seattle: University of Washington Press, 1964.

Articles in Journals, Magazines, and Books

Anderson, Frederick. "Twain Papers: A Fount of Biographical Studies." *Manuscripts* 11 (February 1959): 14–15.

Bell, Robert. "How Mark Twain Comments on Society through the Use of Folklore." *Mark Twain Journal* 11 (1955): 1–8, 24–25.

Blair, Walter. "Mark Twain and the Mind's Ear." In *The American Self: Myth, Ideology and Popular Culture,* edited by Sam Girgus. Albuquerque: University of New Mexico Press, 1981.

Brodwin, Stanley. "Mark Twain's Masks of Satan: The Final Phase." *American Literature* 45 (1973): 206–24.

Budd, Louis J. "A 'Talent for Posturing': The Achievement of Mark Twain's Public Personality." in *The Mythologizing of Mark Twain,* edited by Sara de Saussure Davis and Philip Beidler, with an Introduction by Davis.

Cummings, Sherwood. "Mark Twain's Acceptance of Science." *The Centennial Review* 6 (Summer 1962): 245–61.

———. "Mark Twain's Social Darwinism." *Huntington Library Quarterly* 20 (February 1967): 163–75.

———. "What Is Man? The Scientific Sources." *Essays on Determinism in American Literature* 33 (1965): 108–16.

Davis, John H. "The Dream as Reality: Structure and Meaning in Mark Twain's 'The Great Dark.'" *Mississippi Quarterly* 35, no. 4 (Fall 1982): 407–26.

DeEulis, Marilyn Davis. "Mark Twain's Experiment in Autobiography." *American Literature* 53 (May 1981): 203–13.

Delaney, Paul. "The Dissolving Self: The Narrator of Mark Twain's *Mysterious Stranger* Fragments." *Journal of Narrative Technique* 6 (1976): 53–62.

De Voto, Bernard. "Mark Twain's Papers." *Saturday Review of Literature,* 10 December 1938, pp. 3–9, 14–15.

Ensor, Allison. "Mark Twain's 'The War Prayer': Its Ties to Howells and Hymnology." *Modern Fiction Studies* 16 (1970): 535–39.

Ferguson, John. "Mark Twain's Utopia." *Mark Twain Journal* 19, no. 3 (1978): 1–2.

Fetterley, Judith. "Mark Twain and the Anxiety of Entertainment." *Georgia Review* 33 (1978): 382–91.

Gibson, William M. "Mark Twain and Howells: Anti-Imperialists." *New England Quarterly* 20 (1947): 435–70.

Gribben, Alan. "Autobiography as Property: Mark Twain and His Legend." In *The Mythologizing of Mark Twain,* edited by Sara de Saussure Davis and Philip Beidler, with an Introduction by Davis. Tuscaloosa: The University of Alabama Press, 1984.

———. "Mark Twain, Phrenology and the 'Temperaments': A Study in Pseudo-scientific Influence." *American Quarterly* 24 (March 1972): 45–68.

———. "Removing Mark Twain's Mask: A Decade of Criticism and Scholarship. Part 1." *ESQ* 26, no. 99 (1980): 100–108.

———. "Removing Mark Twain's Mask: A Decade of Criticism and Scholarship. Part 2." *ESQ* 26, no. 100 (1980): 149–71.

———. "Stolen from Books, Tho' Credit Given: Mark Twain's Use of Literary Sources." *Mosaic* 12, no. 4 (1979): 150–55.

Johnson, Ellwood. "Mark Twain's Dream Self in the Nightmare of History." *Mark Twain Journal* 15 (1970): 6–12.

Jones, Daryl E. "The *Hornet* Disaster: Twain's Adaptation in 'The Great Dark.' " *American Literary Realism* 9 (Summer 1976): 243–48.

———. "The Source of 'Everlasting Sunday': Note on Twain's 'Enchanted Sea-Wilderness.' " *Mark Twain Journal* 19 (1977–78): 18–19.

Karnath, David. "Mark Twain's Implicit Theory of the Comic." *Mosaic* 9, no. 4 (1976): 207–18.

———. "The Mysterious Stranger: Its Mode of Thought." *Mark Twain Journal* 19, no. 4 (1975): 4–8.

Ketterer, David. "Power Fantasy in the 'Science Fiction' of Mark Twain." In *Bridges to Fantasy,* edited by George Slusser, Eric Rabkin, and Robert Scholes. Carbondale and Edwardsville: Southern Illinois University Press, 1982.

Klotz, Marun. "Mark Twain and the Socratic Dialogue." *Mark Twain Journal* 11 (Summer 1959): 1–3.

Krutch, Joseph Wood. "The Kremlin Claims Mark Twain." *New York Times* 6, March 1969, pp. 16, 68–69.

Lakin, R. D. "Mark Twain and the Cold War." *Midwest Quarterly* 2 (Winter 1961): 159–67.

Marotti, Maria O. "Mark Twain alle soglie della fantascienza." *Studi Americani* 23–25 (1979): 177–212.

———. "I *Mysterious Stranger Manuscripts:* Un esperimento nel fantastico." In *I Piaceri dell' Immaginazione,* edited and with an Introduction by Biancamaria Pisapia. Rome: Bulzoni Editore, 1984.

Martin, Jay. "Twain and the Image of the Child." In *Harvests of Change.* Englewood Cliffs, N.J.: Prentice-Hall, 1967.

Marx, Leo. "Mr. Eliot, Mr. Trilling, and *Huckleberry Finn.*" *The American Scholar* 22 (1953): 423–40.

———. "The Vernacular Tradition in American Literature: W. Whitman and Mark Twain." *Die Neueren Sprache* 3 (1958): 46–57.

May, John R. "The Gospel According to Philip Traum: Structural Unity in the
    Mysterious Stranger." Studies in Short Fiction 8 (1971): 411–22.
Mendleson, M. "Mark Twain's Unpublished Literary Heritage." *Soviet Review*
    2 (September 1961): 33–53.
Michelson, Bruce. "Deus Ludens: The Shaping of Mark Twain's Mysterious
    Stranger." *Novel* (Fall 1980): 44–56.
Rubin, Louis D., Jr. "How Mark Twain Threw off His Inhibitions and Discovered
    the Vitality of Formless Form." *Sewanee Review* 79 (1971): 426–33.
Scrivner, Buford, Jr., "The Mysterious Stranger: Mark Twain's New Myth of
    the Fall." *Mark Twain Journal* 17, no. 4 (1975): 20–21.
Tanner, Tony. "The Literary Children of James and Clemens." *Nineteenth
    Century Fiction* 16 (December 1961): 205–18.
———. "The Lost America—The Despair of Henry Adams and Mark Twain."
    Modern Age 5 (Summer 1961): 299–310.
———. "Samuel Clemens and the Progress of a Stylistic Rebel." *British Associ-
    ation for American Studies Bulletin* 3 (December 1961): 31–42.
Tuckey, John S. "Mark Twain's Later Dialogue: The 'Me' and the Machine."
    American Literature 41, no. 4 (1969): 532–42.
Tuerk, Richard. "Appearance and Reality in Mark Twain's 'Which Was the
    Dream?,' 'The Great Dark' and 'What Was It?' " *Illinois Quarterly* 40
    (1978): 25–28.
Turner, Arlin. "Seeds of Literary Revolt in the Humor of the Old Southwest."
    Louisiana Historical Quarterly 39 (1956): 143–51.
Wagenknecht, Edward. "The Mark Twain Papers and Henry James: The
    Treacherous Years." *Studies in the Novel* (North Texas State University)
    2: 88–98.
Werge, Thomas. "Mark Twain and the Fall of Adam." *Mark Twain Journal* 15
    (Summer 1970): 5–13.

Critical and Theoretical Works

Auerbach, Erich. *Mimesis*. Translated by Willard Trask. Garden City, N.Y.:
    Doubleday, 1957.
Bakhtin, Mikhail. *The Dialogic Imagination: Four Essays*. Translated by Caryl
    Emerson and Michael Holquist. Austin: University of Texas Press, 1981.
Barthes, Roland. *Mythologies*. Translated by Annette Lavers. New York: Hill
    & Wang. 1957.
———. *Writing Degree Zero*. Translated by Annette Lavers. Boston: Beacon
    Press, 1967.
Bloom, Harold. "Clinamen: Towards a Theory of Fantasy." In *Bridges to Fan-
    tasy*, edited by George Slusser, Eric Rabkin, and Robert Scholes. Car-
    bondale and Edwardsville: Southern Illinois University Press, 1982.

Booth, Wayne C. *The Rhetoric of Fiction*. Chicago and London: The University of Chicago Press, 1961.

Brecht, Bertolt. *Brecht on Theatre: The Development of an Aesthetic*. Translated and edited by John Willett. London: Methuen, 1964.

Campbell, Joseph. *The Mythic Image*. Princeton, N.J.: Princeton University Press, 1974.

Clayton, David. "On Realistic and Fantastic Discourse." In *Bridges to Fantasy*, edited by George Slusser, Eric Rabkin, and Robert Scholes. Carbondale and Edwardsville: Southern Illinois University Press, 1982.

Derrida, Jacques. *Writing and Difference*. Translated by Alan Bass. Chicago: University of Chicago Press, 1978.

Durand, Gilbert. *Les structures anthropologiques de l'imaginaire: Introduction a' l'archétypologie générale*. Paris: Bordas, 1969.

Eco, Umberto. *The Role of the Reader*. Bloomington: Indiana University Press, 1979.

Eliade, Mircea. *Myths, Dreams and Mysteries: The Encounter Between Contemporary Faith and Archaic Realities*. Translated by Philip Mairet. London: Harvill Press, 1960.

Foucault, Michel. "What Is an Author?" In *Language, Counter-Memory, Practice*, translated by Donald Bouchard and Sherry Simon. Ithaca, N.Y.: Cornell University Press, 1977.

Freud, Sigmund. *Beyond the Pleasure Principle*. Translated by James Strachey. New York: Liveright, 1950.

————. *Jokes and Their Relation to the Unconscious*. Translated by James Strachey. New York: Norton, 1963.

————. *Totem and Taboo: Some Points of Agreement Between the Mental Lives of Savages and Neurotics*. Translated by James Strachey. New York: Norton, 1952.

————. *Das Unheimliche: Aufsatze zur literatur*. Frankfurt am Main: S. Fischer, 1963.

Frye, Northrop. *Fables of Identity: Studies in Poetic Mythology*. New York: Harcourt Brace and World, 1963.

————. *The Secular Scripture: A Study of the Structure of Romance*. Cambridge, Mass.: Harvard University Press, 1976.

Genette, Gérard. *Figures III*. Paris: Editions du Seuil, 1976.

————. *Narrative Discourse: An Essay in Method*. Translated by Jane E. Lewin. Ithaca, N.Y.: Cornell University Press, 1980.

Greimas, J. G. *Sémantique Structurale*. Paris: Larousse, 1966.

Hoffmann, Gerhard. "The Fantastic in Fiction: Its 'Reality' Status, Its Historical Development and Its Transformation in Post-modern Narration." *REAL* (1982): 267–365.

Howells, William Dean. *Criticism and Fiction and Other Essays*. New York: New York University Press, 1959.

Iser, Wolfgang. *The Implied Reader: Patterns of Communication in Prose Fiction from Bunyan to Beckett*. Baltimore, Md.: The Johns Hopkins University Press, 1974.

Jakobson, Roman. *Essais de linguistique générale*. Translated and with a Preface by Nicolas Ruwet. Paris: Les Editions de Minuit, 1963.

James, William. *The Principles of Psychology*. Vol. 2. New York: Dover, 1962.

Jung, Carl G. *The Archetypes and the Collective Unconscious*. In *The Collected Works*, vol. 9, part 1. Translated by R. F. C. Hull. London: Routledge and Kegan Paul, 1975.

———. "On the Psychology of the Trickster Figure." In *The Trickster: A Study in American Indian Mythology*, edited by Paul Radin. New York: Philosophical Library, 1956.

Jung, Carl G., with Karl Kerényi. *Essays on a Science of Mythology: The Myths of the Divine Child and the Mysteries of Eleusis*. Translated by R. F. C. Hull. Princeton, N.J.: Princeton University Press, 1969.

Lacan, Jacques. *Ecrits*. Paris: Editions du Seuil, 1966.

Lejeune, Philippe. *Le pacte autobiographique*. Paris: Editions du Seuil, 1975.

Lévi-Strauss, Claude. *Structural Anthropology*. Translated by Claire Jacobson and Brooke Grundfest Schoepf. New York: Basic Books, 1963.

Lotman, Juri. *Antropologia della Cultura*. Milano: Bompiani, 1974.

———. "Primary and Secondary Communication-Modeling Systems," pp. 95–98; "Two Models of Communication," pp. 99–102; "Problems in the Typology of Texts," pp. 119–24; "Problems in the Typology of Culture," pp. 213–22; "Numerical Semantics and Cultural Types," pp. 227–32; and "Myth-Name-Culture" (with Uspenskij, B. A.), pp. 233–52, In *Soviet Semiotics*, edited, translated, and with an introduction by Daniel P. Lucid. Baltimore, Md.: The Johns Hopkins University Press, 1977.

———. *Theses on the Semiotic Study of Culture (as Applied to Slavic Texts)*. Lisse, Netherlands: The Peter de Ridder Press, 1975.

Milner, Max. *La Fantasmagorie*. Paris: Presses Universitaires de France, 1982.

Orlando, Francesco. *Toward a Freudian Theory of Literature: With an Analysis of Racine's "Phèdre."* Translated by Charmaine Lee. Baltimore, Md.: The Johns Hopkins University Press, 1978.

Poulet, Georges. *Les métamorphoses du cercle*. Paris: Plon, 1961.

Propp, Vladimir. *Morphology of the Folktale*. Translated by Laurence Scott. Introduction by Svatava Pirkova-Jakobson, Revised and Edited with a Preface by Louis A. Wagner, New Introduction by Alan Dundes. Austin: University of Texas Press, 1968.

Rabkin, Eric. *The Fantastic in Literature*. Princeton, N.J.: Princeton University Press, 1976.

Saussure, Ferdinand de. *Course in General Linguistics*. Translated by Wade Baskin. New York: McGraw-Hill, 1966.

Scholes, Robert. "The Roots of Science Fiction." In *Science Fiction*, edited by Mark Rose. Englewood Cliffs, N.J.: Prentice-Hall, 1976.

———. *Structural Fabulations*. Notre Dame and London: University of Notre Dame Press, 1975.

Sklovskij, Viktor. "L'art comme procédé" and "La construction de la nouvelle et du roman." In *Théorie de la littérature: Textes des formalistes russes*, edited and translated by Tzvetan Todorov. Preface by Roman Jakobson. Paris: Editions du Seuil, 1965.

———. *O teorii prozy.* Moscow, 1929.

Suleiman, Susan, ed. *The Reader in the Text.* Princeton, N.J.: Princeton University Press, 1980.

Todorov, Tzvetan. *The Fantastic: A Structural Approach to a Literary Genre.* Translated by Richard Howard. Cleveland, Ohio: Press of Case Western Reserve University, 1973.

Tomasevskij, Boris. "Thèmatique." In *Théorie de la littérature: Textes des formalistes russes,* with an Introduction by Tzvetan Todorov. Preface by Roman Jakobson. Paris: Editions du Seuil, 1965.

Tynianov, Juri. "La notion de construction." In *Théorie de la littérature: Textes des formalistes russes,* edited and translated by Tzvetan Todorov. Preface by Roman Jakobson. Paris: Editions du Seuil, 1965.

Vax, Louis. *Les Chefs-d'oeuvre de la littérature fantastique.* Paris: Presses Universitaires de France, 1979.

Index